TABLE OF CONTENTS

Spicy Tomato Sauce

~

page 333

Pastitsio

~

page 37

INTRODUCTION

This cookbook is designed to take the work and worry out of everyday low-fat pasta cooking; to provide delicious, fresh, and filling recipes for family and friends; to use quick, streamlined methods and available ingredients; and, within every recipe, to keep the percentage of calories from fat under 30 percent.

To cooks all over the world, pasta offers one of life's great pleasures. It is a perfect companion for such delights as garlic, olive oil, onions, tomatoes, and flavorful cheeses, to name but a few. This simple staple is also a healthful food. Packed with complex carbohydrates but very little fat, pasta is something we've learned to count on when we're reducing the fat in our diets. The goal for this book was to re-create the silky creaminess of the meals you've known and loved.

THE ART OF THE SAUCE

The process of inventing pasta sauces begins with access to inspiring ingredients. The complex and satisfying flavors in authentic Italian pasta dishes come from using fresh produce in season. Italian cooks will often design a pasta dish based on what they've run across in the market that day. For example, if eggplant or cauliflower is in season, they will think of combining those vegetables with a sturdy pasta like radiatore or gnocchi. Or if they've picked up a head of cabbage, they might decide to toss strips of cabbage with ribbons of fettuccine, a perfect match of ingredient and pasta shape (see "Pasta Pairings" on page 9). Summer weather, and the wonderfully flavorful vegetables that come with it, tend to inspire meatless pasta dishes, especially those made with juicy, ripe tomatoes. Colder weather brings the heartier meat sauces—often made with canned tomatoes, a far more flavorful alternative to using out-of-season fresh tomatoes (see "Tasty Tomatoes," page 6).

A RICH SELECTION

In spite of the place of honor that Italian pasta dishes hold, don't think for a moment that all the recipes in this book are Italian. Although there's a full complement of delicious tomato toppings, including Puttanesca, Amatriciana, and Arrabbiata—as well as Alfredo, Primavera, Pesto, and other favorites—you'll also find sauces flavored with curry, almonds, lemon, chili powder, paprika, dill, or mint; and dishes inspired by Thai, Chinese, Indonesian, and Mexican cuisines. Some of the recipes are adaptations of familiar main dishes (or soups) into pasta-sauce form. We've performed this transformation on, among others, chili, minestrone, chicken parmigiana, and pork and beans.

In the first chapter, Baked Pasta, comes a host of surprises, including a low-fat Chicken Lasagna and a Creamy Penne, Bacon, and Vegetable Bake. And although none of our baked pasta recipes *has* to be made ahead, all of the dishes lend themselves to being prepared in advance and baked or reheated just before serving.

In Poultry Sauces, you'll find fragrant Chicken Sauce with Sage, Turkey Sauce with Orange and Sweet Spices, and a Neapolitan Chicken Sauce with true old-world flavor. In addition to a sturdy Beef and Mushroom Ragù, our Meat Sauces chapter offers Pork Piccata Sauce, Paprikash Sauce, and a creamy Ham and Ricotta Cheese Sauce. On a lighter note, you'll want to sample our Seafood Sauces, such as Provençal Shrimp Sauce and Salmon and Lemon-Dill Sauce. You'll be impressed with the variety of recipes in the Vegetable Sauces chapter. Choices range from creamy sauces—including Artichoke-Parmesan Sauce, Asparagus Cream Sauce, and Vegetable-Cheese Sauce—to highly seasoned Vegetable Agliata (a garlic-lover's delight), Spicy Tomato Sauce, and Green Bean Gremolata Sauce.

The chapter on Pasta Salads tops off the book with more variety still. We borrowed from many culinary traditions and started a few of our own to create our quick, delicious main-dish salads. And for maximum flexibility, you can serve these salads hot, cold, or at room temperature.

Be sure to read the "Secrets of Low-Fat Cooking" pages, which follow, for tips on ingredients and pasta cooking techniques. Then you'll be on your way to enjoying a fabulous succession of tasty, low-fat, family-pleasing pasta dishes.

CONTRIBUTING EDITORS

Sandra Rose Gluck, a New York City chef, has years of experience creating delicious low-fat recipes that are quick to prepare. Her secret for satisfying results is to always aim for great taste and variety. By combining readily available, fresh ingredients with simple cooking techniques, Sandra has created the perfect recipes for today's busy lifestyles.

Grace Young has been the director of a major test kitchen specializing in low-fat and health-related cookbooks for over 12 years. Grace oversees the development, taste testing, and nutritional analysis of every recipe in this book. Her goal is simple: take the work and worry out of low-fat cooking so that you can enjoy delicious, healthy meals every day.

Kate Slate has been a food editor for almost 20 years, and has published thousands of recipes in cookbooks and magazines. As the Editorial Director of this book, Kate combined simple, easy to follow directions with practical cooking tips. The result is guaranteed to make your low-fat cooking as rewarding and fun as it is foolproof.

NUTRITION

Every recipe in this book provides per-serving values for the nutrients listed in the chart at right. The daily intakes listed in the chart are based on those recommended by the USDA and presume a nonsedentary lifestyle. The nutritional emphasis in this book is not only on controlling calories, but on reducing total fat grams. Research has shown that dietary fat metabolizes more easily into body fat than do carbohydrates and protein. In order to control the amount of fat in a given recipe and in your diet in general, no more than 30 percent of the calories should come from fat.

Nutrient	Women	Men
Fat	<65 g	<80 g
Calories	2000	2500
Saturated fat	<20 g	<25 g
Carbohydrate	300 g	375 g
Protein	50 g	65 g
Cholesterol	<300 mg	<300 mg
Sodium	<2400 mg	<2400 mg

These recommended daily intakes are averages used by the Food and Drug Administration and are consistent with the labeling on all food products. Although the values for cholesterol and sodium are the same for all adults, the other intake values vary depending on gender, ideal weight, and activity level. Check with a physician or nutritionist for your own daily intake values.

SECRETS OF LOW-FAT COOKING

PASTA

Thank goodness for pasta—and for the thousands of wonderful ways to serve it. It is perfectly suited to low-fat cooking since it's made with flour and water, not fat. But without some sort of sauce, pasta would be undeniably dull. Just add a simple sauce (chopped raw tomatoes, fresh basil or oregano, and a shimmer of extra-virgin olive oil, for example), and pasta takes its rightful place as one of the world's great and versatile foods, as welcome at a festive dinner party on Saturday evening as it is at the family supper table any night of the week.

Here, in "Secrets of Low-Fat Cooking," we offer helpful hints on cooking pasta properly, selecting an appropriate pasta shape for a sauce, ways to thicken sauces without fat, and working with the most common tomato products.

KEYS TO HEALTHFUL SAUCES

A great pasta sauce should cling to the pasta and stick to your ribs—and of course the taste must be memorable. This is as true of a healthful, low-fat sauce as it is of a high-fat one, and for satisfying results, it takes some ingenuity consisting of equal parts cooking technique and knowledge of

ingredients. We supply both in our recipes, and offer them to you in these pages. In the photograph at right are key components of great pasta sauces: tomatoes in various forms, hot-shot flavor boosters, and low-fat thickeners that can enrich a sauce. We use them all—and when your kitchen is stocked with these ingredients, you may be tempted to improvise your own original sauces, or cook up variations on the recipes in this book.

FABULOUS FLAVORS

Pasta's unassuming taste is the perfect foil for intense flavorings. The fresh vegetables, lean meats, poultry, and seafood that go into our sauces are enhanced with imaginative seasonings. We start by giving our sauces a flavorful foundation: We sizzle up some lean Canadian bacon, steep dried mushrooms in boiling water, or sauté onions, garlic, and bell pepper until they're tender and savory. As the sauce simmers, we add modest amounts of other high-flavor ingredients: pungent brine-cured or pimiento-stuffed olives, piquant capers, freshly grated citrus zest, and fragrant spices. For an outstanding finish, we often splash in some wine—a mellow Marsala, nutty sherry, or crisp, dry white—or drizzle in a few drops of fruity, extra-virgin olive oil. Wine vinegar adds

full flavor as well as tartness; balsamic vinegar has a uniquely rounded, sweetly mellow taste. We're careful to add fresh herbs, too—waiting until the sauce is nearly cooked, do they don't lose their full bouquet.

TASTY TOMATOES

No discussion of pasta sauces would be complete without a mention of tomatoes, which form the basis for so many classic sauces. Among the juiciest and most flavorful of vegetables, tomatoes are a natural for sauce-making. Fresh tomatoes, whether globe or beefsteak, plum or cherry, can be diced, chopped, or puréed to make raw and cooked pasta toppings. The better the tomatoes, the better the sauce—so it's worth hunting down vine-ripened tomatoes at roadside stands and farmers' markets (or in your own backyard, if you have a garden) during the growing season.

Of course, locally grown tomatoes are not available year-round, which is why you'll want to keep ready-to-use tomato products on hand. The canned ones—peeled tomatoes, stewed tomatoes, tomato purées, sauces, and pastes—offer consistently good flavor; we use no-salt-added products for delicately seasoned sauces without excessive

sodium (check the ingredients on the label since not all cans are labeled "no-salt-added"). And don't forget sun-dried tomatoes, with their super-concentrated essence-of-tomato flavor; their pleasant chewiness adds textural interest, too. Use dry-packed tomatoes, rather than oil-packed, for low-fat meals.

MAKING THE SAUCE THICK AND RICH

Pasta sauces can be given a sense of richness and thickness in a number of ways; but if a healthful pasta dinner is your goal, copious quantities of butter, oil, heavy cream, or cheese are not appropriate options. There are several more healthful tricks of the trade. One, very simply, is to reduce the amount of fat used without destroying the nature of the dish. For example, for pesto—which is a savory paste traditionally made thick with a lot of oil, ground nuts, and cheese—we use the same basic ingredients, but lighten the sauce by using less oil (with chicken broth as a stand-in to keep the sauce moist) and smaller quantities of nuts and cheese. The heady flavors of garlic and basil are still there and the lighter sauce is even more pungent and satisfying.

In addition to reducing the oil, cream, or butter in a traditional recipe, we also look for ways to replace the original rich "mouth-feel." One way to do this is to add a starchy ingredient, such as flour or cornstarch, to the sauce. Flour makes a thicker, opaque sauce, while cornstarch produces a lighter, more translucent one. Starchy vegetables such as potatoes or corn can also thicken a sauce slightly with the natural starches they give off while cooking.

Another thickening trick that we use in several recipes is to purée or mash all or some of the solid ingredients (such as beans or vegetables) cooked in the sauce. You can do this with a food processor or blender (regular or hand-held), or with a fork or wooden spoon.

Dairy products add inimitable richness to pasta sauces, and even reduced-fat products will do the job. Among those utilized in our recipes are rich-tasting Neufchâtel, a reduced-fat cream cheese; low-fat and skimmed evaporated milk (smart substitutes for heavy cream); tangy low-fat and non-fat yogurt; and velvety reduced-fat sour cream. Parmesan and other grated sharp cheeses can also give body to a pasta sauce. Use a well-aged cheese, which will contribute plenty of flavor as well as

substance. Naturally, when cooking low-fat meals, you'll want to use full-fat cheeses, such as Parmesan or Cheddar, in moderation.

COOKING PASTA PERFECTLY

You'll enjoy these pasta recipes to the fullest when the pasta itself is cooked to perfection. That means al dente—not soft or limp, but gently resistant when you bite into it. Learn to gauge the proper texture for yourself: Different brands require different cooking times, but generally speaking, pasta imported from Italy tends to take a bit longer than domestic brands. And fresh pasta cooks much faster than dried—sometimes in only the time it takes for the water to come back to a boil after you've added the pasta to the pot.

For 10 ounces of pasta, use a large pot—at least 4 quarts—and bring the water to a rolling boil (cover the pot to speed the process). Salt is optional—our recipes don't call for it. Add the pasta, stir to keep it from clumping together, and return to a boil. Check for doneness by biting a piece of pasta. When it's still a bit chewy, but has no white core remaining in the center, the pasta is done. Drain it well in a colander or strainer before adding the sauce.

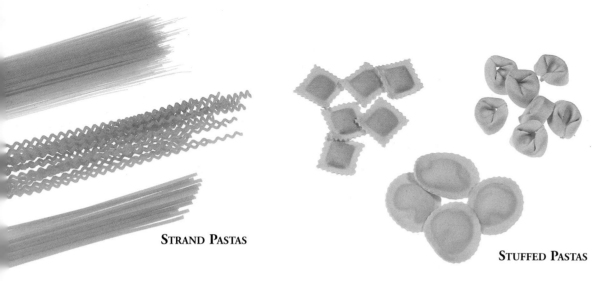

STRAND PASTAS

STUFFED PASTAS

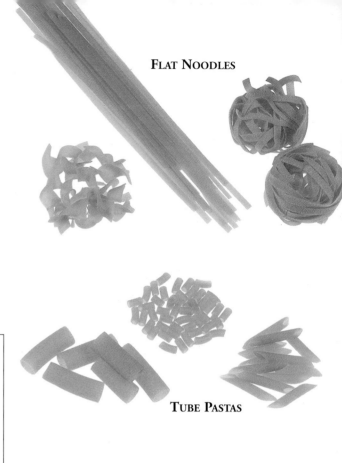

FLAT NOODLES

TUBE PASTAS

SHAPED PASTAS

PASTA PAIRINGS

Traditionally, different types of pasta are matched with certain sauces according to the size and shape of the pasta and the texture and flavor of the sauce. We've observed these "rules" (though not slavishly) in our recipes, suggesting one or more appropriate pastas for each sauce.

On this page you see pastas grouped according to size and shape, and you can always substitute within a group. But feel free to go beyond the guidelines: If you're out of penne, use fettuccine broken into shorter pieces; if you prefer chewy rigatoni to slippery spaghetti, go ahead and make the switch. If your kids are fond of a certain pasta shape, use the shells, elbows, or whatever they prefer as a way of encouraging them to try different sauces.

• A smooth but clingy sauce is ideal for **strand pastas** such as angel hair pasta, spaghetti, long fusilli, and linguine.

• **Stuffed pastas**, almost a meal in themselves, don't require complicated sauce.

• **Flat noodles** like fettuccine and egg noodles are great with creamy sauces.

• **Tube pastas**—ziti and penne, for example—go well with vegetable sauces.

• Chunky sauces are neatly complemented by what we think of as **"sauce-catcher" pastas**: shells, wagon wheels (ruote), radiatore, and other shapes with hollows and gaps to hold the sauce.

• **Pasta twists**, such as rotini and bow ties (farfalle), are among the most versatile pastas and can be served with a wide variety of sauces.

BAKED PASTA

Left, Hearty Macaroni and Cheese. Above, Baked Manicotti.

CHICKEN LASAGNA

SERVES: 4
WORKING TIME: 40 MINUTES
TOTAL TIME: 1 HOUR

Our lasagna is probably as rich-tasting as your family's favorite, but with much less fat. The creamy white sauce is made with low-fat milk, and we use strongly flavored Parmesan cheese so we don't need much. And we grind the chicken breasts in the food processor, which adds less fat than packaged ground chicken would. Serve with a green salad.

9 lasagna noodles (9 ounces)
2 teaspoons olive oil
1 large red onion, finely chopped
1 carrot, finely chopped
4 cloves garlic, minced
¾ pound skinless, boneless chicken breasts, cut into small pieces
½ cup dry white wine
2½ cups canned crushed tomatoes
½ teaspoon dried rosemary
½ teaspoon salt
½ teaspoon freshly ground black pepper
¼ teaspoon red pepper flakes
1¾ cups low-fat (1%) milk
3 tablespoons flour
¼ cup grated Parmesan cheese

1. In a large pot of boiling water, cook the noodles until almost tender. Drain. Transfer to a bowl of cold water to prevent sticking. Meanwhile, in a large nonstick skillet, heat the oil until hot but not smoking over medium heat. Add the onion, carrot, and garlic and cook until the onion is softened, about 5 minutes.

2. In a food processor, process the chicken until coarsely ground. Add the chicken to the skillet and stir until lightly colored, about 2 minutes. Add the wine, increase the heat to high, and cook until the liquid has been reduced by half, about 2 minutes. Stir in the tomatoes, rosemary, salt, ¼ teaspoon of the black pepper, and the red pepper flakes. Return to a boil, reduce to a simmer, and cook, uncovered, for 5 minutes to blend the flavors.

3. Preheat the oven to 400°. In a medium saucepan, whisk the milk into the flour and cook over medium heat, stirring frequently, until slightly thickened, about 5 minutes. Stir in the remaining ¼ teaspoon black pepper.

4. Spray a 9-inch square baking dish with nonstick cooking spray. Dividing the ingredients evenly, build the lasagna in three layers, using the following order: noodles, chicken sauce, white sauce, Parmesan. Bake for 20 minutes, or until bubbling hot. Divide among 4 plates and serve.

FAT: 7G/14%
CALORIES: 473
SATURATED FAT: 3.4G
CARBOHYDRATE: 66G
PROTEIN: 35G
CHOLESTEROL: 57MG
SODIUM: 500MG

*T*he zesty Mexican flavors of hot peppers, lime, and green chilies highlight this creamy casserole, thickened with cornmeal for a deliciously subtle sweetness. A fresh jalapeño adds welcome fire but if unavailable, you may substitute the jarred, pickled variety. Rotini and ruote, other short-shaped pastas, are excellent alternatives to the radiatore.

CREAMY MEXICAN-STYLE RADIATORE

SERVES: 4
WORKING TIME: 25 MINUTES
TOTAL TIME: 45 MINUTES

8 ounces radiatore pasta

2 teaspoons olive oil

1 teaspoon mild chili powder

4 scallions, thinly sliced

1 red bell pepper, diced

1 green bell pepper, diced

1 teaspoon minced jalapeño pepper (use gloves; see tip)

¾ teaspoon dried oregano

1 cup frozen corn kernels, thawed

4-ounce can chopped mild green chilies

1 tablespoon fresh lime juice

2 tablespoons yellow cornmeal

2 cups low-fat (1%) milk

¾ teaspoon salt

¼ teaspoon freshly ground black pepper

4 ounces Monterey Jack cheese, shredded (about 1 cup)

1. Preheat the oven to 350°. Spray a shallow 2½-quart baking dish with nonstick cooking spray. Heat a large pot of water to boiling, and cook the radiatore until just tender. Drain well.

2. Meanwhile, in a large nonstick skillet, heat the oil until hot but not smoking over medium heat. Add the chili powder and cook, stirring constantly, until fragrant, about 30 seconds. Add the scallions, bell peppers, jalapeño, and oregano and cook, stirring occasionally, until the bell peppers are crisp-tender, about 5 minutes. Stir in the corn, chilies with their liquid, and lime juice. Remove from the heat.

3. Place the cornmeal in a large saucepan over medium heat, and gradually whisk in the milk until well combined. Bring to a boil and whisk in the salt and black pepper. Cook, whisking frequently, until the mixture is slightly thickened, about 4 minutes. Stir in ¾ cup of the cheese just until melted, about 1 minute longer. Stir in the vegetable mixture and the radiatore until well combined.

4. Spoon the pasta mixture into the prepared baking dish, sprinkle the remaining ¼ cup cheese on top, and bake for 20 minutes, or until the pasta is piping hot.

Suggested accompaniments: Watercress and sliced red onion salad with a mustard vinaigrette and, for dessert, reduced-calorie chocolate pudding sprinkled with crumbled coconut macaroons.

FAT: 14G/27%
CALORIES: 471
SATURATED FAT: 6.3G
CARBOHYDRATE: 67G
PROTEIN: 21G
CHOLESTEROL: 35MG
SODIUM: 814MG

TIP

Most of the heat in jalapeños and other fresh chili peppers comes from the volatile oils in the seeds and ribs, so for a tamer dish, omit those parts. When working with the peppers, use rubber gloves to protect your hands and keep them away from your face, especially the eyes. Wash hands thoroughly once you're done.

BAKED RIGATONI WITH VEGETABLES

SERVES: 4
WORKING TIME: 25 MINUTES
TOTAL TIME: 55 MINUTES

12 ounces rigatoni pasta
2 teaspoons olive oil
1 large onion, diced
2 cloves garlic, minced
1 red bell pepper, diced
1 cup broccoli florets
1 cup frozen corn kernels
1½ cups no-salt-added tomato sauce
1 cup part-skim ricotta cheese
½ cup low-fat (1%) cottage cheese
2 tablespoons grated Parmesan cheese
½ teaspoon salt
¼ teaspoon freshly ground black pepper
2 tablespoons chopped fresh parsley

1. Preheat the oven to 350°. In a large pot of boiling water, cook the rigatoni until just tender. Drain well and set aside.

2. Meanwhile, in a large nonstick skillet, heat the oil until hot but not smoking over medium heat. Add the onion and garlic and cook, stirring frequently, until the onion is slightly softened, about 5 minutes. Add the bell pepper, broccoli, and corn and cook until the pepper and broccoli are crisp-tender, about 3 minutes longer. Remove from the heat.

3. In a large bowl, stir together the tomato sauce, ricotta, cottage cheese, and Parmesan. Stir in the vegetable mixture, salt, and black pepper. Add the rigatoni and toss well to combine.

4. Spoon the rigatoni mixture into a 12 x 8-inch baking dish. Cover with foil and bake for 30 minutes, or until the casserole is piping hot. Sprinkle with the parsley and serve.

Suggested accompaniments: Escarole and sliced cucumber salad with a nonfat Italian dressing. Follow with fresh pineapple wedges.

FAT: 10G/17%
CALORIES: 558
SATURATED FAT: 4.2G
CARBOHYDRATE: 91G
PROTEIN: 27G
CHOLESTEROL: 22MG
SODIUM: 548MG

1 6

Who can resist this delicious pasta casserole? The sauce is creamy, but we've trimmed the fat by using part-skim ricotta cheese and low-fat cottage cheese. When you buy broccoli, make sure the florets are tight and green, with no yellow patches. Experiment with other vegetables here as well, including zucchini, cauliflower, peas, yellow squash, and lima beans.

*T*he filling for these manicotti is a combination of ground chicken, ricotta cheese, spinach, and seasonings. In the sauce, we take advantage of jarred roasted red peppers to add robust flavor to the tomatoes. You can assemble the dish early in the day and refrigerate. Allow extra time for baking if taking the dish directly from the refrigerator.

CHICKEN, SPINACH, AND RICOTTA MANICOTTI

SERVES: 4
WORKING TIME: 30 MINUTES
TOTAL TIME: 55 MINUTES

12 manicotti shells

¾ pound skinless, boneless chicken breasts, cut into small pieces

3 scallions, coarsely chopped

Two 10-ounce packages frozen chopped spinach, thawed and squeezed dry

1½ cups part-skim ricotta cheese

½ cup plain dried bread crumbs

1 teaspoon dried marjoram

⅛ teaspoon nutmeg

3 tablespoons grated Parmesan cheese

1 cup canned no-salt-added stewed tomatoes, drained

¼ cup jarred roasted red peppers, rinsed and drained

1½ teaspoons dried basil

¼ teaspoon hot pepper sauce

1. Preheat the oven to 375°. Spray an 11 x 9-inch baking dish with nonstick cooking spray. In a large pot of boiling water, cook the manicotti until just tender. Drain well and rinse under cold water.

2. Meanwhile, in a food processor, process the chicken until coarsely ground. In a medium bowl, combine the ground chicken, scallions, spinach, ricotta, bread crumbs, marjoram, nutmeg, and 2 tablespoons of the Parmesan, stirring to blend thoroughly. Spoon the chicken mixture into a pastry bag with no tip attached (or use a sturdy plastic bag; see tip). Pipe the chicken mixture into the manicotti shells and place them in the prepared baking dish.

3. In a food processor or blender, combine the tomatoes, roasted peppers, basil, and hot pepper sauce and purée until smooth. Spoon the sauce on top of the filled manicotti and cover the baking dish with foil. Bake for 25 to 30 minutes, or until the manicotti are piping hot and firm to the touch. Sprinkle with the remaining 1 tablespoon Parmesan; let sit for 10 minutes before serving.

Helpful hint: You can use the same chicken filling with store-bought won ton wrappers to make ravioli.

Fill a sturdy plastic bag with the chicken mixture. Twist the top of the bag closed, and snip off a bottom corner. Squeezing the top and sides of the bag, pipe the filling into each end of the cooked manicotti.

FAT: 12G/19%
CALORIES: 560
SATURATED FAT: 6G
CARBOHYDRATE: 89G
PROTEIN: 49G
CHOLESTEROL: 81MG
SODIUM: 506MG

OLD-FASHIONED NOODLE PUDDING

SERVES: 4
WORKING TIME: 20 MINUTES
TOTAL TIME: 40 MINUTES

We've converted this very traditional baked noodle pudding, also known as a kugel, by using reduced-fat dairy products: cottage cheese, sour cream, and milk. For added richness and a little texture, we've tossed in a few spoonfuls of chopped pecans. Leftovers would be delicious served cold or at room temperature.

8 ounces wide egg noodles
2 teaspoons vegetable oil
2 large onions, diced
1 Granny Smith apple, cored and diced
1 teaspoon sugar
1½ cups low-fat (1%) cottage cheese
½ cup low-fat (1%) milk
3 tablespoons snipped fresh dill
3 tablespoons coarsely chopped pecans
2 tablespoons light sour cream
2 tablespoons all-purpose flour
1 whole egg
1 egg white, lightly beaten
½ teaspoon salt
¼ teaspoon freshly ground black pepper

1. Heat a large pot of water to boiling, and cook the noodles until just tender. Drain well. Transfer to a large bowl. Meanwhile, preheat the oven to 400°. Spray a 2-quart baking dish with nonstick cooking spray.

2. In a large nonstick skillet, heat the oil until hot but not smoking over medium heat. Add the onions and cook, stirring frequently, until the onions begin to brown, about 5 minutes. Stir in the apple and sugar and cook until the onions are golden brown and the apple is tender, 12 to 15 minutes longer. Remove from the heat and cool slightly.

3. Add the onion and apple mixture to the noodles. Stir in the cottage cheese, milk, dill, pecans, sour cream, flour, egg, egg white, salt, and pepper until well combined. Spoon the noodle mixture into the prepared baking dish and bake for 15 minutes, or until the top is lightly golden.

Suggested accompaniments: Marinated cucumber salad with a parsley vinaigrette. Follow with sliced peaches flavored with ginger, and sautéed with a little brown sugar and lemon juice.

FAT: 12G/24%
CALORIES: 453
SATURATED FAT: 2.7G
CARBOHYDRATE: 63G
PROTEIN: 24G
CHOLESTEROL: 114MG
SODIUM: 678MG

CHEESE-TOPPED BAKED ZITI WITH CHUNKY VEGETABLES

SERVES: 4
WORKING TIME: 20 MINUTES
TOTAL TIME: 1 HOUR

The rich finish for this family-pleasing casserole is a topping of part-skim ricotta cheese, accented with a dusting of Parmesan.

8 ounces ziti pasta

1 large onion, cut into 1-inch chunks

3 cloves garlic, minced

⅔ cup reduced-sodium chicken broth, defatted, or reduced-sodium vegetable broth

2 carrots, cut into ½-inch-thick slices

2 zucchini, halved lengthwise and cut into ½-inch-thick slices

1 yellow bell pepper, cut into ½-inch squares

14½-ounce can no-salt-added stewed tomatoes, chopped with their juices

¾ teaspoon dried oregano

½ teaspoon salt

½ teaspoon freshly ground black pepper

1 cup part-skim ricotta cheese

¼ cup grated Parmesan cheese

1. Preheat the oven to 425°. In a large pot of boiling water, cook the ziti until just tender. Drain well and set aside.

2. Meanwhile, in a Dutch oven, combine the onion, garlic, and ⅓ cup of the broth. Cover and cook over medium heat, stirring occasionally, until the onion is softened, about 7 minutes.

3. Stir in the carrots, zucchini, bell pepper, tomatoes and their juices, the oregano, salt, black pepper, and remaining ⅓ cup broth. Cover again and cook, stirring frequently, until the carrots are crisp-tender, about 7 minutes. Remove from the heat. Stir in the ziti until well combined.

4. Spoon the mixture into an 11 x 7-inch baking dish, cover with foil, and bake for 15 minutes, or until the pasta is piping hot. Uncover, spoon the ricotta on top, sprinkle the Parmesan over, and bake for 12 minutes longer, or until the cheese is lightly browned.

Helpful hints: Use any mix of vegetables according to the season—green beans, broccoli, cauliflower, squash, and so on. Mix the ziti and the cooked vegetables together in the baking dish earlier in the day, and then bake just before serving, allowing a little extra cooking time if transferring the dish directly from the refrigerator to the oven.

FAT: 8G/17%
CALORIES: 401
SATURATED FAT: 4.2G
CARBOHYDRATE: 65G
PROTEIN: 20G
CHOLESTEROL: 23MG
SODIUM: 590MG

MEDITERRANEAN BAKED PASTA

SERVES: 4
WORKING TIME: 20 MINUTES
TOTAL TIME: 50 MINUTES

12 ounces lasagna noodles, broken into fourths

1¾ cups low-fat (1%) cottage cheese

⅔ cup part-skim ricotta cheese

⅔ cup evaporated low-fat or skimmed milk

1 cup canned no-salt-added tomatoes, chopped with their juices

3 tablespoons no-salt-added tomato paste

1 whole egg, lightly beaten

2 egg whites, lightly beaten

2 tablespoons grated Parmesan cheese

1 teaspoon ground cinnamon

½ teaspoon salt

½ teaspoon freshly ground black pepper

1 cup frozen Italian flat green beans

⅓ cup chopped fresh mint

1. Preheat the oven to 350°. Spray an 11 x 7-inch ceramic or glass baking dish with nonstick cooking spray. In a large pot of boiling water, cook the lasagna noodles until tender. Drain well.

2. Meanwhile, in a food processor, combine the cottage cheese, ricotta, and evaporated milk and process until smooth and creamy, about 1 minute. Transfer to a large bowl and stir in the tomatoes, tomato paste, whole egg, egg whites, Parmesan, cinnamon, salt, and pepper. Fold in the green beans and mint. Add the cooked pasta and transfer the mixture to the prepared baking dish. Bake for about 30 minutes, or until set and slightly crisped.

Helpful hint: If fresh mint is not available, try ½ teaspoon dried oregano (another favorite Greek herb) as a substitute.

FAT: 9G/15%
CALORIES: 560
SATURATED FAT: 3.7G
CARBOHYDRATE: 82G
PROTEIN: 37G
CHOLESTEROL: 79MG
SODIUM: 878MG

Greek pastitsio is the inspiration here, but our creamy sauce is far lighter than the original.

FARFALLE WITH BROCCOLI AND TWO CHEESES

SERVES: 4
WORKING TIME: 15 MINUTES
TOTAL TIME: 40 MINUTES

5 cups broccoli florets

8 ounces farfalle (bow-tie) pasta

1 cup low-fat (1%) cottage cheese

3 tablespoons flour

2 cups low-fat (1%) milk

4 ounces smoked Gouda cheese, shredded (about 1 cup)

3 scallions, minced

½ teaspoon dry mustard

½ teaspoon salt

½ teaspoon freshly ground black pepper

1. Preheat the oven to 400°. Spray a 13 x 9-inch baking dish with nonstick cooking spray. Heat a large pot of water to boiling, and cook the broccoli until crisp-tender, about 3 minutes. Reserve the boiling water for the pasta and, with a slotted spoon, transfer the broccoli to a colander. Drain, rinse under cold water, and drain again. Cook the farfalle in the reserved boiling water until just tender. Drain well. Transfer the broccoli and farfalle to a large bowl.

2. Meanwhile, in a blender or food processor, purée the cottage cheese until very smooth, about 1 minute. Set aside.

3. Place the flour in a medium saucepan over medium heat, and gradually whisk in the milk until well combined. Bring to a boil and cook, whisking frequently, until the mixture is slightly thickened, about 3 minutes. Whisk in the cottage cheese purée, ¾ cup of the Gouda, the scallions, mustard, salt, and pepper. Add the cheese mixture to the farfalle and broccoli and toss to combine.

4. Spoon the pasta mixture into the prepared baking dish, sprinkle the remaining ¼ cup Gouda on top, and bake for 20 minutes, or until the top is lightly golden. Spoon the farfalle mixture onto 4 plates and serve.

Suggested accompaniments: Mixed bell pepper salad with an oregano vinaigrette. Follow with whole apples baked in a little red wine and sprinkled with cinnamon.

FAT: 13G/25%
CALORIES: 487
SATURATED FAT: 6.7G
CARBOHYDRATE: 63G
PROTEIN: 32G
CHOLESTEROL: 93MG
SODIUM: 849MG

Our choice for cheese in this soothing, creamy sauce is low-fat cottage cheese, puréed until smooth, and made all the more flavorful by the addition of delightfully assertive smoked Gouda. In a pinch, you could substitute regular Gouda or Cheddar (smoked or not). And instead of the farfalle, you may use penne, ruote, medium rigatoni, or ziti.

Baked ham adds smoky flavor to these spinach-stuffed lasagna rolls. Be sure the ham is cut very thin so there is enough to fill the eight rolls and, for even heating, place the lasagna rolls in the baking dish equally spaced so the sauce will bubble around them. You may fill the rolls earlier in the day and then, shortly before serving, add the tomatoes and sauce and bake.

SPINACH LASAGNA ROLLS

SERVES: 4
WORKING TIME: 25 MINUTES
TOTAL TIME: 50 MINUTES

8 lasagna noodles (8 ounces)

2 teaspoons olive oil

1 medium onion, finely chopped

3 cloves garlic, minced

10-ounce package frozen chopped spinach, thawed and squeezed dry

¾ cup part-skim ricotta cheese

¼ cup grated Parmesan cheese

½ teaspoon salt

¼ teaspoon black pepper

1 egg white, lightly beaten

3 ounces very thinly sliced baked ham, cut into strips

14½-ounce can no-salt-added stewed tomatoes, chopped with their juices

1 can (8 ounces) no-salt-added tomato sauce

3 tablespoons chopped fresh parsley

1. Heat a large pot of water to boiling, and cook the noodles until just tender. Drain. Transfer to a bowl of cold water to prevent sticking. Meanwhile, preheat the oven to 400°. Spray an 11 x 7-inch baking dish with nonstick cooking spray.

2. In a large nonstick skillet, heat the oil until hot but not smoking over low heat. Add the onion and garlic and cook, stirring frequently, until the onion has softened, about 7 minutes. Stir in the spinach and cook until the spinach is heated through, about 4 minutes. Transfer to a large bowl and cool slightly. Stir in the ricotta, Parmesan, salt, pepper, and egg white until well combined.

3. Lay the noodles flat and spread 3 tablespoons of the spinach mixture on top of each (see tip; top photo). Arrange the ham on top of the spinach mixture and tightly roll up each noodle (middle photo). Place the rolls, seam-sides down, in the prepared baking dish (bottom photo).

4. Spoon the tomatoes with their juices and the tomato sauce around the lasagna rolls, cover with foil, and bake for 15 minutes. Uncover and bake for 5 minutes longer, or until the sauce is bubbly and the filling is hot. Place the lasagna rolls on 4 plates, spoon some sauce on top, sprinkle with the parsley, and serve.

Suggested accompaniments: Chilled white wine, and a salad with cherry tomatoes, escarole, and cucumbers in a reduced-fat Italian dressing.

FAT: 11G/22%
CALORIES: 445
SATURATED FAT: 4.4G
CARBOHYDRATE: 63G
PROTEIN: 25G
CHOLESTEROL: 31MG
SODIUM: 846MG

BROCCOLI-MUSHROOM LASAGNA

SERVES: 8
WORKING TIME: 35 MINUTES
TOTAL TIME: 1 HOUR 30 MINUTES

Although this lasagna tastes rich, it's remarkably low in fat since we've used one-percent cottage cheese and reduced-fat cream cheese (Neufchâtel), mixed with grated Parmesan for a flavor boost. If desired, assemble the lasagna a day ahead, cover, and refrigerate until you're ready to bake. Be sure to let the lasagna stand for fifteen minutes before cutting so the slices will be firmer.

20 lasagna noodles

3 cups sliced mushrooms

1 cup shredded carrots

3 cloves garlic, minced

½ teaspoon dried rosemary

Two 10-ounce packages frozen chopped broccoli, thawed and drained

16-ounce can no-salt-added whole tomatoes, drained and coarsely chopped

Two 16-ounce containers low-fat (1%) cottage cheese

3 ounces reduced-fat cream cheese (Neufchâtel)

2 egg whites

¼ cup grated Parmesan cheese

¼ teaspoon white pepper

Two 8-ounce cans no-salt-added tomato sauce

14½-ounce can no-salt-added stewed tomatoes, chopped with their juices

¼ cup no-salt-added tomato paste

1 teaspoon dried basil

8 ounces part-skim mozzarella cheese, shredded (about 2 cups)

1. In a large pot of boiling water, cook the noodles until almost tender. Drain. Transfer to a bowl of cold water to prevent sticking. Meanwhile, spray a large nonstick skillet with nonstick cooking spray, then place over medium-high heat. Add the mushrooms, carrots, garlic, and rosemary and cook, stirring, until the mushrooms are tender, about 5 minutes. Add the broccoli and tomatoes and cook until the liquid evaporates, about 6 minutes. Set aside.

2. Preheat the oven to 400°. In a blender or food processor, purée the cottage cheese, cream cheese, egg whites, 2 tablespoons of the Parmesan, and the pepper until smooth. In a medium bowl, stir together the tomato sauce, stewed tomatoes, tomato paste, and basil.

3. In a 13 x 9-inch baking dish, spread ½ cup of the tomato sauce. Lay 4 lasagna noodles on top, overlapping slightly. Spoon one-third of the cheese purée, then one-third of the vegetables over. Top with 4 noodles and 1½ cups sauce. Sprinkle 1 cup of the mozzarella over. Top with 4 more noodles, another one-third of the purée, and one-third of the vegetables. Top with 4 noodles. Add the remaining purée, vegetables, and noodles. Spoon the remaining sauce over. Cover with foil and bake for 40 minutes. Remove the foil, sprinkle the remaining 1 cup mozzarella and 2 tablespoons Parmesan over, and bake for 15 minutes longer, or until the cheese is melted.

Suggested accompaniment: Fresh fruit cup with vanilla nonfat yogurt.

FAT: 11G/19%
CALORIES: 518
SATURATED FAT: 5.8G
CARBOHYDRATE: 70G
PROTEIN: 37G
CHOLESTEROL: 31MG
SODIUM: 756MG

CREAMY PENNE, BACON, AND VEGETABLE BAKE

SERVES: 4
WORKING TIME: 15 MINUTES
TOTAL TIME: 40 MINUTES

3 cups broccoli florets
2 red bell peppers, diced
8 ounces penne pasta
1½ cups low-fat (1%) cottage cheese
1 cup evaporated skimmed milk
⅔ cup part-skim ricotta cheese
¼ cup plus 2 tablespoons grated Parmesan cheese
2 tablespoons flour
1 egg
¼ cup chopped fresh parsley
½ teaspoon freshly ground black pepper
2 ounces Canadian bacon, diced

1. Preheat the oven to 375°. In a large pot of boiling water, cook the broccoli and bell peppers until crisp-tender, about 2 minutes. Reserve the boiling water for the penne and, with a slotted spoon, transfer the vegetables to a colander to drain. Rinse under cold water and drain again. Cook the penne in the reserved boiling water until just tender. Drain well. Return the penne, broccoli, and bell peppers to the cooking pot and set aside.

2. In a blender or food processor, purée the cottage cheese, evaporated milk, ricotta, ¼ cup of the Parmesan, the flour, and egg until smooth, about 1 minute. Add the parsley and black pepper and purée until well combined. Pour the purée over the penne mixture, add the bacon, and toss well to combine.

3. Spray a 2-quart baking dish with nonstick cooking spray. Spoon the penne mixture into the prepared baking dish, cover with foil, and bake for 15 to 20 minutes, or until the casserole is bubbly and piping hot. Remove the foil, sprinkle the remaining 2 tablespoons Parmesan over, and bake for 4 minutes longer, or until the cheese is lightly golden.

Suggested accompaniments: Tossed green salad with a basil vinaigrette, and assorted reduced-fat cookies with hazelnut coffee for dessert.

FAT: 10G/18%
CALORIES: 511
SATURATED FAT: 4.9G
CARBOHYDRATE: 66G
PROTEIN: 39G
CHOLESTEROL: 85MG
SODIUM: 854MG

This flavorful baked version of spaghetti carbonara captures all the richness of the original, but with much less fat. Low-fat cheeses and lean Canadian bacon are the secrets. You can assemble the casserole several hours ahead and refrigerate it, allowing a little extra baking time for the chilled dish. Buy Parmesan in chunks and store in the freezer, then freshly grate as needed.

The trick that turns this manicotti into a low-fat meal is the substitution of mashed potatoes for some of the cheese in the stuffing. Chopped pork, nonfat ricotta, bread crumbs, egg white, and Parmesan go into the filling as well; fresh basil adds a pesto-like flavor. Serve the manicotti with a light side dish, such as steamed zucchini and summer squash.

BAKED PORK MANICOTTI

SERVES: 4
WORKING TIME: 30 MINUTES
TOTAL TIME: 1 HOUR

½ pound all-purpose potatoes,
peeled and cut into 8 wedges
each

12 manicotti shells (8 ounces)

14½-ounce can no-salt-added
stewed tomatoes

8-ounce can no-salt-added
tomato sauce

¾ cup packed basil leaves,
chopped

¾ teaspoon salt

⅛ teaspoon freshly ground black
pepper

½ pound well-trimmed pork
tenderloin, cut into 1-inch cubes

3 scallions, finely chopped

½ cup fresh bread crumbs (from
1 slice of bread)

1 cup nonfat ricotta cheese

1 egg white

6 tablespoons grated Parmesan
cheese

1. In a large pot of boiling water, cook the potatoes until firm-tender, about 10 minutes. With a slotted spoon, transfer the potatoes to a medium bowl and mash. Bring the water back to a boil, add the manicotti shells, and cook until almost tender. Drain, rinse under cold water, and drain again.

2. Meanwhile, preheat the oven to 425°. Spray a 13 x 9-inch baking dish with nonstick cooking spray. In a medium bowl, combine the stewed tomatoes, tomato sauce, ¼ cup of the basil, ¼ teaspoon of the salt, and the pepper. Spoon one-third of the sauce into the prepared baking dish.

3. Place the pork, scallions, and the remaining ½ cup basil in a food processor and process until the mixture is the size of small peas. Add the mashed potatoes, bread crumbs, ricotta, egg white, 4 tablespoons of the Parmesan, and the remaining ½ teaspoon salt and process until just combined. Pipe the mixture into the manicotti shells with a pastry bag or a sturdy plastic bag (see tip).

4. Arrange the manicotti in the baking dish and spoon the remaining sauce on top. Cover tightly with foil and bake for 30 minutes, or until heated through. Divide the manicotti among 4 plates, sprinkle the remaining 2 tablespoons Parmesan over, and serve.

TIP

If you don't have a pastry bag, use a heavy-duty plastic bag to fill the manicotti. Spoon the mixture into the bag, then snip off one of the lower corners. Place the open tip in the pasta shell and squeeze the bag to pipe in the filling.

FAT: 6G/11%
CALORIES: 477
SATURATED FAT: 2.3G
CARBOHYDRATE: 68G
PROTEIN: 35G
CHOLESTEROL: 43MG
SODIUM: 731MG

BAKED CINCINNATI CHILI

SERVES: 4
WORKING TIME: 25 MINUTES
TOTAL TIME: 50 MINUTES

Ohio's famous chili is unique: Seasoned with both sweet and hot spices, it's served over spaghetti and topped with Cheddar.

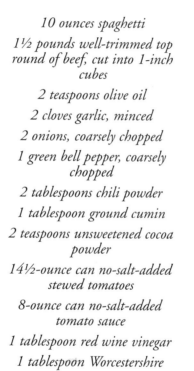

10 ounces spaghetti

1½ pounds well-trimmed top round of beef, cut into 1-inch cubes

2 teaspoons olive oil

2 cloves garlic, minced

2 onions, coarsely chopped

1 green bell pepper, coarsely chopped

2 tablespoons chili powder

1 tablespoon ground cumin

2 teaspoons unsweetened cocoa powder

14½-ounce can no-salt-added stewed tomatoes

8-ounce can no-salt-added tomato sauce

1 tablespoon red wine vinegar

1 tablespoon Worcestershire sauce

¾ teaspoon salt

½ teaspoon hot pepper sauce

¼ cup grated Cheddar cheese

1. In a large pot of boiling water, cook the spaghetti until just tender. Drain well.

2. Preheat the oven to 400°. Spray a shallow 3-quart casserole with nonstick cooking spray. Place the beef in a food processor and process until the size of small peas.

3. Meanwhile, in a large nonstick skillet, heat the oil until hot but not smoking over medium heat. Add the garlic, onions, and bell pepper and cook, stirring, until the onion is tender, about 8 minutes. Stir in the chili powder, cumin, and cocoa powder and cook until fragrant, about 1 minute. Stir in the stewed tomatoes, tomato sauce, vinegar, Worcestershire sauce, salt, and hot pepper sauce; bring to a simmer, stir in the chopped beef, and cook until heated through, about 2 minutes.

4. In a large bowl, combine the beef mixture and spaghetti and add to the prepared casserole. Cover with foil and bake for 20 minutes, or until the chili is piping hot. Remove the foil, sprinkle the cheese over, and bake 5 minutes, or until the cheese is melted. Divide among 4 plates and serve.

Helpful hint: You can prepare the beef mixture up to one day in advance and refrigerate it in a covered container. Reheat the beef mixture while you cook the spaghetti.

FAT: 13G/18%
CALORIES: 639
SATURATED FAT: 4G
CARBOHYDRATE: 77G
PROTEIN: 54G
CHOLESTEROL: 105MG
SODIUM: 681MG

OLD-FASHIONED CHICKEN NOODLE CASSEROLE

SERVES: 4
WORKING TIME: 40 MINUTES
TOTAL TIME: 1 HOUR

8 ounces wide egg noodles

13¾-ounce can reduced-sodium chicken broth, defatted

3 carrots, quartered lengthwise and sliced

2 shallots or 1 small onion, finely chopped

1 tablespoon no-salt-added tomato paste

1 teaspoon paprika

¾ teaspoon dried thyme

¾ pound skinless, boneless chicken breasts, cut into 1-inch chunks

½ pound green beans, cut into 2-inch pieces

¼ cup flour

½ cup reduced-fat sour cream

¼ teaspoon salt

¼ cup plain dried bread crumbs

1. Preheat the oven to 375°. In a large pot of boiling water, cook the noodles until just tender. Drain well. Spray an 11 x 7-inch baking dish with nonstick cooking spray. Spoon the noodles into the prepared baking dish.

2. Meanwhile, in a medium saucepan, combine the broth, carrots, shallots, tomato paste, paprika, and thyme. Bring to a boil over medium heat. Add the chicken and green beans, reduce to a simmer, and cook until the beans are crisp-tender and the chicken is cooked through, about 5 minutes.

3. In a jar with a tight-fitting lid, combine the flour and ⅓ cup of water and shake until smooth. Whisk the flour mixture into the chicken mixture and cook until slightly thickened, about 2 minutes. Remove the saucepan from the heat and stir in the sour cream and salt. Add the chicken mixture to the noodles, stirring to combine. Sprinkle the bread crumbs on top and spray the bread crumbs with nonstick cooking spray. Cover the dish loosely with foil and bake for 20 minutes. Uncover, and bake for 7 minutes, or until the top is golden and the noodle mixture is bubbling hot.

Helpful hints: Don't use nonfat sour cream instead of the reduced-fat; the nonfat product can turn rubbery when cooked. The casserole can be assembled earlier in the day, refrigerated, and reheated in the oven just before serving, adding several minutes to the baking time.

FAT: 8G/16%
CALORIES: 474
SATURATED FAT: 2.9G
CARBOHYDRATE: 65G
PROTEIN: 35G
CHOLESTEROL: 113MG
SODIUM: 584MG

This is an easy mid-week dinner—chicken, a creamy sauce, vegetables, and noodles, all in one dish.

Cider vinegar adds a nice bite to the lean lamb filling, while low-fat cottage cheese and skim milk thickened with a little flour create the rich-tasting, cheesy topping in this Greek favorite. A final dusting of Parmesan followed by a quick run under the broiler imparts an appetizing, golden glow. Small macaroni, bow ties, or ziti may be substituted for the shells.

PASTITSIO

SERVES: 8
WORKING TIME: 30 MINUTES
TOTAL TIME: 1 HOUR 10 MINUTES

16 ounces small pasta shells

2 teaspoons olive oil

1 medium onion, chopped

2 cloves garlic, minced

1 pound lean ground lamb
(see tip)

¾ pound eggplant, peeled and
cut into ½-inch cubes

¼ cup dark raisins or currants

1½ teaspoons dried oregano

¾ teaspoon salt

½ teaspoon cinnamon

Two 8-ounce cans no-salt-added
tomato sauce

2 teaspoons cider vinegar

1 cup skim milk

3 tablespoons flour

1½ cups low-fat (1%) cottage
cheese

¼ teaspoon white pepper

¼ cup grated Parmesan cheese

1 tablespoon chopped fresh
parsley

1. In a large pot of boiling water, cook the pasta until just tender. Drain well and set aside. Meanwhile, in a large nonstick skillet, heat the oil until hot but not smoking over medium heat. Add the onion and garlic and cook, stirring frequently, until the onion is softened, about 7 minutes. Add the lamb, eggplant, raisins, 1¼ teaspoons of the oregano, the salt, and cinnamon and cook, stirring frequently, until the lamb is browned, about 12 minutes. Remove from the heat and stir in the tomato sauce and vinegar. Set aside.

2. Meanwhile, preheat the oven to 400°. In a blender or food processor, purée the milk and flour until smooth. Transfer to a small saucepan, bring to a boil over medium heat, and cook, whisking constantly, until the mixture is slightly thickened, about 4 minutes. Remove from the heat. In a blender or food processor, purée the cottage cheese, pepper, and remaining ¼ teaspoon oregano until smooth. Stir the cheese purée into the milk mixture until combined.

3. Spray a 3-quart baking dish with nonstick cooking spray. Spoon half of the pasta into the prepared dish and top with half of the lamb mixture. Repeat with the remaining pasta and lamb. Spoon the white sauce over, cover with foil, and bake for 30 minutes. Preheat the broiler. Remove the foil, sprinkle the Parmesan over, and broil for 3 minutes, or until golden. Sprinkle with the parsley and serve.

Suggested accompaniment: Strawberries rolled in confectioners' sugar.

FAT: 8G/16%
CALORIES: 421
SATURATED FAT: 2.4G
CARBOHYDRATE: 60G
PROTEIN: 28G
CHOLESTEROL: 42MG
SODIUM: 500MG

TIP

To grind your own lamb at home, purchase a pound of lean, boneless lamb. Cut into ¼-inch cubes and place in a food processor. Process the lamb with on-off pulses until finely ground, scraping down the sides of the bowl with a rubber spatula as needed.

SOUTHWESTERN SHELLS WITH CHICKEN AND CORN

SERVES: 6
WORKING TIME: 20 MINUTES
TOTAL TIME: 40 MINUTES

This hearty dish is a real showstopper, packed with tender chunks of chicken, plump corn, and the bite of salsa and chilies, all in a silky cheese sauce.

Using pre-shredded cheese makes this dish even easier to prepare.

You may adjust the heat in this casserole to suit your taste, depending on your choice of hot or mild salsa.

12 ounces medium pasta shells

½ pound skinless, boneless chicken breasts, cut into ½-inch pieces

2 tablespoons flour

2 teaspoons vegetable oil

12-ounce can evaporated skimmed milk

8 ounces shredded Monterey Jack cheese (about 2 cups)

1½ cups frozen corn kernels

⅔ cup chopped scallions

½ cup good-quality prepared thick and chunky salsa

4-ounce can chopped mild green chilies

¼ teaspoon salt

¼ teaspoon freshly ground black pepper

1. Preheat the oven to 375°. Spray a 2½-quart baking dish with non-stick cooking spray. Heat a large pot of water to boiling, and cook the pasta shells until just tender. Drain well, rinse under cold water, and drain again. Transfer to a large bowl.

2. Meanwhile, in a medium bowl, combine the chicken and flour and toss to coat. In a large nonstick skillet, heat the oil until hot but not smoking over medium-high heat. Add the chicken and cook, stirring frequently, until browned on all sides, about 3 minutes.

3. Reduce the heat to medium-low, very gradually add the evaporated milk, and cook, stirring constantly, until the milk begins to simmer, about 3 minutes. Continue to cook, stirring occasionally, until the mixture is slightly reduced, about 1 minute longer. Remove from the heat and stir in 1 cup of the cheese, the corn, scallions, salsa, green chilies with their liquid, salt, and pepper. Add the chicken mixture to the pasta shells and toss well to combine.

4. Spoon the pasta mixture into the prepared baking dish, sprinkle the remaining 1 cup cheese on top, and bake for 20 to 25 minutes, or until the top is golden brown. Spoon the pasta mixture onto 6 plates and serve.

Suggested accompaniments: Zucchini salad dressed with a lime vinaigrette, and a dessert of warmed flour tortillas filled with poached apples and raisins sweetened with a little apricot jam.

FAT: 15G/26%
CALORIES: 517
SATURATED FAT: 7.2G
CARBOHYDRATE: 64G
PROTEIN: 32G
CHOLESTEROL: 64MG
SODIUM: 741MG

Baked Fusilli with Mushroom Sauce

SERVES: 4
WORKING TIME: 25 MINUTES
TOTAL TIME: 40 MINUTES

10 ounces short fusilli pasta

2 teaspoons olive oil

6 shallots, minced

3 cloves garlic, minced

1 red bell pepper, diced

1 pound mushrooms, thinly sliced

½ pound fresh shiitake mushrooms, trimmed and thinly sliced

3 tablespoons brandy

3 tablespoons flour

2 cups reduced-sodium chicken broth, defatted

½ teaspoon dried rosemary

¼ teaspoon salt

¼ teaspoon freshly ground black pepper

⅓ cup light sour cream

2 tablespoons chopped fresh parsley

2 tablespoons grated Parmesan cheese

1. Preheat the oven to 450°. Spray an 11 x 7-inch baking dish with nonstick cooking spray. Heat a large pot of water to boiling, and cook the fusilli until just tender. Drain well. Transfer to a large bowl.

2. Meanwhile, in a large nonstick skillet, heat the oil until hot but not smoking over medium heat. Add the shallots and garlic and cook, stirring frequently, until softened, about 4 minutes. Add the bell pepper and cook, stirring frequently, until softened, about 3 minutes. Stir in all the mushrooms. Cover and cook, stirring occasionally, until the mushrooms are tender, about 5 minutes.

3. Stir in the brandy and cook, uncovered, until the liquid has evaporated, about 1 minute. Stir in the flour until well combined. Gradually stir in the broth. Add the rosemary, salt, and black pepper and cook until the mixture is slightly thickened, about 2 minutes longer. Remove from the heat and stir in the sour cream and parsley. Add the mushroom mixture to the fusilli and toss to combine.

4. Spoon the pasta mixture into the prepared baking dish, sprinkle the Parmesan on top, and bake for 15 minutes, or until the top is lightly golden. Spoon the fusilli mixture onto 4 plates and serve.

Suggested accompaniments: Sliced tomatoes with chopped parsley, mixed lettuce salad with a white wine vinaigrette, and chunky applesauce sprinkled with cinnamon afterward.

FAT: 8G/16%
CALORIES: 447
SATURATED FAT: 2.3G
CARBOHYDRATE: 72G
PROTEIN: 18G
CHOLESTEROL: 9MG
SODIUM: 519MG

A little brandy gives our mushroom sauce wonderful depth of flavor—the alcohol evaporates during cooking. For extra richness, we've mixed regular white mushrooms with full-flavored shiitakes, a mushroom originally from the Far East now being cultivated in this country. If shiitakes are unavailable, just toss in another half pound of regular mushrooms.

First printing. Printed in U.S.A.

TIME-LIFE is a trademark of Time Warner Inc. U.S.A.

ISBN 0-7370-0002-3

CIP data available upon application.
Librarian, Time-Life Books
2000 Duke Street
Alexandria, VA 22314

PASTA LIGHT

Over 200 Great Taste - Low Fat Pasta Recipes

TIME®
LIFE
BOOKS

ALEXANDRIA, VIRGINIA

HEARTY MACARONI AND CHEESE

SERVES: 6
WORKING TIME: 15 MINUTES
TOTAL TIME: 45 MINUTES

Low-fat cottage cheese and low-fat milk transform this supper-round-the-kitchen-table favorite into a good nutritional choice. To make mealtime easier, you may assemble the dish earlier in the day and refrigerate; allow a little extra baking time if taking directly from the refrigerator. For a browner top, run the baked casserole under the broiler for two to three minutes.

12 ounces elbow macaroni

1½ cups low-fat (1%) cottage cheese

1 tablespoon all-purpose flour

1½ cups low-fat (1%) milk

½ teaspoon salt

¼ teaspoon freshly ground black pepper

¼ teaspoon cayenne pepper

6 ounces Cheddar cheese, shredded (about 1½ cups)

⅔ cup thinly sliced scallions

2 tablespoons Dijon mustard

2 tablespoons plain dried bread crumbs

1 teaspoon vegetable oil

1. Preheat the oven to 375°. Spray a shallow 1½-quart baking dish with nonstick cooking spray. Heat a large pot of water to boiling, and cook the macaroni until just tender. Drain well. Transfer to a large bowl.

2. Meanwhile, in a blender or food processor, purée the cottage cheese until smooth, about 1 minute. Set aside.

3. Place the flour in a large saucepan over medium heat, and gradually whisk in the milk. Bring to a boil and whisk in the salt, pepper, and cayenne. Cook, whisking constantly, until the mixture is slightly thickened, about 4 minutes. Whisk in the cottage cheese purée, 1¼ cups of the Cheddar, the scallions, and mustard until well combined. Cook, whisking constantly, just until the Cheddar has melted, about 1 minute longer. Add the cheese mixture to the macaroni and toss to combine.

4. Spoon the macaroni mixture into the prepared baking dish and sprinkle the remaining ¼ cup Cheddar on top. Sprinkle the bread crumbs over the cheese, drizzle the oil over, and bake for 25 minutes, or until the top is crusty and lightly browned.

Suggested accompaniments: Steamed asparagus with diced red bell pepper in a dill vinaigrette. For dessert, apricot halves broiled with a dollop of berry preserves and garnished with toasted sliced almonds.

FAT: 13G/28%
CALORIES: 421
SATURATED FAT: 7G
CARBOHYDRATE: 51G
PROTEIN: 24G
CHOLESTEROL: 34MG
SODIUM: 763MG

Roasted Vegetable Lasagna

SERVES: 4
WORKING TIME: 30 MINUTES
TOTAL TIME: 1 HOUR

The smoky succulence of roasted bell peppers and two kinds of summer squash give this meatless lasagna great depth of flavor. In warm weather, you could grill the vegetables over an outdoor fire. Placing the cooked lasagna noodles in a bowl of cold water keeps them from sticking together and tearing—saving wear and tear on the cook's temper as well.

9 lasagna noodles (9 ounces)

⅔ cup reduced-sodium chicken broth, defatted

3 tablespoons red wine vinegar

3 tablespoons no-salt-added tomato paste

¾ teaspoon dried oregano

½ teaspoon salt

¼ teaspoon freshly ground black pepper

2 zucchini, cut lengthwise into ¼-inch-thick slices

2 yellow summer squash, cut lengthwise into ¼-inch-thick slices

2 red bell peppers, cut into 1-inch-wide strips

Two 8-ounce cans no-salt-added tomato sauce

1½ cups shredded part-skim mozzarella cheese (6 ounces)

1. In a large pot of boiling water, cook the noodles until just tender. Drain well and transfer to a large bowl of cold water.

2. Preheat the broiler. In a large bowl, combine ⅓ cup of the broth, the vinegar, 1 tablespoon of the tomato paste, ¼ teaspoon of the oregano, ¼ teaspoon of the salt, and the black pepper. Add the zucchini and squash, stirring to combine. Place the zucchini, squash, and bell peppers on the broiler rack and broil 6 inches from the heat, turning occasionally, for 9 minutes, or until the zucchini and squash are tender and the bell pepper skins are blackened. When cool enough to handle, peel the pepper strips.

3. Preheat the oven to 375°. Spray an 11 x 7-inch baking dish with nonstick cooking spray. In a large bowl, combine the tomato sauce and the remaining ⅓ cup broth, 2 tablespoons tomato paste, ½ teaspoon oregano, and ¼ teaspoon salt.

4. Spoon 2 tablespoons of the tomato sauce onto the bottom of the baking dish. Make 2 layers, using the following order of ingredients: 3 noodles (the noodles will come up the ends of the baking dish), half of the vegetables, 1 cup of the sauce, ½ cup of the cheese. Make a final layer: 3 noodles, the remaining sauce, and the remaining cheese. Bake the lasagna for 20 minutes, or until bubbling hot. Let stand for 5 minutes, divide among 4 bowls, and serve.

FAT: 9G/19%
CALORIES: 439
SATURATED FAT: 4.5G
CARBOHYDRATE: 69G
PROTEIN: 23G
CHOLESTEROL: 25MG
SODIUM: 622MG

COUSCOUS-STUFFED PEPPER HALVES

SERVES: 4
WORKING TIME: 20 MINUTES
TOTAL TIME: 45 MINUTES

It's a particular pleasure to serve these stuffed peppers because the filling is so easy to prepare. Instead of rice, red and green bell peppers are filled with couscous, a tiny pasta that requires just 5 minutes of steeping. Raisins, shredded carrots, and cubes of mozzarella are mixed into the couscous. Tender leaf lettuce tossed with sweet red onions would go well with this dish.

2 red bell peppers, stemmed and halved lengthwise

2 green bell peppers, stemmed and halved lengthwise

4 cloves garlic, minced

2 carrots, shredded

¾ teaspoon salt

½ teaspoon ground ginger

1½ cups couscous

⅓ cup raisins

6 ounces part-skim mozzarella cheese, cut into ½-inch cubes

14½-ounce can no-salt-added stewed tomatoes, chopped with their juices

8-ounce can no-salt-added tomato sauce

¼ cup chopped fresh mint or basil

1. In a large pot of boiling water, cook the bell peppers for 3 minutes to blanch. Drain.

2. Preheat the oven to 375°. In a medium saucepan, bring 3 cups of water to a boil. Add the garlic, carrots, salt, and ginger and boil for 1 minute. Add the couscous, remove from the heat, cover, and let stand until tender, about 5 minutes. Stir in the raisins and mozzarella and set aside.

3. In a 13 x 9-inch glass baking dish, combine the stewed tomatoes, tomato sauce, and mint. Add the bell peppers, cut-sides up, and spoon in the couscous filling. Cover with foil and bake for about 20 minutes, or until the peppers are tender and the sauce is piping hot. Divide the pepper halves among 4 plates, spoon the tomato sauce over, and serve.

Helpful hint: To prepare the bell peppers for stuffing, use a paring knife to cut around the stem of each pepper. Gently remove the stems and cut the peppers in half. Discard the seeds and ribs.

FAT: 8G/14%
CALORIES: 506
SATURATED FAT: 4.4G
CARBOHYDRATE: 88G
PROTEIN: 23G
CHOLESTEROL: 25MG
SODIUM: 669MG

WAGON WHEELS WITH SPINACH-BASIL SAUCE

SERVES: 4
WORKING TIME: 30 MINUTES
TOTAL TIME: 50 MINUTES

Whenever luxurious bunches of basil are available—that's the ideal time to prepare this recipe. The wagon wheels add a whimsical touch, but fusilli, rigatoni, or ziti would be equally tasty. We scatter pine nuts over the top for crunch and flavor, but because of their high fat content, we use them sparingly. Store the pine nuts in the freezer for up to six months.

1 red bell pepper, diced

8 ounces ruote (wagon wheel) pasta

2 tablespoons flour

2½ cups low-fat (1%) milk

½ cup chopped fresh basil

4 cloves garlic, minced

¼ teaspoon cayenne pepper

10-ounce package frozen chopped spinach, thawed and squeezed dry

1 large tomato, halved, seeded, and coarsely chopped

1 cup grated Parmesan cheese

2 tablespoons pine nuts

3 ounces part-skim mozzarella cheese, shredded (about ¾ cup)

2 tablespoons plain dried bread crumbs

1. In a large pot of boiling water, cook the bell pepper until just crisp-tender, about 2 minutes. Reserve the boiling water for the ruote and, with a slotted spoon, transfer the pepper to a colander to drain. Cook the ruote in the reserved boiling water until just tender. Drain well. Return the ruote and bell pepper to the cooking pot and set aside.

2. Meanwhile, preheat the oven to 375°. Place the flour in a large saucepan over medium heat, and gradually whisk in the milk. Bring to a boil and cook, whisking frequently, until the mixture is slightly thickened, about 5 minutes.

3. Whisk in the basil, garlic, and cayenne and cook until the flavors have blended, about 4 minutes longer. Remove from the heat and stir in the spinach, tomato, and Parmesan. Pour the spinach sauce over the ruote mixture and toss well to combine.

4. Spray a 2-quart baking dish with nonstick cooking spray. Spoon the ruote mixture into the prepared baking dish. Scatter the pine nuts over, cover with foil, and bake for 15 minutes, or until the casserole is piping hot. Remove the foil, sprinkle the mozzarella over, and dust with the bread crumbs. Bake for 5 minutes longer, or until the the cheese is melted and the crumbs are golden.

Suggested accompaniment: Plum halves drizzled with honey and broiled.

FAT: 15G/26%
CALORIES: 512
SATURATED FAT: 7.5G
CARBOHYDRATE: 65G
PROTEIN: 31G
CHOLESTEROL: 34MG
SODIUM: 639MG

CHICKEN TETRAZZINI

SERVES: 4
WORKING TIME: 20 MINUTES
TOTAL TIME: 35 MINUTES

In this classic baked dish with a light mushroom cream sauce and browned chicken strips, we've added almonds for flavor and crunch.

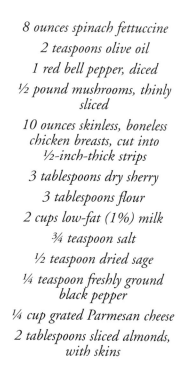

8 ounces spinach fettuccine

2 teaspoons olive oil

1 red bell pepper, diced

½ pound mushrooms, thinly sliced

10 ounces skinless, boneless chicken breasts, cut into ½-inch-thick strips

3 tablespoons dry sherry

3 tablespoons flour

2 cups low-fat (1%) milk

¾ teaspoon salt

½ teaspoon dried sage

¼ teaspoon freshly ground black pepper

¼ cup grated Parmesan cheese

2 tablespoons sliced almonds, with skins

1. Heat a large pot of water to boiling, and cook the fettuccine until just tender. Drain well. Transfer to a large bowl. Meanwhile, preheat the oven to 425°. Spray an 11 x 7-inch baking dish with nonstick cooking spray.

2. In a large nonstick skillet, heat the oil until hot but not smoking over medium heat. Add the bell pepper and cook, stirring frequently, until almost tender, about 5 minutes. Stir in the mushrooms and cook until the mushrooms are tender, about 5 minutes. Add the chicken and cook, stirring frequently, until the chicken is lightly browned, about 3 minutes.

3. Add the sherry and cook until the liquid has almost evaporated, about 2 minutes. Stir in the flour until well combined. Gradually add the milk. Cook, stirring frequently, until the mixture is slightly thickened and the chicken is cooked through, about 2 minutes longer. Stir in the salt, sage, black pepper, and 2 tablespoons of the Parmesan. Add the chicken mixture to the fettuccine and toss well to combine.

4. Spoon the pasta mixture into the prepared baking dish, sprinkle the almonds and remaining 2 tablespoons Parmesan on top, and bake for 15 minutes, or until the top is lightly crisped.

Suggested accompaniments: Cauliflower salad with a red wine vinaigrette, and halved red grapes topped with vanilla nonfat yogurt for dessert.

FAT: 11G/21%
CALORIES: 465
SATURATED FAT: 3G
CARBOHYDRATE: 56G
PROTEIN: 33G
CHOLESTEROL: 104MG
SODIUM: 657MG

HOME-STYLE BAKED ZITI

SERVES: 8
WORKING TIME: 30 MINUTES
TOTAL TIME: 55 MINUTES

12 ounces ziti
2 teaspoons olive oil
1 large onion, minced
3 cloves garlic, minced
2 carrots, minced
1 rib celery, minced
6 ounces extra-lean ground beef
4 ounces lean ground pork
½ cup dry white wine
2 tablespoons flour
½ cup low-fat (1%) milk
Three 8-ounce cans no-salt-added tomato sauce
¾ teaspoon dried oregano
½ teaspoon dried rosemary
½ teaspoon salt
¼ teaspoon freshly ground black pepper
4 ounces shredded part-skim mozzarella cheese (about 1 cup)
¼ cup grated Parmesan cheese

1. Heat a large pot of water to boiling, and cook the ziti until just tender. Drain well. Transfer to a large bowl. Meanwhile, in a large nonstick skillet, heat the oil until hot but not smoking over medium heat. Add the onion and garlic and cook, stirring frequently, until the onion has softened, about 7 minutes. Add the carrots and celery and cook until the vegetables have softened, about 5 minutes longer.

2. Preheat the oven to 400°. Spray a shallow 3-quart baking dish with nonstick cooking spray. Stir the beef and pork into the vegetable mixture and cook, stirring frequently, until no longer pink, about 4 minutes. Add the wine and cook until the liquid has almost evaporated, about 5 minutes longer. Stir in the flour until well combined. Gradually stir in the milk and cook until the mixture is slightly thickened, about 4 minutes. Stir in the tomato sauce, oregano, rosemary, salt, and pepper and cook until the flavors have blended, about 4 minutes longer. Add the meat mixture to the ziti and toss well to combine.

3. Spoon the ziti mixture into the prepared baking dish and bake for 10 minutes. Sprinkle the mozzarella and Parmesan on top and bake for 5 minutes longer, or until the cheese has melted and the pasta is piping hot.

Suggested accompaniments: Crusty peasant bread, and a fresh fruit cup.

FAT: 11G/27%
CALORIES: 365
SATURATED FAT: 4.2G
CARBOHYDRATE: 46G
PROTEIN: 19G
CHOLESTEROL: 34MG
SODIUM: 314MG

This tasty ziti benefits from two kinds of ground meat—it would also be delicious made with all ground beef.

Chopped fresh mint and several colorful vegetables perk up the filling of this all-time pasta winner. If fresh mint is not available, you may substitute two teaspoons of dried. Stuffed shells are a good choice for a party because they can be prepared a day in advance. Refrigerate the shells and sauce separately, and then assemble and bake as directed.

SAVORY STUFFED SHELLS

SERVES: 4
WORKING TIME: 20 MINUTES
TOTAL TIME: 50 MINUTES

*24 large pasta shells
(10 ounces)*

2 teaspoons olive oil

2 cloves garlic, minced

1 red bell pepper, finely diced

1 carrot, finely chopped

*10-ounce package frozen
chopped spinach, thawed and
squeezed dry*

¼ cup chopped fresh mint

1 cup part-skim ricotta cheese

*1 cup low-fat (1%) cottage
cheese*

½ teaspoon sugar

½ teaspoon salt

*½ teaspoon freshly ground
black pepper*

*14½-ounce can stewed
tomatoes, chopped with their
juices*

*Two 8-ounce cans no-salt-
added tomato sauce*

*2 tablespoons no-salt-added
tomato paste*

1. Heat a large pot of water to boiling, and cook the pasta shells until just tender. Drain well, rinse under cold water, and drain again. Meanwhile, preheat the oven to 400°.

2. In a large nonstick skillet, heat the oil until hot but not smoking over medium heat. Add the garlic and cook, stirring frequently, until fragrant, about 1 minute. Stir in the bell pepper and carrot and cook, stirring occasionally, until the vegetables have softened, about 5 minutes. Stir in the spinach and mint and cook until the spinach is heated through, about 3 minutes longer. Transfer to a large bowl and cool slightly. Stir in the ricotta, cottage cheese, sugar, salt, and black pepper.

3. In a 13 x 9-inch baking dish, stir together the stewed tomatoes with their juices, tomato sauce, and tomato paste. Spoon the cheese mixture into a pastry bag with no tip attached (or use a sturdy plastic bag, see tip). Pipe the cheese mixture into the shells and place the shells on top of the sauce in the baking dish.

4. Spoon some of the sauce over the shells, cover with foil, and bake for 20 minutes. Uncover and bake for 10 minutes longer, or until the shells are piping hot. Place the stuffed shells in 4 shallow bowls, spoon some sauce on top, and serve.

Suggested accompaniments: A green salad with mushrooms in a balsamic vinaigrette. For dessert, mixed melon balls drizzled with honey.

FAT: 10G/17%
CALORIES: 517
SATURATED FAT: 3.9G
CARBOHYDRATE: 81G
PROTEIN: 28G
CHOLESTEROL: 21MG
SODIUM: 935MG

TIP

If you don't own a pastry bag, spoon the filling into a large, sturdy plastic bag. Twist the top of the bag closed, and snip off one bottom corner with scissors. Squeezing the bag gently, pipe the filling evenly into the pasta shells.

BAKED MANICOTTI

SERVES: 4
WORKING TIME: 35 MINUTES
TOTAL TIME: 55 MINUTES

8 manicotti shells (5 ounces)

19-ounce can chick-peas, rinsed and drained

1½ cups jarred roasted red peppers, rinsed and drained

3 cloves garlic, peeled

3 tablespoons plain dried bread crumbs

2 tablespoons whole unblanched almonds

1 tablespoon no-salt-added tomato paste

1½ teaspoons ground cumin

¾ teaspoon dried oregano

½ teaspoon salt

¼ teaspoon cayenne pepper

14½-ounce can no-salt-added stewed tomatoes

8-ounce can no-salt-added tomato sauce

¾ teaspoon ground coriander

1 cup shredded part-skim mozzarella cheese (4 ounces)

1 tablespoon chopped fresh parsley (optional)

1. In a large pot of boiling water, cook the manicotti until just tender. Drain well.

2. Preheat the oven to 425°. In a food processor, combine the chick-peas, roasted peppers, garlic, bread crumbs, almonds, tomato paste, cumin, oregano, salt, and cayenne and process until almost smooth but with some texture.

3. In an 11 x 7-inch glass baking dish, combine the stewed tomatoes, the tomato sauce, and coriander. Spoon the chick-pea mixture into a pastry bag with no tip attached. Pipe the chick-pea mixture into the cooked manicotti shells. Transfer the filled shells to the baking dish and spoon some of the sauce over. Cover with foil and bake for 20 minutes, or until the manicotti are piping hot and the sauce is bubbly. Uncover, sprinkle the mozzarella over, and bake for about 4 minutes, or until the cheese is melted. Divide among 4 plates, sprinkle the parsley over, and serve.

Helpful hint: Instead of using a pastry bag, you can fill a sturdy plastic bag with the filling, snip off one of the bottom corners, and pipe the filling into the manicotti shells.

FAT: 10G/22%
CALORIES: 415
SATURATED FAT: 3.3G
CARBOHYDRATE: 62G
PROTEIN: 20G
CHOLESTEROL: 16MG
SODIUM: 744MG

Instead of a fat-laden filling of meat or cheese (or both), these pasta tubes are stuffed with a robust mixture of chick-peas, roasted peppers, bread crumbs, almonds, and tomato paste. The manicotti are baked atop coriander-scented tomato sauce and crowned with part-skim mozzarella. Serve the pasta with sautéed zucchini and red onions, and a lettuce-and-radish salad.

POULTRY SAUCES

Left, Garlic Chicken Sauce.
Above, Chunky Chicken and Vegetable Sauce.

SPAGHETTI CACCIATORE

SERVES: 4
WORKING TIME: 25 MINUTES
TOTAL TIME: 30 MINUTES

2 tablespoons olive oil

1 ounce Canadian bacon, finely chopped

6 ounces skinless, boneless chicken breasts, cut into ½-inch chunks

1 large onion, minced

4 cloves garlic, minced

¼ pound mushrooms, thinly sliced

¼ pound fresh shiitake mushrooms, trimmed and thinly sliced

2 tablespoons brandy

2½ cups canned crushed tomatoes

1 teaspoon dried rosemary

½ teaspoon freshly ground black pepper

3 tablespoons chopped fresh parsley

10 ounces spaghetti

1. In a large nonstick skillet, heat 2 teaspoons of the oil until hot but not smoking over medium heat. Add the bacon and cook, stirring frequently, until lightly browned, about 4 minutes. With a slotted spoon, transfer the bacon to a plate. In the same pan, heat 1 tablespoon oil until hot but not smoking over medium heat. Add the chicken and cook, stirring frequently, until golden brown, about 4 minutes. With a slotted spoon, transfer the chicken to the plate with the bacon.

2. Start heating a large pot of water to boiling for the pasta. In the same skillet, heat the remaining 1 teaspoon oil until hot but not smoking over medium heat. Add the onion and garlic and cook, stirring frequently, until the onion begins to brown, about 7 minutes. Add the mushrooms and cook until the mushrooms begin to soften, about 2 minutes. Add the brandy, increase the heat to high, and cook until the liquid has evaporated, about 1 minute. Add the tomatoes, rosemary, and pepper and cook until slightly thickened, about 5 minutes. Add the chicken, bacon, and parsley and cook until the chicken is cooked through, about 2 minutes longer.

3. Meanwhile, cook the spaghetti in the boiling water until just tender. Drain well. Transfer the chicken mixture to a large bowl, add the spaghetti, and toss to combine. Spoon the spaghetti cacciatore onto 4 plates and serve.

Suggested accompaniment: Escarole salad with a lemon vinaigrette.

FAT: 10G/19%
CALORIES: 462
SATURATED FAT: 1.5G
CARBOHYDRATE: 68G
PROTEIN: 24G
CHOLESTEROL: 28MG
SODIUM: 383MG

W*e've used Canadian bacon for depth, and two kinds of mushrooms to give this sauce a wonderfully earthy flavor. Shiitake mushrooms, sold in specialty markets and some supermarkets, should be trimmed of their stems before using. If unavailable, use all regular mushrooms. This sauce can be made a day ahead, then reheated on the stovetop or in the microwave.*

FETTUCCINE WITH CHICKEN, ASPARAGUS, AND PEAS

SERVES: 4
WORKING TIME: 15 MINUTES
TOTAL TIME: 25 MINUTES

To create this rich (yet low-fat) sauce, we've thickened it with a little cornstarch and stirred in light sour cream—off the heat to avoid separation. Although you may use frozen asparagus, tender fresh spears from early spring are best. Select bright green, firm stalks with tight tips. If stalks still seem tough after trimming the ends, peel them with a vegetable peeler.

1 tablespoon Oriental sesame oil

1 red bell pepper, cut into thin strips

6 ounces skinless, boneless chicken breasts, cut into ¼-inch-wide strips

6 scallions, cut diagonally into ½-inch pieces

½ pound asparagus, trimmed and cut into 1-inch pieces

¾ cup reduced-sodium chicken broth, defatted

2 teaspoons fresh lemon juice

1 teaspoon grated lemon zest

½ teaspoon salt

½ teaspoon dried thyme

⅔ cup frozen peas

2 teaspoons cornstarch

2 tablespoons light sour cream

10 ounces fettuccine

¼ cup grated Parmesan cheese

1. Start heating a large pot of water to boiling for the pasta. In a large nonstick skillet, heat the oil until hot but not smoking over medium heat. Add the bell pepper and cook, stirring frequently, until crisp-tender, about 3 minutes. Add the chicken and scallions, stirring to coat. Add the asparagus, broth, lemon juice, lemon zest, salt, and thyme and cook until the asparagus is crisp-tender, about 1 minute. Stir in the peas and cook until the peas are heated through, about 1 minute.

2. In a cup, combine the cornstarch and 1 tablespoon of water and stir to blend. Bring the chicken mixture to a boil over medium-high heat, stir in the cornstarch mixture, and cook, stirring constantly, until the mixture is slightly thickened and the chicken is cooked through, about 1 minute longer. Remove from the heat and stir in the sour cream.

3. Meanwhile, cook the fettuccine in the boiling water until just tender. Drain well. Transfer the chicken mixture to a large bowl, add the fettuccine and Parmesan, and toss to combine. Spoon the fettuccine mixture into 4 shallow bowls and serve.

Suggested accompaniments: Garlic toast, and orange sorbet sprinkled with melon liqueur for dessert.

FAT: 8G/17%
CALORIES: 423
SATURATED FAT: 2.3G
CARBOHYDRATE: 63G
PROTEIN: 25G
CHOLESTEROL: 31MG
SODIUM: 550MG

LEMON CHICKEN SAUCE

SERVES: 4
WORKING TIME: 30 MINUTES
TOTAL TIME: 30 MINUTES

10 ounces medium strand pasta, such as perciatelli, linguine, or spaghetti

2 teaspoons olive oil

3 shallots or scallions, finely chopped

1 clove garlic, minced

¾ pound skinless, boneless chicken thighs, cut into ½-inch chunks

½ teaspoon salt

½ teaspoon ground ginger

¼ teaspoon freshly ground black pepper

1 cup reduced-sodium chicken broth, defatted

1 teaspoon grated lemon zest

3 tablespoons fresh lemon juice

⅓ cup snipped fresh dill

1 cup frozen peas

2 tablespoons reduced-fat cream cheese (Neufchâtel)

1½ teaspoons cornstarch mixed with 1 tablespoon water

1. In a large pot of boiling water, cook the pasta until just tender. Drain well.

2. Meanwhile, in a large nonstick skillet, heat the oil until hot but not smoking over medium heat. Add the shallots and garlic and cook, stirring frequently, until the shallots are tender, about 2 minutes. Add the chicken, sprinkle with the salt, ginger, and pepper, and cook, stirring frequently, until the chicken is no longer pink, about 3 minutes.

3. Stir the broth, lemon zest, lemon juice, and dill into the pan and bring to a boil. Reduce to a simmer and cook until the chicken is cooked through, about 2 minutes. Stir in the peas and cream cheese and cook just until the peas are heated through and the cream cheese is melted, about 2 minutes. Stir in the cornstarch mixture and cook, stirring, until the sauce is slightly thickened, about 1 minute. Toss the sauce with the hot pasta, divide among 4 bowls, and serve.

Helpful hint: Be sure to grate the lemon zest before squeezing the lemon. Any extra lemon zest can be frozen for future use.

FAT: 8G/16%
CALORIES: 450
SATURATED FAT: 2.2G
CARBOHYDRATE: 63G
PROTEIN: 30G
CHOLESTEROL: 74MG
SODIUM: 573MG

L*emon, dill, and green peas, used together in a single dish, carry an unmistakable suggestion of spring. And a delicate sauce made with reduced-fat cream cheese keeps this dish light. Any sort of long pasta would work with this sauce; perciatelli (shown here) looks like thick spaghetti but the strands are actually hollow in the middle.*

FUSILLI AND TURKEY STIR-FRY

SERVES: 4
WORKING TIME: 20 MINUTES
TOTAL TIME: 30 MINUTES

¼ cup reduced-sodium chicken broth, defatted

3 tablespoons reduced-sodium soy sauce

2 tablespoons maple syrup

2 tablespoons cider vinegar

2 teaspoons cornstarch

½ teaspoon ground ginger

½ teaspoon red pepper flakes

2 tablespoons coarsely chopped pecans

1 tablespoon vegetable oil

½ pound turkey cutlets, cut into ¼-inch-wide strips

2 cups cut butternut squash (2-by-¼-inch pieces)

3 cloves garlic, minced

1 leek, halved lengthwise and cut into 1-inch pieces

1 rib celery, cut into 2-inch julienne

2 tablespoons chopped fresh parsley

8 ounces long fusilli pasta

1. Start heating a large pot of water to boiling for the pasta. In a small bowl, combine the broth, soy sauce, maple syrup, vinegar, cornstarch, ginger, and pepper flakes and stir to blend. Set aside. Place the pecans in a large nonstick skillet over low heat, and cook, stirring constantly, until lightly toasted, about 5 minutes. Transfer to a plate. Wipe the skillet with paper towels.

2. In the same skillet, heat the oil until hot but not smoking over medium-high heat. Add the turkey and cook, stirring constantly, until the turkey is lightly browned, about 3 minutes. With a slotted spoon, transfer the turkey to the plate with the pecans.

3. Add the squash to the pan and cook, stirring frequently, until lightly browned and almost tender, about 4 minutes. Reduce the heat to medium. Add the garlic, leek, and celery and cook, stirring frequently, until the leek and celery are crisp-tender, about 4 minutes. Stir the broth mixture again and add to the pan. Stir in the pecans and turkey and cook, stirring constantly, until the turkey is cooked through, about 1 minute longer. Stir in the parsley.

4. Meanwhile, cook the fusilli in the boiling water until just tender. Drain well. Transfer the turkey mixture to a large bowl, add the fusilli, and toss to combine. Spoon the pasta mixture onto a platter and serve.

Suggested accompaniment: Spinach salad with a poppy seed vinaigrette.

FAT: 7G/15%
CALORIES: 422
SATURATED FAT: .9G
CARBOHYDRATE: 66G
PROTEIN: 24G
CHOLESTEROL: 35MG
SODIUM: 541MG

A delicious combination of robust "winter" flavors—butternut squash, maple syrup, and pecans—comes together beautifully in this colorful stir-fry. Although butternut is available all year round, its best months are from early fall through winter. Instead of the long fusilli, linguine or spaghetti would also work well with this sauce.

CHICKEN AND RUOTE WITH SUN-DRIED TOMATOES

SERVES: 4
WORKING TIME: 20 MINUTES
TOTAL TIME: 30 MINUTES

This simply made sauce is deliciously fragrant—be sure to use dry-pack sun-dried tomatoes, not jarred ones that are packed in oil.

¼ cup sun-dried (not oil-packed) tomato halves

¾ cup boiling water

2 teaspoons olive oil

1 medium red onion, coarsely chopped

3 cloves garlic, slivered

6 ounces mushrooms, cut into quarters

6 ounces skinless, boneless chicken breasts, cut into ½-inch chunks

½ cup dry white wine

2 tablespoons Dijon mustard

¾ teaspoon dried oregano

3 tablespoons light sour cream

2 tablespoons chopped fresh parsley

10 ounces ruote (wagon wheel) pasta

1. In a small bowl, combine the sun-dried tomatoes and boiling water. Let stand until the tomatoes have softened, about 20 minutes. Drain, reserving the soaking liquid, and thinly sliver the tomatoes.

2. Meanwhile, start heating a large pot of water to boiling for the pasta. In a large nonstick skillet, heat the oil until hot but not smoking over medium heat. Add the onion and garlic and cook, stirring frequently, until the onion has softened, about 7 minutes. Add the mushrooms and chicken and cook, stirring frequently, until the chicken is golden brown, about 4 minutes.

3. Add the wine, increase the heat to high, and cook until the liquid has almost evaporated and the chicken is cooked through, about 2 minutes longer. Stir in the tomatoes and their soaking liquid, the mustard, and oregano and bring to a boil. Remove from the heat and stir in the sour cream and parsley.

4. Meanwhile, cook the ruote in the boiling water until just tender. Drain well. Transfer the chicken mixture to a large bowl, add the ruote, and toss to combine. Spoon the pasta mixture onto 4 plates and serve.

Suggested accompaniments: Shredded carrot and celery salad with a black pepper vinaigrette, followed by mixed berries topped with a dollop of vanilla nonfat yogurt and sprinkled with nutmeg.

FAT: 6G/13%
CALORIES: 426
SATURATED FAT: 1.4G
CARBOHYDRATE: 65G
PROTEIN: 22G
CHOLESTEROL: 28MG
SODIUM: 273MG

FAJITA-STYLE FETTUCCINE

SERVES: 4
WORKING TIME: 25 MINUTES
TOTAL TIME: 25 MINUTES

8 ounces fettuccine

¾ pound skinless, boneless chicken breasts, cut into ¼-inch-wide strips

3 cloves garlic, minced

1 red bell pepper, slivered

1 medium red onion, slivered

⅓ cup fresh lemon juice

¼ cup chopped fresh cilantro or parsley

2 teaspoons cornstarch

1 teaspoon dried oregano

1 teaspoon dried basil

½ teaspoon ground cumin

½ teaspoon freshly ground black pepper

¼ teaspoon salt

1 tablespoon olive oil

⅓ cup reduced-sodium chicken broth, defatted

1. In a large pot of boiling water, cook the pasta until just tender. Drain.

2. Meanwhile, in a medium bowl, combine the chicken, garlic, bell pepper, onion, lemon juice, 2 tablespoons of the cilantro, the cornstarch, oregano, basil, cumin, black pepper, and salt and toss gently to coat thoroughly.

3. In a large nonstick skillet, heat the oil until hot but not smoking over medium-high heat. Add the chicken mixture and cook, stirring frequently, until the chicken is cooked through and the vegetables are tender, about 5 minutes.

4. Add the broth and cook, stirring constantly, until the mixture just comes to a simmer, about 1 minute longer. Remove from the heat. Stir in the remaining 2 tablespoons cilantro. Place the pasta on 4 plates, spoon the chicken and vegetables on top, and serve.

Suggested accompaniments: Hearts of romaine lettuce with a nonfat blue cheese dressing. For dessert, lemon ice sprinkled with toasted coconut.

FAT: 7G/17%
CALORIES: 381
SATURATED FAT: 1.2G
CARBOHYDRATE: 50G
PROTEIN: 29G
CHOLESTEROL: 103MG
SODIUM: 262MG

For a new twist on the original Texas fajita, we've substituted chicken for skirt steak, and pasta for tortillas.

PENNE WITH CHICKEN, CORN, AND BROCCOLI

SERVES: 4
WORKING TIME: 30 MINUTES
TOTAL TIME: 30 MINUTES

This sunny pasta dinner is a real "pantry shelf" meal: You probably have most of the ingredients on hand. If there's no fresh broccoli in the house, substitute frozen, or switch to frozen green beans, adjusting the cooking time as necessary. Rinsed, drained, canned corn (1¾ cups) can be used instead of frozen. Flexibility is a key to quick cooking, and many vegetables are interchangeable.

8 ounces penne pasta

1 tablespoon vegetable oil

½ pound skinless, boneless, chicken breasts, cut into 1-inch chunks

1 onion, coarsely chopped

1 clove garlic, minced

2 cups broccoli florets

10-ounce package frozen corn kernels

1¼ cup reduced-sodium chicken broth, defatted

1 teaspoon dried basil

¼ teaspoon red pepper flakes

½ teaspoon salt

1 teaspoon cornstarch mixed with 1 tablespoon water

¼ cup grated Parmesan cheese

1. In a large pot of boiling water, cook the pasta until just tender. Drain well.

2. Meanwhile, in a large nonstick skillet, heat the oil until hot but not smoking over medium heat. Add the chicken and cook, stirring, until the chicken is lightly browned, about 5 minutes. With a slotted spoon, transfer the chicken to a plate.

3. Add the onion and garlic to the pan and cook, stirring, until the onion is softened, about 4 minutes. Add the broccoli, corn, broth, basil, red pepper flakes, and salt and bring to a boil. Reduce the heat to a simmer and cook until the broccoli is crisp-tender, about 5 minutes. Stir the cornstarch mixture into the broccoli mixture. Return the chicken to the skillet. Bring to a boil and cook, stirring, until the sauce is slightly thickened and the chicken is cooked through, about 1 minute.

4. Transfer the mixture to a large bowl, add the pasta, and toss to combine. Divide the pasta mixture among 4 plates, sprinkle with the Parmesan, and serve.

Helpful hint: When buying frozen vegetables, squeeze the box between your fingers: The contents should feel loose and "crunchy." If the package has been thawed and refrozen at some point, it may feel like a solid block of ice and the vegetables may not taste as fresh.

FAT: 7G/15%
CALORIES: 434
SATURATED FAT: 1.8G
CARBOHYDRATE: 66G
PROTEIN: 28G
CHOLESTEROL: 37MG
SODIUM: 628MG

F*or*
richness without
excessive fat, we've
added small amounts
of Cheddar and
Parmesan to the flour-
based "cream" sauce,
made with low-fat
milk. Flavorful chili
powder and garlic add
a hint of warmth. For
a different pasta shape,
substitute ruote, penne,
or medium shells.

CREAMY RIGATONI WITH CHICKEN AND SPINACH

SERVES: 4
WORKING TIME: 20 MINUTES
TOTAL TIME: 30 MINUTES

2 tablespoons all-purpose flour

2¼ cups low-fat (1%) milk

¾ teaspoon mild chili powder

½ teaspoon salt

½ teaspoon freshly ground black pepper

1 tablespoon olive oil

2 cloves garlic, minced

½ pound skinless, boneless chicken breasts, cut into 1-inch chunks

10-ounce package frozen chopped spinach, thawed and squeezed dry (see tip)

2 ounces Cheddar cheese, shredded (about ½ cup)

3 tablespoons grated Parmesan cheese

10 ounces rigatoni pasta

1. Start heating a large pot of water to boiling for the pasta. Place the flour in a large saucepan over medium heat, and gradually whisk in the milk. Bring to a boil and whisk in the chili powder, salt, and pepper. Cook, whisking constantly, until the mixture is slightly thickened, about 5 minutes. Remove from the heat.

2. In a large nonstick skillet, heat the oil until hot but not smoking over medium heat. Add the garlic and cook, stirring frequently, until fragrant, about 1 minute. Add the chicken and cook, stirring frequently, until the chicken is lightly browned, about 3 minutes. Add the spinach, stirring to coat. Stir in the milk mixture, Cheddar, and Parmesan and cook until the Cheddar has melted and the chicken is cooked through, about 2 minutes longer.

3. Meanwhile, cook the rigatoni in the boiling water until just tender. Drain well. Transfer the chicken mixture to a large bowl, add the rigatoni, and toss to combine. Spoon the pasta mixture onto 4 plates and serve.

Suggested accompaniments: Iced lime-flavored seltzer, sliced Italian bread and, for dessert, canned apricots topped with a dollop of light sour cream and sprinkled with cinnamon.

TIP

To prepare frozen spinach, thaw according to package directions, and then squeeze out excess liquid (this prevents a watery sauce). Work over a bowl as you squeeze the spinach, one handful at a time. If you wish, use the liquid for flavoring soups, sauces, and stir-fries.

FAT: 13G/22%
CALORIES: 523
SATURATED FAT: 5.4G
CARBOHYDRATE: 67G
PROTEIN: 34G
CHOLESTEROL: 56MG
SODIUM: 599MG

LONG FUSILLI WITH PORCINI AND CHICKEN

SERVES: 4
WORKING TIME: 35 MINUTES
TOTAL TIME: 40 MINUTES

Porcini mushrooms are pricier than other dried mushrooms, but you'll find that a small amount goes a long way. Instead of whole dried porcini, you can buy a bag of small dried mushroom pieces, which are quite reasonably priced. Follow this fragrant pasta entrée with a refreshing dessert of citrus fruit—oranges, tangerines, or, for a more exotic touch, kumquats.

½ ounce dried mushrooms, preferably porcini
1 cup boiling water
2 teaspoons olive oil
1 large onion, finely chopped
3 cloves garlic, minced
1 large carrot, finely chopped
1 cup reduced-sodium chicken broth, defatted
½ pound skinless, boneless chicken thighs, cut into ½-inch pieces
¼ cup no-salt-added tomato paste
½ teaspoon dried rosemary
½ teaspoon salt
¼ teaspoon freshly ground black pepper
10 ounces long fusilli
3 tablespoons grated Parmesan cheese

1. In a small bowl, combine the dried mushrooms and boiling water and let stand until the mushrooms have softened, about 10 minutes. Scoop the dried mushrooms from their soaking liquid, reserving the liquid, then rinse and coarsely chop the mushrooms. Strain the liquid through a paper towel-lined sieve and set aside.

2. Meanwhile, in a large nonstick skillet, heat the oil until hot but not smoking over medium heat. Add the onion and garlic and cook, stirring occasionally, until the onion is softened, about 7 minutes. Add the carrot and ¼ cup of the broth and cook, stirring frequently, until softened, about 5 minutes.

3. Add the chicken, stirring to coat. Add the tomato paste, mushrooms, the reserved soaking liquid, the remaining ¾ cup broth, the rosemary, salt, and pepper and bring to a boil. Reduce to a simmer and cook until the sauce is slightly thickened and the chicken is cooked through, about 5 minutes.

4. Meanwhile, in a large pot of boiling water, cook the fusilli until just tender. Drain well. Transfer the pasta to a large bowl, add the sauce, and toss to combine. Add the Parmesan, toss again, spoon into 4 pasta bowls, and serve.

Helpful hint: Seal dried mushrooms in a plastic bag (their aroma is quite powerful), and store them in the freezer.

FAT: 7G/15%
CALORIES: 432
SATURATED FAT: 1.8G
CARBOHYDRATE: 67G
PROTEIN: 25G
CHOLESTEROL: 50MG
SODIUM: 581MG

SMOKED TURKEY, JACK CHEESE, AND PEPPER SAUCE

SERVES: 4
WORKING TIME: 30 MINUTES
TOTAL TIME: 30 MINUTES

For a memorable macaroni-and-cheese variation, try this lively stovetop casserole. Instead of Cheddar or American cheese, the velvety sauce is rich with melted jalapeño jack. Cubes of smoked turkey and apple, corn kernels, and bell pepper squares give the dish a confetti-like quality. A salad of sliced cucumbers and sweet red onions would offer a pleasant contrast to the pasta.

10 ounces shaped pasta, such as orecchiette or farfalle (bow ties)

1 tablespoon olive oil

4 scallions, thinly sliced

1 red bell pepper, cut into ½-inch squares

1 green bell pepper, cut into ½-inch squares

6 ounces unsliced smoked turkey, cut into ½-inch cubes

1 Granny Smith apple, cored and cut into ½-inch cubes

2 tablespoons flour

2 cups low-fat (1%) milk

¼ teaspoon salt

1 cup frozen corn kernels

1 cup shredded jalapeño jack cheese (4 ounces)

1. In a large pot of boiling water, cook the pasta until just tender. Drain well.

2. Meanwhile, in a large nonstick skillet, heat the oil until hot but not smoking over medium heat. Add the scallions and cook until softened, about 2 minutes. Add the bell peppers and cook, stirring frequently, until crisp-tender, about 4 minutes.

3. Add the turkey and apple to the pan and cook, stirring frequently, until the apple is crisp-tender, about 3 minutes. Stir in the flour until well combined. Gradually add the milk. Stir in the salt and cook, stirring constantly, until the sauce is slightly thickened and no floury taste remains, about 5 minutes. Add the corn and cheese and cook just until the corn is heated through and the cheese is melted, about 2 minutes. Toss the sauce with the hot pasta and serve.

Helpful hint: For a milder meal, substitute regular Monterey jack cheese for the jalapeño jack (the latter is studded with bits of chili pepper).

FAT: 17G/26%
CALORIES: 588
SATURATED FAT: 7G
CARBOHYDRATE: 81G
PROTEIN: 31G
CHOLESTEROL: 57MG
SODIUM: 826MG

CHICKEN AND MUSHROOM SAUCE

SERVES: 4
WORKING TIME: 35 MINUTES
TOTAL TIME: 35 MINUTES

There's subtle sophistication in this unique sauce, perhaps because the mushrooms pick up the delicate bouquet of the white wine and sherry.

10 ounces medium strand pasta, such as long fusilli, linguine, or spaghetti

2 teaspoons olive oil

¼ cup plus 2 tablespoons coarsely chopped pancetta or Canadian bacon (2 ounces)

¾ pound skinless, boneless chicken breasts, cut into ½-inch chunks

1 onion, minced

3 cloves garlic, minced

½ pound mushrooms, thinly sliced

¼ cup dry white wine

3 tablespoons dry sherry

1 cup reduced-sodium chicken broth, defatted

2 tablespoons no-salt-added tomato paste

½ teaspoon salt

½ teaspoon dried rosemary

¼ teaspoon freshly ground black pepper

⅓ cup plus 1 tablespoon chopped fresh parsley

2 tablespoons reduced-fat sour cream

1. In a large pot of boiling water, cook the pasta until just tender. Drain well.

2. Meanwhile, in a large nonstick skillet, heat the oil until hot but not smoking over medium heat. Add the pancetta and cook until slightly crisp, about 3 minutes. Add the chicken and cook, stirring frequently, until lightly browned and cooked through, about 4 minutes. With a slotted spoon, transfer the chicken to a plate.

3. Add the onion and garlic to the pan and cook, stirring frequently, until the onion is softened, about 7 minutes. Add the mushrooms and cook, stirring frequently, until tender, about 4 minutes. Add the wine and sherry, increase the heat to high, and cook until almost evaporated, about 2 minutes.

4. Stir the broth, tomato paste, salt, rosemary, and pepper into the pan and bring to a boil. Reduce the heat to medium, return the chicken to the pan, and cook until heated through, about 1 minute. Remove from the heat, stir in ⅓ cup of the parsley and the sour cream. Toss the sauce with the hot pasta, sprinkle the remaining 1 tablespoon parsley over, and serve.

Helpful hint: You can substitute additional white wine or chicken broth for the sherry, if you like.

FAT: 7G/14%
CALORIES: 466
SATURATED FAT: 1.6G
CARBOHYDRATE: 63G
PROTEIN: 36G
CHOLESTEROL: 59MG
SODIUM: 570MG

SPAGHETTI WITH CHUNKY TURKEY SAUSAGE SAUCE

SERVES: 12
WORKING TIME: 35 MINUTES
TOTAL TIME: 1 HOUR

1 tablespoon olive oil

1½ pounds turkey sausage, casings removed, cut into ½-inch-thick slices

2 large onions, cut into 1-inch chunks

6 cloves garlic, minced

4 carrots, cut into ½-inch-thick slices

1 pound mushrooms, quartered

3½ pounds plum tomatoes, coarsely chopped

Three 8-ounce cans tomato sauce

2 teaspoons dried oregano

1 teaspoon salt

2 pounds spaghetti

2 zucchini, cut into ½-inch chunks

1. In a large Dutch oven, heat the oil until hot but not smoking over medium heat. Add the sausage and cook, stirring frequently, until browned and cooked through, about 7 minutes. With a slotted spoon, transfer the sausage to a plate and set aside.

2. Add the onions and garlic to the pan and cook, stirring frequently, until the onions are golden brown, about 10 minutes. Add the carrots and cook until the carrots are tender, about 7 minutes. Add the mushrooms and cook until the mushrooms are tender, about 5 minutes. Stir in the tomatoes, tomato sauce, oregano, and salt and bring to a boil. Return the sausage to the pan. Reduce to a simmer, cover, and cook until the sauce is slightly thickened, about 15 minutes.

3. Meanwhile, in a large pot of boiling water, cook the spaghetti until just tender. Drain, return to the cooking pot, and cover to keep warm.

4. Stir the zucchini into the sauce. Cover again and cook until the zucchini is just tender, 5 to 7 minutes longer. Pour the sauce over the spaghetti and toss well to combine. Divide the spaghetti mixture among 12 shallow bowls and serve.

Suggested accompaniments: Garlic bread. For dessert, sliced navel oranges topped with a strawberry purée.

FAT: 9G/18%
CALORIES: 471
SATURATED FAT: 2.1G
CARBOHYDRATE: 77G
PROTEIN: 23G
CHOLESTEROL: 30MG
SODIUM: 927MG

You can easily freeze half of the savory sauce for another party and then reheat it, tossing it with a pound of pasta.

CHICKEN CHOW MEIN

SERVES: 4
WORKING TIME: 20 MINUTES
TOTAL TIME: 25 MINUTES

This variation on the Chinese-American favorite uses fettuccine rather than higher-fat crispy fried noodles, but is still crunchy with vegetables and water chestnuts. The flavors remain pure Asian—a tangy combination of soy, ginger, and hoisin sauce. If Napa cabbage is not available, substitute shredded romaine lettuce.

¼ cup reduced-sodium soy sauce

2 tablespoons hoisin sauce

1 tablespoon dry sherry

½ teaspoon ground ginger

½ teaspoon hot pepper sauce

2 tablespoons vegetable oil

½ pound skinless, boneless chicken breasts, cut into ¼-inch-wide strips

4 cloves garlic, minced

½ cup sliced scallions

2 tablespoons minced fresh ginger

1 red bell pepper, diced

1 rib celery, thinly sliced

¼ pound mushrooms, thinly sliced

2 cups ¼-inch-wide shredded Napa cabbage

½ cup sliced water chestnuts, rinsed and drained

8 ounces fettuccine

1. Start heating a large pot of water to boiling for the pasta. In a small bowl, combine the soy sauce, hoisin sauce, sherry, ground ginger, and hot pepper sauce and stir to blend. Set aside.

2. In a large nonstick skillet, heat the oil until hot but not smoking over medium heat. Add the chicken and cook, stirring frequently, until golden brown, about 4 minutes. With a slotted spoon, transfer the chicken to a plate.

3. Add the garlic, scallions, and fresh ginger to the pan and cook, stirring frequently, until the scallions are tender, about 2 minutes. Stir in the bell pepper, celery, and mushrooms and cook until the bell pepper is crisp-tender, about 4 minutes. Add the cabbage and water chestnuts, cover, and cook until the cabbage has wilted, about 4 minutes. Stir the soy sauce mixture again and add to the pan. Add the chicken and cook, uncovered, stirring frequently, until the chicken is cooked through, about 1 minute longer.

4. Meanwhile, cook the fettuccine in the boiling water until just tender. Drain well. Transfer the chicken mixture to a large bowl, add the fettuccine, and toss to combine. Spoon the chicken chow mein onto a platter and serve.

Suggested accompaniments: Fortune cookies, and fresh pineapple or orange wedges.

FAT: 10G/22%
CALORIES: 414
SATURATED FAT: 1.6G
CARBOHYDRATE: 55G
PROTEIN: 24G
CHOLESTEROL: 87MG
SODIUM: 939MG

CURRIED CHICKEN SAUCE

SERVES: 4
WORKING TIME: 30 MINUTES
TOTAL TIME: 30 MINUTES

The sunstruck colors of this inventive dish are matched by its vibrant flavor. The unconventional pairing of curry sauce and pasta may startle traditionalists, but just persuade them to sample a forkful of this warmly seasoned cream sauce with flavorful vegetables and they'll willingly forgo tradition for once.

10 ounces shaped pasta, such as farfalle (bow ties) or orecchiette

1 tablespoon olive oil

2 scallions, thinly sliced

1 red bell pepper, cut into ½-inch squares

1 green bell pepper, cut into ½-inch squares

2 carrots, halved lengthwise and thinly sliced

¾ pound skinless, boneless chicken breasts, cut into ½-inch chunks

1 cup reduced-sodium chicken broth, defatted

¾ cup plain nonfat yogurt

3 tablespoons reduced-fat sour cream

2 tablespoons flour

1 tablespoon no-salt-added tomato paste

2 teaspoons curry powder

½ teaspoon ground ginger

1. In a large pot of boiling water, cook the pasta until just tender. Drain well.

2. Meanwhile, in a large nonstick skillet, heat the oil until hot but not smoking over medium heat. Add the scallions, bell peppers, and carrots and cook, stirring frequently, until the carrots are crisp-tender, about 5 minutes. Add the chicken and cook until no longer pink, about 2 minutes. Add the broth and bring to a boil. Reduce to a simmer.

3. Meanwhile, in a small bowl, combine the yogurt, sour cream, flour, tomato paste, curry powder, and ginger. Stir the yogurt mixture into the simmering broth and cook, stirring constantly, until slightly thickened and no floury taste remains, about 3 minutes. Toss the sauce with the hot pasta and serve.

Helpful hint: Combining the yogurt and sour cream with flour keeps the dairy products from curdling when the mixture is added to the simmering broth. Still, you should be careful not to bring the mixture to a boil after adding the yogurt mixture.

FAT: 7G/13%
CALORIES: 482
SATURATED FAT: 1.7G
CARBOHYDRATE: 68G
PROTEIN: 34G
CHOLESTEROL: 54MG
SODIUM: 257MG

SPICY SAUSAGE AND BEAN SAUCE

SERVES: 4
WORKING TIME: 20 MINUTES
TOTAL TIME: 45 MINUTES

Though the resemblance may escape American eyes, radiatore pasta was inspired by the shape of an Italian radiator—which makes it a perfect match for a spicy warming sauce! Keep in mind the spicy heat of the main dish and offer cool accompaniments such as a lightly dressed salad and tall, cold drinks.

1 tablespoon olive oil

10 ounces hot Italian-style turkey sausage, casings removed

10 ounces shaped pasta, such as radiatore or rotini

1 red onion, coarsely chopped

1 red bell pepper, diced

2 cloves garlic, minced

2 teaspoons chili powder

28-ounce can no-salt-added tomatoes, chopped with their juices

16-ounce can pinto beans, rinsed and drained

4½-ounce can chopped mild green chilies, drained

½ teaspoon dried oregano

¼ teaspoon freshly ground black pepper

1. In a large nonstick skillet, heat 2 teaspoons of the oil until hot but not smoking over medium heat. Crumble the sausage into the pan and cook, stirring, until cooked through, 6 to 7 minutes. With a slotted spoon, transfer the sausage to a plate.

2. In a large pot of boiling water, cook the pasta until just tender. Drain well.

3. Meanwhile, add the remaining 1 teaspoon oil to the skillet. Add the onion, bell pepper, and garlic and cook, stirring, until the onion begins to soften, 4 to 5 minutes. Add the chili powder and cook until fragrant, about 30 seconds. Return the sausage to the pan and add the tomatoes, beans, green chilies, oregano, and black pepper. Bring the mixture to a boil, reduce to a simmer, cover, and cook until the sauce is slightly thickened, about 15 minutes.

4. Toss the sauce with the hot pasta, divide among 4 bowls, and serve.

Helpful hint: To prepare the sausage for this recipe, slit the casings lengthwise with the tip of a sharp knife, then peel off the casings with your fingers.

FAT: 13G/21%
CALORIES: 551
SATURATED FAT: 2.8G
CARBOHYDRATE: 82G
PROTEIN: 28G
CHOLESTEROL: 38MG
SODIUM: 891MG

RADIATORE WITH CHICKEN, ZUCCHINI, AND FETA CHEESE

SERVES: 4
WORKING TIME: 20 MINUTES
TOTAL TIME: 30 MINUTES

The ruffles of radiatore are perfect for holding this chunky sauce, which is vibrantly flavored with red wine vinegar and feta cheese. Fresh dill adds an aromatic seasoning. Feta, a Greek cheese, is traditionally made from sheep's or goat's milk, and is usually crumbly with a tangy taste. Just a small amount adds loads of flavor.

1 tablespoon flour
½ teaspoon freshly ground black pepper
¼ teaspoon salt
½ pound skinless, boneless chicken breasts, cut into ½-inch-wide strips
1 tablespoon olive oil
5 cloves garlic, slivered
2 zucchini, halved lengthwise and thinly sliced
1 red bell pepper, diced
¼ cup red wine vinegar
1 tomato, cut into thin strips
3 tablespoons snipped fresh dill
¾ teaspoon dried oregano
2 tablespoons light sour cream
8 ounces radiatore pasta
3 ounces feta cheese, crumbled

1. Start heating a large pot of water to boiling for the pasta. On a plate, combine the flour, ¼ teaspoon of the black pepper, and salt. Dredge the chicken in the flour mixture, shaking off the excess. In a large nonstick skillet, heat the oil until hot but not smoking over medium heat. Add the chicken and cook, stirring frequently, until golden brown, about 4 minutes. With a slotted spoon, transfer the chicken to a plate.

2. Add the garlic, zucchini, and bell pepper to the pan and cook, stirring frequently, until the bell pepper is tender, about 5 minutes. Sprinkle the vinegar over the vegetables. Stir in the tomato, ½ cup of water, dill, oregano, and remaining ¼ teaspoon black pepper. Bring to a boil over medium-high heat, reduce to a simmer, cover, and cook until the mixture is flavorful and slightly thickened, about 4 minutes. Add the chicken and cook, uncovered, until the chicken is cooked through, about 1 minute longer. Remove from the heat and stir in the sour cream.

3. Meanwhile, cook the radiatore in the boiling water until just tender. Drain well. Transfer the chicken mixture to a large bowl, add the radiatore, and toss to combine. Add the feta cheese and toss again. Spoon the pasta mixture into 4 shallow bowls and serve.

Suggested accompaniments: French baguette and, for dessert, a reduced-calorie lemon pudding garnished with blueberries.

FAT: 11G/24%
CALORIES: 421
SATURATED FAT: 4.5G
CARBOHYDRATE: 55G
PROTEIN: 26G
CHOLESTEROL: 54MG
SODIUM: 289MG

SWEET AND SAVORY CHICKEN SAUCE

SERVES: 4
WORKING TIME: 30 MINUTES
TOTAL TIME: 35 MINUTES

Apple, banana, and raisins, combined with chicken in a creamy curry sauce, make an unexpected and delicious pasta topping.

10 ounces shaped pasta, such as small shells or ruote (wagon wheels)

1 tablespoon olive oil

¾ pound skinless, boneless chicken breasts, cut into ½-inch chunks

1 red Delicious apple, cored and diced

1 onion, coarsely diced

2 cloves garlic, minced

1 teaspoon curry powder

1¼ cups reduced-sodium chicken broth, defatted

1 firm-ripe banana, cut into ¼-inch slices

¼ cup golden raisins

¾ teaspoon salt

½ cup evaporated skimmed milk

2 teaspoons cornstarch

2 teaspoons fresh lemon juice

¼ cup chopped fresh parsley

1. In a large pot of boiling water, cook the pasta until just tender. Drain well.

2. Meanwhile, in a large nonstick skillet, heat 2 teaspoons of the oil until hot but not smoking over medium heat. Add the chicken and cook, stirring, until browned, about 5 minutes. With a slotted spoon, transfer the chicken to a plate.

3. Add the remaining 1 teaspoon oil to the skillet. Add the apple, onion, and garlic and cook, stirring, until the onion begins to soften, 4 to 5 minutes. Add the curry powder and cook, stirring, until fragrant, about 30 seconds. Add the broth, banana, raisins, and salt and bring to boil. Reduce to a simmer, cover, and cook until the banana is softened but not mushy, about 5 minutes.

4. In a small bowl, combine the evaporated milk with the cornstarch. Stir the cornstarch mixture into the skillet and cook, stirring constantly, until the sauce is slightly thickened, about 1 minute. Return the chicken to the pan and cook until the chicken is heated through, about 1 minute. Stir in the lemon juice. Toss the sauce with the hot pasta, divide among 4 bowls, sprinkle the parsley over, and serve.

Helpful hint: You can use another favorite apple variety instead of the Delicious apple; pick a red-skinned type for a touch of color.

FAT: 6G/10%
CALORIES: 517
SATURATED FAT: 1G
CARBOHYDRATE: 82G
PROTEIN: 33G
CHOLESTEROL: 51MG
SODIUM: 689MG

CHICKEN PARMIGIANA SAUCE

SERVES: 4
WORKING TIME: 25 MINUTES
TOTAL TIME: 30 MINUTES

10 ounces rigatoni

½ cup grated Parmesan cheese

2 tablespoons flour

¼ teaspoon freshly ground black pepper

10 ounces skinless, boneless chicken breasts, cut crosswise into ½-inch-wide strips

1 tablespoon olive oil

1½ cups canned no-salt-added tomatoes, chopped with their juices

½ cup reduced-sodium chicken broth, defatted

1 tablespoon no-salt-added tomato paste

½ cup chopped fresh basil

¾ teaspoon salt

¼ teaspoon hot pepper sauce

1. In a large pot of boiling water, cook the pasta until just tender. Drain well.

2. Meanwhile, on a sheet of waxed paper, combine 2 tablespoons of the Parmesan, the flour, and pepper. Dredge the chicken in the Parmesan mixture, patting the mixture onto the chicken.

3. In a large nonstick skillet, heat the oil until hot but not smoking over medium heat. Add the chicken and cook, turning the pieces as they brown, until browned all over, about 5 minutes. Add the tomatoes, broth, tomato paste, basil, salt, and hot pepper sauce and bring to a boil. Reduce to a simmer and cook until the sauce is slightly thickened and the chicken is cooked through, about 3 minutes.

4. Toss the sauce with the hot pasta and the remaining 6 tablespoons Parmesan. Divide among 4 bowls and serve.

Helpful hint: Freshly grated Italian Parmesan (which says "Parmigiano-Reggiano" on the rind) will make a big flavor difference in this recipe, and in any recipe calling for Parmesan cheese.

FAT: 9G/18%
CALORIES: 460
SATURATED FAT: 2.8G
CARBOHYDRATE: 62G
PROTEIN: 32G
CHOLESTEROL: 49MG
SODIUM: 743MG

While it's not loaded with cheese (which is high in fat), this pasta sauce is full of potent Parmesan flavor.

CHICKEN ARRABBIATA SAUCE

SERVES: 4
WORKING TIME: 30 MINUTES
TOTAL TIME: 40 MINUTES

The Italian word "arrabbiata" means "furious" and refers here to the peppery heat of the sauce. Whole chicken breasts are traditionally cooked in this type of sauce, but we've used chunks of chicken instead, along with rigatoni. For dessert, serve palate-cooling portions of Italian lemon or orange ice with fresh fruit.

1 tablespoon olive oil
¾ pound skinless, boneless, chicken breasts, cut into ½-inch chunks
10 ounces rigatoni
1 onion, diced
2 cloves garlic, minced
28-ounce can tomatoes in purée
1 tablespoon minced fresh ginger
¾ teaspoon dried rosemary
½ teaspoon salt
¼ teaspoon red pepper flakes
2 tablespoons capers, rinsed and drained
1 tablespoon balsamic vinegar

1. In a large nonstick skillet, heat 2 teaspoons of the oil until hot but not smoking over medium heat. Add the chicken and cook, stirring, until browned, about 5 minutes. With a slotted spoon, transfer the chicken to a plate.

2. In a large pot of boiling water, cook the pasta until just tender. Drain well.

3. Meanwhile, add the remaining 1 teaspoon oil to the skillet. Add the onion and garlic and cook, stirring, until the onion is softened, about 4 minutes. Stir in the tomatoes, ginger, rosemary, salt, and red pepper flakes. Cover and cook until the sauce is richly flavored and slightly thickened, 10 to 12 minutes.

4. Return the chicken to the pan along with the capers and vinegar and cook until the chicken is heated through, about 1 minute. Toss the sauce with the hot pasta, divide among 4 plates, and serve.

Helpful hint: Red pepper flakes are small bits of dried hot red chili peppers. Start with a tiny pinch and add more gradually if you don't want too "furious" a sauce.

FAT: 6G/12%
CALORIES: 460
SATURATED FAT: 0.9G
CARBOHYDRATE: 70G
PROTEIN: 31G
CHOLESTEROL: 49MG
SODIUM: 761MG

CHICKEN, PROSCIUTTO, AND ARTICHOKE SAUCE

SERVES: 4
WORKING TIME: 40 MINUTES
TOTAL TIME: 40 MINUTES

For a country-style Italian dinner, we've started with a handful of chopped prosciutto, the super-savory Italian ham that can add rich flavor to a sauce in seconds. The chicken, tomatoes, carrots, and artichokes all benefit from this big-time taste booster. The large lasagna noodles, broken into smaller pieces, resemble squares of country-style homemade pasta.

1 tablespoon olive oil

¼ cup plus 2 tablespoons coarsely chopped prosciutto or Canadian bacon (2 ounces)

2 carrots, quartered lengthwise and thinly sliced

1 rib celery, quartered lengthwise and thinly sliced

10 ounces lasagna noodles, broken crosswise into thirds

9-ounce package frozen artichoke hearts, thawed and coarsely chopped

½ cup dry red wine

1 cup canned no-salt-added tomatoes, chopped with their juices

1 cup reduced-sodium chicken broth, defatted

½ teaspoon salt

¼ teaspoon dried thyme

¾ pound skinless, boneless chicken breasts, cut into ½-inch chunks

1 cup frozen peas

1½ teaspoons cornstarch mixed with 1 tablespoon water

1. In a large nonstick skillet, heat the oil until hot but not smoking over medium heat. Add the prosciutto and cook, stirring frequently, until lightly crisped, about 3 minutes. Add the carrots and celery and cook, stirring frequently, until the carrots are softened, about 5 minutes.

2. In a large pot of boiling water, cook the pasta until just tender. Drain well.

3. Meanwhile, add the artichokes to the skillet and cook, stirring frequently, until the artichokes are tender, about 15 minutes. Add the wine, increase the heat to high, and cook until the wine has almost evaporated, about 2 minutes. Add the tomatoes, broth, salt, and thyme and bring to a boil. Reduce the heat to a simmer, add the chicken, and cook until the chicken is just barely cooked through, about 3 minutes.

4. Add the peas to the skillet, return to a boil, and stir in the cornstarch mixture. Cook, stirring constantly, until the sauce is slightly thickened, about 1 minute. Toss the sauce with the hot pasta, divide among 4 bowls, and serve.

Helpful hint: If you like the flavor of celery, don't throw away the leafy tops. Chop them and use them as a flavoring or garnish, as you would parsley.

FAT: 8G/14%
CALORIES: 510
SATURATED FAT: 1.5G
CARBOHYDRATE: 71G
PROTEIN: 38G
CHOLESTEROL: 61MG
SODIUM: 837MG

SOUTHWESTERN CHICKEN SAUCE

SERVES: 4
WORKING TIME: 20 MINUTES
TOTAL TIME: 45 MINUTES

1 tablespoon olive oil

½ pound skinless, boneless chicken breasts, cut into ½-inch chunks

1 red bell pepper, diced

1 green bell pepper, diced

1 cup sliced scallions

1 clove garlic, minced

1 teaspoon ground cumin

1½ cups reduced-sodium chicken broth, defatted

10-ounce package frozen corn kernels, thawed

2 cups diced plum tomatoes or canned no-salt-added tomatoes, chopped with their juices

1 teaspoon salt

10 ounces shaped pasta, such as ruote (wagon wheels) or medium shells

1 teaspoon cornstarch

¼ cup reduced-fat sour cream

½ cup diced avocado

½ cup chopped fresh cilantro or basil

1. In a large nonstick skillet, heat 2 teaspoons of the oil until hot but not smoking over medium heat. Add the chicken and cook, stirring, until browned, about 5 minutes. With a slotted spoon, transfer the chicken to a plate.

2. Add the remaining 1 teaspoon oil to the skillet. Add the bell peppers, scallions, and garlic and cook, stirring frequently, until the peppers begin to soften, about 5 minutes. Add the cumin and cook, stirring, until fragrant, about 30 seconds. Add 1¼ cups of the broth, the corn, tomatoes, and salt and bring to a boil. Reduce to a simmer, cover, and cook until the sauce is slightly thickened, about 10 minutes.

3. Meanwhile, in a large pot of boiling water, cook the pasta until just tender. Drain well.

4. In a small bowl, combine the remaining ¼ cup broth and the cornstarch. Stir the cornstarch mixture into the skillet along with the sour cream. Cook, stirring constantly, until the sauce is slightly thickened, about 1 minute. Return the chicken to the pan, stir in the avocado and cilantro, and cook until the chicken is heated through, about 1 minute. Toss the sauce with the hot pasta, divide among 4 bowls, and serve.

Helpful hint: Add a pinch of cayenne pepper (with the cumin in step 2), if you like your pasta sauce spicy.

FAT: 11G/19%
CALORIES: 521
SATURATED FAT: 2.4G
CARBOHYDRATE: 80G
PROTEIN: 29G
CHOLESTEROL: 38MG
SODIUM: 829MG

A Southwestern sauce is the perfect topping for whimsical wagon-wheel pasta. Although the flavors of tomatoes, garlic, cumin, and cilantro may remind you of chili, this dish is not too spicy; on the contrary, the avocado and sour cream bring a particularly mellow quality to the sauce. If you serve a salad with this, garnish the greens with some oven-toasted tortilla triangles.

PASTA SHELLS WITH SAUSAGE AND MUSHROOMS

SERVES: 4
WORKING TIME: 35 MINUTES
TOTAL TIME: 40 MINUTES

½ ounce dried mushrooms, preferably porcini

1½ cups boiling water

10 ounces medium pasta shells

2 teaspoons olive oil

½ pound Italian-style turkey sausage, casings removed

4 shallots or scallions, finely chopped

2 cloves garlic, minced

1 large yellow or red bell pepper, cut into 1-inch squares

½ pound fresh mushrooms, thickly sliced

1 large tomato, coarsely chopped

½ teaspoon salt

⅓ cup grated Parmesan cheese

1. In a small bowl, combine the dried mushrooms and boiling water and let stand until softened, about 10 minutes. Remove the dried mushrooms from their soaking liquid, reserving the liquid. Rinse and coarsely chop the mushrooms. Strain the liquid through a paper towel-lined sieve and set aside.

2. In a large pot of boiling water, cook the pasta shells until just tender. Drain well.

3. Meanwhile, in a large nonstick skillet, heat 1 teaspoon of the oil until hot but not smoking over medium heat. Crumble the sausage into the pan and cook until lightly golden, about 3 minutes. With a slotted spoon, transfer the sausage to a plate. Add the shallots and garlic to the pan and cook, stirring frequently, until the shallots are softened, about 2 minutes.

4. Add the remaining 1 teaspoon oil to the pan along with the bell pepper, fresh mushrooms, and dried mushrooms and cook, stirring occasionally, until the pepper and fresh mushrooms are tender, about 5 minutes. Stir in the tomato, reserved mushroom soaking liquid, and salt. Return the sausage to the pan and simmer until the sausage is cooked through, about 4 minutes. Toss with the pasta and Parmesan, divide the mixture among 4 plates, and serve.

FAT: 12G/24%
CALORIES: 455
SATURATED FAT: 3.4G
CARBOHYDRATE: 65G
PROTEIN: 24G
CHOLESTEROL: 36MG
SODIUM: 782MG

The savory sauce for this delicious pasta dish pays double homage to the Italian passion for mushrooms—dried mushrooms (use Italian porcini if you can) are paired with fresh white button mushrooms to simulate the taste and texture of fresh porcini. The turkey sausage offers a light alternative to traditional pork sausage.

*T*he mild, licorice-like flavor of fresh fennel is nicely complemented by the orange juice and basil in this soul-warming dish. Fennel is available from the fall through the spring. Look for bulbs free of discoloration, and stalks with dark green feathery fronds. Refrigerate, in a plastic bag, for up to four days. Celery may be substituted for the fennel for a similar texture.

PENNE WITH CHICKEN, FENNEL, AND PINE NUTS

SERVES: 4
WORKING TIME: 25 MINUTES
TOTAL TIME: 35 MINUTES

2 tablespoons olive oil

6 ounces skinless, boneless chicken breasts, cut into ½-inch chunks

1 large onion, coarsely chopped

3 cloves garlic, minced

1 small fennel bulb, cut into ½-inch chunks (about 2 cups; see tip)

½ cup orange juice

1 teaspoon grated orange zest

2 cups chopped tomatoes

½ cup reduced-sodium chicken broth, defatted

3 tablespoons chopped fresh basil

¾ teaspoon salt

¼ teaspoon cayenne pepper

2 teaspoons cornstarch

1 tablespoon pine nuts

10 ounces penne pasta

1. In a large nonstick skillet, heat 1 tablespoon of the oil until hot but not smoking over medium heat. Add the chicken and cook, stirring frequently, until golden brown, about 4 minutes. With a slotted spoon, transfer the chicken to a plate.

2. Start heating a large pot of water to boiling for the pasta. In the same skillet, heat the remaining 1 tablespoon oil until hot but not smoking over medium heat. Add the onion and garlic. Cook, stirring frequently, until the onion is caramelized, about 10 minutes.

3. Add the fennel to the onion mixture, stirring to coat. Stir in the orange juice and zest. Cover and cook, stirring occasionally, until the fennel is tender, about 10 minutes. Stir in the tomatoes, broth, basil, salt, and cayenne and cook, uncovered, stirring frequently, until slightly thickened, about 5 minutes. In a cup, combine the cornstarch and 1 tablespoon of water, stir to blend, and stir into the fennel mixture. Add the chicken and pine nuts, bring to a boil over medium-high heat, and cook, stirring constantly, until the chicken is cooked through, about 1 minute longer.

4. Meanwhile, cook the penne in the boiling water until just tender. Drain well. Transfer the chicken mixture to a large bowl, add the penne, and toss to combine. Spoon the penne mixture into 4 shallow bowls and serve.

Suggested accompaniment: Baked Bartlett pears stuffed with currants.

FAT: 10G/20%
CALORIES: 459
SATURATED FAT: 1.5G
CARBOHYDRATE: 70G
PROTEIN: 22G
CHOLESTEROL: 25MG
SODIUM: 589MG

TIP

To prepare fresh fennel, cut the stalks from the bulb, and trim the stem end and any tough outer sections from the bulb. Cut the bulb crosswise into ½-inch-thick slices, then cut the slices into ½-inch chunks.

SWEET AND SAVORY GROUND TURKEY SAUCE

SERVES: 4
WORKING TIME: 25 MINUTES
TOTAL TIME: 35 MINUTES

Turkey's light flavor is perfect for this intriguingly tangy "meat" sauce. For the healthiest meal, be sure to get lean ground turkey—skinless breast meat only—or cut up a piece of turkey breast and grind it yourself in the food processor. Chili sauce and Dijon mustard do their bit for the spicy side, while honey and orange juice balance things out with sweet and tart notes.

10 ounces medium tube pasta, such as ziti or penne

1 tablespoon olive oil

4 scallions, thinly sliced

3 cloves garlic, minced

1 green bell pepper, cut into ½-inch squares

1 carrot, quartered lengthwise and thinly sliced

10 ounces lean ground turkey

14½-ounce can no-salt-added stewed tomatoes

½ cup reduced-sodium chicken broth, defatted

¼ cup orange juice

¼ cup chili sauce

1 tablespoon Dijon mustard

1 tablespoon honey

½ teaspoon dried sage

½ teaspoon salt

½ teaspoon freshly ground black pepper

1 teaspoon cornstarch mixed with 1 tablespoon water

1. In a large pot of boiling water, cook the pasta until just tender. Drain well.

2. Meanwhile, in a large nonstick skillet, heat the oil until hot but not smoking over medium heat. Add the scallions and garlic and cook, stirring, until the scallions are softened, about 2 minutes. Add the bell pepper and carrot and cook, stirring frequently, until the pepper and carrot are softened, about 5 minutes. Crumble in the turkey and cook until no longer pink, about 4 minutes.

3. Add the tomatoes, broth, orange juice, chili sauce, mustard, honey, sage, salt, and black pepper to the pan and bring to a boil. Reduce to a simmer, cover, and cook until the sauce is richly flavored, about 5 minutes. Return to a boil, stir in the cornstarch mixture, and cook, stirring constantly, until the sauce is slightly thickened, about 1 minute. Toss the sauce with the hot pasta, divide among 4 bowls, and serve.

Helpful hint: You can make the sauce a day ahead; its flavors will blend and mellow with time. Reheat it over medium-low heat, adding a little chicken broth or water if it is too thick.

FAT: 10G/18%
CALORIES: 491
SATURATED FAT: 2G
CARBOHYDRATE: 76G
PROTEIN: 24G
CHOLESTEROL: 52MG
SODIUM: 761MG

CHICKEN AND POTATOES WITH PENNE

SERVES: 4
WORKING TIME: 15 MINUTES
TOTAL TIME: 25 MINUTES

Combining potatoes and pasta is a traditional northern Italian touch that adds both heartiness and texture to this fresh-tasting dish.

6 ounces penne or other tubular pasta

2 teaspoons olive oil

1 ounce Canadian bacon, diced

1 large onion, diced

½ pound all-purpose potatoes, peeled and cut into ½-inch dice

1 pound skinless, boneless chicken breasts, cut into 1-inch chunks

½ pound mushrooms, thinly sliced

2 tablespoons fresh lemon juice

¾ teaspoon salt

½ teaspoon dried rosemary

1 cup chopped plum tomatoes

1. In a large pot of boiling water, cook the pasta until just tender. Drain, return the pasta to the cooking pot, and cover to keep warm.

2. Meanwhile, in a large nonstick skillet, heat the oil until hot but not smoking over medium heat. Add the bacon and onion and cook, stirring frequently, until the onion begins to soften, about 5 minutes. Stir in the potatoes, cover, and cook for 5 minutes.

3. Stir in the chicken, mushrooms, lemon juice, salt, rosemary, and ½ cup of water. Bring to a boil over medium-high heat, reduce to a simmer, cover, and cook until the chicken is cooked through and the potatoes are tender, adding a little more water if the mixture seems dry, about 8 minutes longer.

4. Stir in the tomatoes, pour the sauce over the pasta, and toss to combine. Spoon the chicken-pasta mixture onto 4 plates and serve.

Suggested accompaniment: Thinly sliced navel oranges sprinkled with orange liqueur for dessert.

FAT: 5G/12%
CALORIES: 386
SATURATED FAT: 1G
CARBOHYDRATE: 48G
PROTEIN: 36G
CHOLESTEROL: 69MG
SODIUM: 597MG

ORIENTAL CHICKEN WITH NOODLES

SERVES: 4
WORKING TIME: 25 MINUTES
TOTAL TIME: 30 MINUTES

8-ounce can pineapple chunks
in unsweetened juice

¼ cup low-sodium ketchup

2 tablespoons cider vinegar

2 tablespoons reduced-sodium
soy sauce

1 tablespoon firmly packed
light brown sugar

2 teaspoons cornstarch

2 tablespoons peanut oil

½ pound skinless, boneless
chicken breasts, cut into
½-inch chunks

3 cloves garlic, minced

2 tablespoons minced fresh
ginger

1 rib celery, thinly sliced

1 large carrot, thinly sliced

2 cups diagonally cut
bok choy (2-inch pieces)

3 scallions, thinly sliced

8 ounces lasagna noodles,
broken into eighths

1. Start heating a large pot of water to boiling for the pasta. Drain the pineapple, reserving ½ cup of the juice. Set the pineapple aside. In a small bowl, combine the reserved ½ cup pineapple juice, ketchup, vinegar, soy sauce, brown sugar, and cornstarch. Stir to blend and set aside.

2. In a large nonstick skillet, heat 1 tablespoon of the oil until hot but not smoking over medium heat. Add the chicken and cook, stirring frequently, until the chicken is lightly browned, about 3 minutes. Add the garlic and ginger and cook, stirring frequently, until fragrant, about 1 minute. Stir in the remaining 1 tablespoon oil, the celery, carrot, and bok choy and cook until the vegetables are crisp-tender, about 4 minutes.

3. Stir the ketchup mixture again and add to the pan. Stir in the reserved pineapple and cook, stirring constantly, until the vegetables are coated and the sauce is slightly thickened, about 2 minutes longer. Stir in the scallions.

4. Meanwhile, cook the lasagna noodles in the boiling water until just tender. Drain well. Transfer the chicken mixture to a large bowl, add the noodles, and toss to combine. Spoon the noodle mixture into 4 shallow bowls and serve.

Suggested accompaniments: Sesame bread sticks, and a fresh fruit cup sprinkled with chopped crystallized ginger for dessert.

FAT: 9G/19%
CALORIES: 424
SATURATED FAT: 1.5G
CARBOHYDRATE: 65G
PROTEIN: 22G
CHOLESTEROL: 33MG
SODIUM: 496MG

B*reaking up the lasagna noodles creates a new pasta shape that goes well with the crunchy slices of bok choy.*

NEAPOLITAN CHICKEN SAUCE

SERVES: 4
WORKING TIME: 25 MINUTES
TOTAL TIME: 30 MINUTES

Dishes from Naples are typically lavished with robust, garlicky tomato sauce and topped with mozzarella. In fact, the classic pizza is a Neapolitan invention. This bountiful main dish includes both the sauce and the cheese, along with chunks of chicken and Italian sausage. The flavors of garlic and fennel—dominant seasonings in the sausage—suffuse the entire dish.

10 ounces fine strand pasta, such as spaghettini or capellini

3 ounces sweet or hot Italian pork sausage, casings removed

1 cup reduced-sodium chicken broth, defatted

10 ounces skinless, boneless chicken breasts, cut into ½-inch chunks

4 cloves garlic, minced

14½-ounce can no-salt-added stewed tomatoes, chopped with their juices

2 tablespoons no-salt-added tomato paste

½ cup chopped fresh parsley

½ teaspoon freshly ground black pepper

¼ teaspoon salt

1 cup frozen peas, thawed

¾ cup shredded part-skim mozzarella cheese (3 ounces)

1. In a large pot of boiling water, cook the pasta until just tender. Drain well.

2. Meanwhile, crumble the sausage into a large nonstick skillet. Add ¼ cup of the broth and cook over medium heat, stirring, until the sausage is no longer pink, about 4 minutes. Add the chicken and garlic and cook, stirring occasionally, until the chicken is no longer pink, about 4 minutes.

3. Stir the tomatoes, tomato paste, parsley, pepper, salt, and the remaining ¾ cup broth into the pan and bring to a boil. Reduce to a simmer and cook until the chicken is cooked through and the sauce is flavorful, about 3 minutes. Add the peas and cook just until heated through, about 2 minutes. Toss the sauce with the hot pasta, sprinkle the mozzarella over, and serve.

Helpful hints: To prepare the sausage for this recipe, slit the casings lengthwise with the tip of a sharp knife, then peel off the casings with your fingers. If you prefer, use Italian-style turkey sausage instead of pork sausage.

FAT: 12G/20%
CALORIES: 541
SATURATED FAT: 5G
CARBOHYDRATE: 68G
PROTEIN: 38G
CHOLESTEROL: 70MG
SODIUM: 648MG

GARLIC CHICKEN SAUCE

SERVES: 4
WORKING TIME: 25 MINUTES
TOTAL TIME: 30 MINUTES

Garlic lovers will applaud this assertive sauce laced with pungent slivers of sautéed garlic. The sauce is made with roasted-pepper purée to ensure a thick, "clingy" coating for the pasta strands; anchovy paste lends a savory kick. For a trattoria-style dinner, accompany the pasta with grissini (thin, crisp bread sticks) and follow it with a colorful tossed salad.

10 ounces medium strand pasta, such as linguine, spaghetti, or long fusilli

1 cup jarred roasted red peppers, rinsed and drained

1 tablespoon olive oil

1 onion, finely chopped

6 cloves garlic, slivered

1 red bell pepper, cut into ½-inch squares

¾ pound skinless, boneless chicken breasts, cut into ½-inch chunks

1 cup reduced-sodium chicken broth, defatted

½ cup chopped fresh basil

1 tablespoon anchovy paste, or 2 tablespoons grated Parmesan cheese

1. In a large pot of boiling water, cook the pasta until just tender. Drain well.

2. Meanwhile, in a food processor, process the jarred roasted peppers to a smooth purée; set aside. In a large nonstick skillet, heat the oil until hot but not smoking over medium heat. Add the onion and garlic and cook, stirring frequently, until the onion is softened, about 7 minutes. Add the bell pepper and cook, stirring frequently, until the bell pepper is crisp-tender, about 4 minutes.

3. Add the chicken to the pan and cook until no longer pink, about 2 minutes. Stir the puréed peppers into the skillet along with the broth, basil, and anchovy paste. Simmer until the chicken is just cooked through, about 2 minutes. Toss the sauce with the hot pasta, divide among 4 bowls, and serve.

Helpful hint: Keep a watchful eye on the garlic as it sautés; scorched garlic has an unpleasant, bitter flavor.

FAT: 6G/12%
CALORIES: 452
SATURATED FAT: 1G
CARBOHYDRATE: 65G
PROTEIN: 32G
CHOLESTEROL: 52MG
SODIUM: 442MG

CHICKEN ALFREDO

SERVES: 4
WORKING TIME: 20 MINUTES
TOTAL TIME: 30 MINUTES

8 ounces fettuccine

3 tablespoons flour

¾ teaspoon salt

½ teaspoon freshly ground black pepper

¾ pound skinless, boneless chicken breasts, cut into 1-inch chunks

2 teaspoons olive oil

1 cup low-fat (1%) milk

2 tablespoons reduced-fat cream cheese (Neufchâtel)

¼ teaspoon nutmeg

½ cup frozen peas

¼ cup grated Parmesan cheese

2 tablespoons sliced scallions or snipped fresh chives

1. In a large pot of boiling water, cook the fettuccine until tender. Drain well, reserving ⅓ cup of the cooking water.

2. Meanwhile, on a sheet of waxed paper, combine 2 tablespoons of the flour, ¼ teaspoon of the salt, and ¼ teaspoon of the pepper. Dredge the chicken in the flour mixture, shaking off the excess.

3. In a large nonstick skillet, heat the oil until hot but not smoking over medium heat. Add the chicken and cook, stirring, until lightly browned, about 2 minutes. Add the remaining 1 tablespoon flour and stir until the chicken is coated. Gradually add the milk, stirring until smooth. Add the cream cheese, reserved ⅓ cup pasta water, the nutmeg, remaining ½ teaspoon salt, and remaining ¼ teaspoon pepper. Bring to a boil, reduce to a simmer, cover, and cook until the sauce is slightly thickened and the chicken is cooked through, about 5 minutes.

4. Add the peas and cook, uncovered, just until the peas are warmed through, about 1 minute. Transfer to a large bowl, add the fettuccine and Parmesan, and toss to combine. Spoon the fettuccine mixture onto 4 plates, sprinkle the scallions over, and serve.

Helpful hint: For playful variations, replace the fettuccine with bow-tie, rotelle, or even multi-colored radiatore pasta.

If there was ever a name associated with high fat, "Alfredo" is it. But surprise—with low-fat wizardry, we've created a delicious and nutritionally sensible dish by using low-fat milk instead of heavy cream, with a touch of reduced-fat cream cheese for richness.

FAT: 10G/20%
CALORIES: 433
SATURATED FAT: 3.5G
CARBOHYDRATE: 51G
PROTEIN: 34G
CHOLESTEROL: 115MG
SODIUM: 651MG

TURKEY SAUSAGE AND SPINACH SAUCE

SERVES: 4
WORKING TIME: 30 MINUTES
TOTAL TIME: 30 MINUTES

Pasta with sausage and cream sauce might not sound like a healthy, low-fat main dish, but you may be surprised when you read the ingredients for this recipe. The sausage is made from turkey, the smooth sauce is based on low-fat milk and Neufchâtel (reduced-fat cream cheese), and there's a generous portion of spinach in every serving.

10 ounces shaped pasta, such as farfalle (bow ties) or orecchiette

2 teaspoons olive oil

½ pound Italian-style turkey sausage, casings removed

1 red onion, finely chopped

4 cloves garlic, minced

10-ounce package frozen chopped spinach, thawed and squeezed dry

1 cup evaporated low-fat milk

2 tablespoons reduced-fat cream cheese (Neufchâtel)

¼ teaspoon freshly ground black pepper

⅓ cup grated Parmesan cheese

1. In a large pot of boiling water, cook the pasta until just tender. Drain well.

2. Meanwhile, in a large nonstick skillet, heat the oil until hot but not smoking over medium heat. Crumble in the sausage and cook until no longer pink, about 3 minutes. Add the onion and garlic and cook, stirring frequently, until the onion is softened, about 7 minutes.

3. Stir the spinach into the skillet and cook until heated through, about 2 minutes. Add the milk, cream cheese, and pepper and cook, stirring frequently, until slightly thickened, about 4 minutes.

4. Toss the sauce with the hot pasta and the Parmesan. Divide among 4 bowls and serve.

Helpful hints: To prepare the sausage for this recipe, slit the casings lengthwise with the tip of a sharp knife, then peel off the casings with your fingers. If you can't find evaporated low-fat milk, use evaporated skimmed milk instead.

FAT: 14G/24%
CALORIES: 518
SATURATED FAT: 4.3G
CARBOHYDRATE: 69G
PROTEIN: 29G
CHOLESTEROL: 50MG
SODIUM: 660MG

RAGÙ OF CHICKEN

SERVES: 4
WORKING TIME: 25 MINUTES
TOTAL TIME: 40 MINUTES

Ragù, as it is made in Bologna, is a rich meat sauce finished with a spoonful of cream. Here's a lighter version to enjoy.

1 tablespoon olive oil

6 tablespoons finely diced Canadian bacon (2 ounces)

¾ pound ground chicken

10 ounces medium strand pasta, such as linguine or spaghetti

1 onion, diced

2 carrots, diced

2 ribs celery, diced

1 clove garlic, minced

¼ cup Marsala wine or dry red wine

28-ounce can no-salt-added crushed tomatoes

½ teaspoon dried oregano

½ teaspoon dried thyme

½ teaspoon salt

2 teaspoons flour

½ cup low-fat (1%) milk

1. In a large nonstick skillet, heat 2 teaspoons of the oil until hot but not smoking over medium heat. Add the Canadian bacon and cook, stirring, until the bacon is browned, about 2 minutes. Add the chicken and cook, stirring to break up the meat, until the chicken is cooked through, about 5 minutes. With a slotted spoon, transfer the chicken and bacon to a plate.

2. In a large pot of boiling water, cook the pasta until just tender. Drain well.

3. Meanwhile, add the remaining 1 teaspoon oil to the skillet and add the onion, carrots, celery, and garlic. Cook, stirring, until the onion begins to soften, about 4 minutes. Return the chicken and bacon to the skillet along with the Marsala and cook until the Marsala is almost evaporated, about 1 minute. Stir in the tomatoes, oregano, thyme, and salt and bring to boil. Reduce the heat to a simmer, cover, and cook until richly flavored, about 12 minutes.

4. In a small bowl, combine the flour and milk. Stir the milk mixture into the skillet and cook, stirring constantly, until the sauce is slightly thickened, about 1 minute. Toss the sauce with the hot pasta, divide among 4 bowls, and serve.

FAT: 14G/23%
CALORIES: 548
SATURATED FAT: 3.1G
CARBOHYDRATE: 74G
PROTEIN: 31G
CHOLESTEROL: 79MG
SODIUM: 621MG

TURKEY AND BASIL PESTO

SERVES: 4
WORKING TIME: 20 MINUTES
TOTAL TIME: 40 MINUTES

1 tablespoon olive oil

¾ pound skinless, boneless turkey breast, cut into ½-inch chunks

10 ounces all-purpose potatoes, diced

3 cloves garlic, minced

2¼ cups reduced-sodium chicken broth, defatted

1 cup packed fresh basil leaves

½ teaspoon salt

¼ teaspoon freshly ground black pepper

10 ounces egg noodles

10-ounce package frozen peas, thawed

⅓ cup grated Parmesan cheese

¼ cup reduced-fat sour cream

1. In a large nonstick skillet, heat 2 teaspoons of the oil until hot but not smoking over medium heat. Add the turkey and cook, stirring, until browned, about 5 minutes. With a slotted spoon, transfer the turkey to a plate.

2. Add the remaining 1 teaspoon oil to the skillet. Add the potatoes and garlic and cook, stirring, until the garlic is fragrant, about 1 minute. Stir in the broth, basil, salt, and pepper and bring to a boil. Reduce to a simmer, cover, and cook until the potatoes are tender, about 20 minutes.

3. Meanwhile, in a large pot of boiling water, cook the noodles until just tender. Drain well.

4. Transfer the potato-basil mixture to a blender or food processor and process to a smooth purée. Return the purée to the skillet along with the turkey. Add the peas, all but 1 tablespoon of the Parmesan, and the sour cream and cook over medium heat until heated through, about 3 minutes. Toss the sauce with the hot pasta. Divide among 4 bowls, sprinkle with the remaining 1 tablespoon Parmesan, and serve.

Helpful hint: We've used curly egg noodles here, but you can use flat noodles instead.

Instead of copious quantities of oil, cheese, and nuts, this basil pesto is thickened with puréed potatoes.

FAT: 12G/18%
CALORIES: 595
SATURATED FAT: 3.6G
CARBOHYDRATE: 80G
PROTEIN: 43G
CHOLESTEROL: 130MG
SODIUM: 864MG

Boneless chicken breasts are a key ingredient in quick dinners, and when you flatten them slightly and cut them into narrow strips, they cook even faster. For a delightful sweet-and-sour quality, the base for this chicken and vegetable sauce is made from tomatoes accented with vinegar, brown sugar, raisins, and orange zest.

CHICKEN AND BROCCOLI SAUCE

SERVES: 4
WORKING TIME: 35 MINUTES
TOTAL TIME: 35 MINUTES

Place the chicken breasts between two sheets of plastic wrap or waxed paper and pound the thicker end lightly with a meat pounder or the flat side of small skillet.

1 tablespoon olive oil

¾ pound skinless, boneless chicken breasts, lightly pounded (see tip) and cut crosswise into ¼-inch-wide strips

10 ounces medium tube pasta, such as penne rigate, penne, or ziti

1 red onion, sliced

1 red bell pepper, cut into thin strips

2 cloves garlic, minced

3 cups diced plum tomatoes or canned no-salt-added tomatoes, chopped with their juices

1½ cups reduced-sodium chicken broth, defatted

¼ cup golden raisins

½ teaspoon grated orange zest

½ teaspoon salt

¼ teaspoon freshly ground black pepper

4 cups small broccoli florets

1 teaspoon cornstarch

2 teaspoons firmly packed light brown sugar

1 tablespoon balsamic vinegar

1. In a large nonstick skillet, heat 2 teaspoons of the oil until hot but not smoking over medium heat. Add the chicken and cook, stirring, until lightly browned, about 5 minutes. With a slotted spoon, transfer the chicken to a plate.

2. In a large pot of boiling water, cook the pasta until just tender. Drain well.

3. Meanwhile, add the remaining 1 teaspoon oil to the skillet. Add the onion, bell pepper, and garlic and cook, stirring, until the onion begins to soften, about 4 minutes. Add the tomatoes, broth, raisins, orange zest, salt, and black pepper and bring to a boil. Reduce to a simmer and cook until the sauce is slightly reduced, about 5 minutes. Return to a boil and add the broccoli. Reduce to a simmer and cook until the broccoli is tender, about 5 minutes.

4. In a small bowl, combine the cornstarch, brown sugar, and vinegar. Return the chicken to the pan and stir in the cornstarch mixture. Bring to a boil and cook, stirring, until the sauce is slightly thickened and the chicken is heated through, about 1 minute. Toss the sauce with the hot pasta and serve.

Helpful hint: Freezing the chicken breasts for about 15 minutes (after pounding them) will make them easier to cut.

FAT: 6G/10%
CALORIES: 524
SATURATED FAT: 1G
CARBOHYDRATE: 82G
PROTEIN: 37G
CHOLESTEROL: 49MG
SODIUM: 595MG

CHUNKY CHICKEN AND VEGETABLE SAUCE

SERVES: 4
WORKING TIME: 25 MINUTES
TOTAL TIME: 40 MINUTES

With a full complement of hearty vegetables, including potatoes, carrots, parsnips, leek, and garlic, this pasta dish captures the warm and comforting flavors of chicken stew. Rather than pouring in cream to enrich the sauce, however, we've used one of the best fat-cutting tricks around—puréeing some of the cooked vegetables to thicken the broth.

1 tablespoon olive oil

¾ pound skinless, boneless chicken breasts, cut into ½-inch chunks

½ pound red potatoes, cut into ¼-inch dice

2 carrots, cut into ¼-inch dice

2 parsnips, cut into ¼-inch dice

1 cup sliced leek or diced onion

2 cloves garlic, minced

2¾ cups reduced-sodium chicken broth, defatted

¾ teaspoon dried thyme

½ teaspoon salt

¼ teaspoon freshly ground black pepper

10 ounces small tube pasta, such as elbow macaroni or ditalini

1 cup frozen peas, thawed

⅓ cup reduced-fat sour cream

1. In a large nonstick skillet, heat 2 teaspoons of the oil until hot but not smoking over medium heat. Add the chicken and cook, stirring, until browned, about 5 minutes. With a slotted spoon, transfer the chicken to a plate.

2. Add the remaining 1 teaspoon oil to the skillet and add the potatoes, carrots, parsnips, leek, and garlic. Cook, stirring, until the potatoes are lightly browned, about 5 minutes. Add the broth, thyme, salt, and pepper and bring to boil. Reduce the heat to a simmer, cover, and cook until the vegetables are tender and the sauce is slightly thickened, about 15 minutes.

3. Meanwhile, in large pot of boiling water, cook the pasta until just tender. Drain well.

4. Transfer about 1 cup of the vegetable-broth mixture to a food processor or blender and process to a smooth purée. Return the purée and the chicken to the skillet along with the peas and cook until the chicken and peas are heated through, about 2 minutes. Toss the sauce with the hot pasta. Divide among 4 bowls, top with a dollop of the sour cream, and serve.

Helpful hint: Instead of puréeing 1 cup of the soup in a food processor or blender (step 4), you can use a hand blender to purée some of the vegetables right in the skillet.

FAT: 9G/14%
CALORIES: 581
SATURATED FAT: 2.3G
CARBOHYDRATE: 88G
PROTEIN: 37G
CHOLESTEROL: 56MG
SODIUM: 799MG

CHICKEN AND BASIL-PEPPER CREAM SAUCE

SERVES: 4
WORKING TIME: 25 MINUTES
TOTAL TIME: 25 MINUTES

Roasted red peppers perk up any dish, and there's no reason to go without when you can buy them in jars, all ready to go. (Look for roasted red peppers in the Italian or gourmet foods section of your supermarket.) The peppers are puréed, along with evaporated milk and broth, to make a rosy, robust sauce for pasta, chicken, and green beans.

10 ounces shaped pasta, such as radiatore or rotini

½ pound green beans, cut into 2-inch lengths

1 tablespoon olive oil

¾ pound skinless, boneless chicken breasts, cut into ½-inch chunks

8-ounce jar roasted red peppers, drained

1 clove garlic, minced

¾ cup reduced-sodium chicken broth, defatted

¾ cup evaporated skimmed milk

¼ cup packed fresh basil leaves

¾ teaspoon salt

¼ teaspoon freshly ground black pepper

1 teaspoon cornstarch

¼ cup grated Parmesan cheese

1. In a large pot of boiling water, cook the pasta until just tender. Add the green beans for the last 2 minutes of cooking time. Drain well.

2. Meanwhile, in a large nonstick skillet, heat 2 teaspoons of the oil until hot but not smoking over medium heat. Add the chicken and cook, stirring, until browned, about 5 minutes. With a slotted spoon, transfer the chicken to a plate.

3. Add the remaining 1 teaspoon oil to the skillet. Add the roasted peppers and garlic and cook, stirring, until the garlic is fragrant, about 1 minute. Stir in the broth, ½ cup of the evaporated milk, the basil, salt, and black pepper and bring to a boil. Reduce to a simmer and cook until slightly thickened, about 3 minutes. Transfer the mixture to a food processor and process to a smooth purée.

4. In a small bowl, combine the remaining ¼ cup evaporated milk with the cornstarch. Return the basil-pepper purée to the skillet along with the chicken and the cornstarch mixture. Bring to a boil over medium heat and cook, stirring, until the sauce is slightly thickened, about 1 minute. Toss the sauce with the hot pasta and green beans. Divide among 4 plates, sprinkle the Parmesan over, and serve.

Helpful hint: You can substitute broccoli for the green beans, if you like.

FAT: 7G/13%
CALORIES: 497
SATURATED FAT: 1.9G
CARBOHYDRATE: 69G
PROTEIN: 36G
CHOLESTEROL: 55MG
SODIUM: 850MG

CHICKEN SAUCE WITH SAGE

SERVES: 4
WORKING TIME: 20 MINUTES
TOTAL TIME: 40 MINUTES

1 tablespoon olive oil

1 onion, diced

2 cloves garlic, minced

¾ pound ground chicken

½ cup dry white wine

1½ cups reduced-sodium chicken broth, defatted

½ pound cremini or button mushrooms, quartered

2 cups diced plum tomatoes or canned no-salt-added tomatoes, chopped with their juices

1½ teaspoons dried sage

1 small bay leaf

1 teaspoon salt

½ teaspoon sugar

¼ teaspoon freshly ground black pepper

10 ounces shaped pasta, such as medium shells or ruote (wagon wheels)

3 tablespoons grated Parmesan cheese

1. In a large nonstick skillet, heat the oil until hot but not smoking over medium heat. Add the onion and garlic and cook, stirring frequently, until the onion begins to soften, about 4 minutes. Add the chicken and cook, stirring to break up the meat, until the chicken is no longer pink, about 5 minutes.

2. Add the wine to the skillet and cook until almost evaporated, about 1 minute. Add the broth, mushrooms, tomatoes, sage, bay leaf, salt, sugar, and pepper and bring to a boil. Reduce the heat to a simmer, cover, and cook until the sauce is richly flavored and thickened, about 20 minutes.

3. Meanwhile, in a large pot of boiling water, cook the pasta until just tender. Drain well.

4. Toss the sauce with the hot pasta. Divide among 4 plates, sprinkle the Parmesan over, and serve.

Helpful hint: If you like, grind the chicken at home: Cut ¾ pound skinless, boneless chicken breast into chunks and process it in a food processor until finely ground, about 30 seconds.

Pasta, ground meat, and tomatoes can add up to the same old spaghetti dinner—or they can be transformed into something far more interesting. Here, for instance, we use ground chicken and plum tomatoes for a light, fresh-tasting dish. A good measure of aromatic sage adds a Tuscan note.

FAT: 14G/25%
CALORIES: 503
SATURATED FAT: 3.3G
CARBOHYDRATE: 65G
PROTEIN: 29G
CHOLESTEROL: 74MG
SODIUM: 918MG

SAUTÉED CHICKEN WITH PESTO FETTUCCINE

SERVES: 4
WORKING TIME: 20 MINUTES
TOTAL TIME: 30 MINUTES

U*p*

*with carbos, down
with fat: This pesto is
thickened with puréed
potatoes rather than
copious quantities of
oil and cheese.*

6 ounces all-purpose potatoes,
peeled and thinly sliced

¾ teaspoon salt

3 cloves garlic, peeled

1½ cups packed fresh basil
leaves

⅔ cup reduced-sodium chicken
broth, defatted

4 teaspoons olive oil

2 tablespoons pine nuts

1 tablespoon balsamic or red
wine vinegar

8 ounces fettuccine

½ teaspoon dried rosemary

⅛ teaspoon cayenne pepper

4 skinless, boneless chicken
breast halves (about 1 pound
total)

2 tablespoons flour

1. In a medium saucepan of boiling water, cook the potatoes with ¼ teaspoon of the salt until the potatoes are firm-tender, about 10 minutes. Add the garlic for the last 2 minutes of cooking time. Drain well. In a food processor, combine the basil, broth, 1 teaspoon of the oil, the pine nuts, vinegar, and ¼ teaspoon of the salt and process to a smooth purée. Add the drained potatoes and garlic and process just until smooth, about 30 seconds.

2. In a large pot of boiling water, cook the fettuccine until just tender. Drain well. In a large bowl, toss the pasta with the basil mixture.

3. Meanwhile, in a small bowl, stir together the rosemary, cayenne, and the remaining ¼ teaspoon salt. Rub the herb mixture into the chicken breasts. On a sheet of waxed paper, dredge the chicken in the flour, shaking off the excess.

4. In a large nonstick skillet, heat the remaining 1 tablespoon oil until hot but not smoking over medium heat. Add the chicken and cook until browned and cooked through, about 5 minutes per side. Divide the fettuccine among 4 plates. Slice the chicken on the diagonal and serve alongside the pasta.

Helpful hint: Save a few sprigs of basil for garnishing the finished dish.

FAT: 9G/29%
CALORIES: 271
SATURATED FAT: 1.3G
CARBOHYDRATE: 19G
PROTEIN: 31G
CHOLESTEROL: 66MG
SODIUM: 601MG

COUSCOUS WITH CHICKEN AND VEGETABLES

SERVES: 4
WORKING TIME: 20 MINUTES
TOTAL TIME: 35 MINUTES

2 teaspoons olive oil

1 large onion, diced

4 cloves garlic, minced

*2 carrots, cut into ½-inch-
thick slices*

*6 ounces skinless, boneless
chicken thighs, cut into
½-inch chunks*

1 teaspoon curry powder

½ teaspoon ground ginger

¼ teaspoon cinnamon

¼ teaspoon salt

⅛ teaspoon cayenne pepper

⅛ teaspoon ground allspice

*⅛ teaspoon freshly ground
black pepper*

*1 yellow summer squash,
halved lengthwise and cut into
½-inch-thick slices*

*1 zucchini, halved lengthwise
and cut into ½-inch-thick slices*

*1 cup reduced-sodium chicken
broth, defatted*

⅔ cup couscous

¼ cup chopped fresh cilantro

1. In a large nonstick skillet, heat the oil until hot but not smoking over medium heat. Add the onion and garlic and cook, stirring frequently, until the onion is softened, about 7 minutes.

2. Stir in the carrots and cook, stirring frequently, until the carrots are well coated, about 2 minutes. Add the chicken and cook, stirring frequently, until the chicken is no longer pink, about 2 minutes. Stir in the curry powder, ginger, cinnamon, salt, cayenne, allspice, and black pepper and cook, stirring constantly, until the mixture is fragrant, about 1 minute.

3. Stir in the yellow squash, zucchini, broth, and ½ cup of water and bring to a boil. Add the couscous and cook, stirring frequently, until the liquid is absorbed and the chicken is cooked through, about 5 minutes longer. Stir in the cilantro and serve.

Suggested accompaniments: Sesame flat breads, sliced cucumbers with an herbed yogurt dressing, and blood oranges or nectarines for dessert.

FAT: 4G/14%
CALORIES: 250
SATURATED FAT: .8G
CARBOHYDRATE: 37G
PROTEIN: 15G
CHOLESTEROL: 35MG
SODIUM: 353MG

This simple dish—which is a snap to prepare—will fill the kitchen with the aroma of sweet spices.

CHICKEN, PINE NUT, AND BASIL SAUCE

SERVES: 4
WORKING TIME: 20 MINUTES
TOTAL TIME: 30 MINUTES

You know there's a tasty dish in the making when basil and pine nuts are paired. Here, they're puréed with cream cheese and broth to make a delicious sauce. The perfect pasta for such a dish is one that has crevices to catch the sauce—twisty rotini, ruffly radiatore, and cavatappi are some good choices. A crisp salad completes the meal.

10 ounces shaped pasta, such as rotini or radiatore

1 tablespoon olive oil

¾ pound skinless, boneless chicken breasts, cut into ½-inch chunks

2 cloves garlic, minced

13¾-ounce can reduced-sodium chicken broth, defatted

½ cup coarsely chopped sun-dried (not oil-packed) tomatoes

½ teaspoon salt

¼ teaspoon red pepper flakes

¾ cup packed fresh basil leaves

2 tablespoons reduced-fat cream cheese (Neufchâtel)

1 tablespoon pine nuts

1. In a large pot of boiling water, cook the pasta until just tender. Drain well.

2. Meanwhile, in a large nonstick skillet, heat 2 teaspoons of the oil until hot but not smoking over medium heat. Add the chicken and cook, stirring, until browned, about 5 minutes. With a slotted spoon, transfer the chicken to a plate.

3. Add the remaining 1 teaspoon oil and the garlic to the skillet and cook until the garlic is softened, about 1 minute. Add all but ¼ cup of the broth, the sun-dried tomatoes, salt, and red pepper flakes and bring to a boil. Reduce the heat to a simmer and cook until the tomatoes are very soft, about 8 minutes.

4. Meanwhile, in a food processor or blender, combine the reserved ¼ cup broth, the basil, cream cheese, and pine nuts and process to a smooth purée. Stir the purée into the skillet. Return the chicken to the pan and cook until the sauce is smooth and creamy and the chicken is heated through, 2 to 3 minutes. Toss the sauce with the hot pasta, divide among 4 bowls, and serve.

Helpful hint: To store fresh basil, place the stems in a glass or jar of water; cover the leaves loosely with a plastic bag and refrigerate.

FAT: 8G/15%
CALORIES: 471
SATURATED FAT: 1.9G
CARBOHYDRATE: 64G
PROTEIN: 34G
CHOLESTEROL: 53MG
SODIUM: 617MG

123

ossing this colorful stir-fry with pasta—instead of serving it with rice— lends a new twist to an Asian classic. The light sauce, based on cornstarch-thickened broth, melds the pasta, chicken, and crisp-tender vegetables into a harmonious whole. We call for fettuccine, but just about any ribbon-shaped pasta noodle would work in this recipe.

ASIAN CHICKEN SAUCE

SERVES: 4
WORKING TIME: 35 MINUTES
TOTAL TIME: 35 MINUTES

10 ounces fettuccine

2 teaspoons vegetable oil

10 ounces skinless, boneless chicken thighs, cut into ½-inch chunks

6 scallions, thinly sliced

2 cloves garlic, minced

1 red bell pepper, cut into ½-inch squares

3 carrots, cut into 2 x ¼-inch julienne strips

¾ teaspoon ground ginger

½ pound snow peas, strings removed (see tip) and halved crosswise

1 cup reduced-sodium chicken broth, defatted

2 tablespoons reduced-sodium soy sauce

¼ teaspoon salt

1½ teaspoons cornstarch mixed with 1 tablespoon water

1. In a large pot of boiling water, cook the pasta until just tender. Drain well.

2. Meanwhile, in a large nonstick skillet, heat the oil until hot but not smoking over medium heat. Add the chicken, scallions, and garlic and cook, stirring, until coated, about 1 minute. Add the bell pepper, carrots, and ginger and cook, stirring frequently, until the chicken and vegetables are just cooked through, about 5 minutes.

3. Add the snow peas to the pan and cook until the snow peas are slightly softened, about 2 minutes. Add the broth, soy sauce, and salt and bring to a boil. Stir in the cornstarch mixture and cook, stirring constantly, until slightly thickened, about 1 minute.

4. Toss the sauce with the hot pasta and serve.

Helpful hint: If you're a big fan of ginger, you could add about 1 tablespoon grated fresh ginger to this recipe (with the ground ginger in step 2).

TIP

To prepare fresh snow peas for cooking, trim the stem end and pull off the string along the straight side.

FAT: 8G/16%
CALORIES: 450
SATURATED FAT: 1.6G
CARBOHYDRATE: 65G
PROTEIN: 28G
CHOLESTEROL: 126MG
SODIUM: 677MG

MEXICAN CHICKEN AND SALSA PASTA

SERVES: 4
WORKING TIME: 20 MINUTES
TOTAL TIME: 20 MINUTES

There's a jar in your kitchen that will make quick and tasty pasta sauce, but it's not what you might expect—it's lively tomato salsa. Salsa, enhanced with additional cumin and cilantro, turns spaghettini, chicken, and corn into a meal worthy of a fiesta. Toss an accompanying salad with a cooling yogurt dressing.

8 ounces spaghettini

2 teaspoons vegetable oil

1 pound skinless, boneless chicken breasts, cut crosswise into 1-inch-wide strips

1 teaspoon ground cumin

1½ cups mild or medium-hot prepared salsa

10-ounce package frozen corn kernels

2 tablespoons chopped fresh cilantro or parsley

1. In a large pot of boiling water, cook the spaghettini until just tender. Drain well.

2. Meanwhile, in a large nonstick skillet, heat the oil until hot but not smoking over medium heat. Add the chicken and cook, turning once, until the chicken is golden brown, about 5 minutes. Add the cumin and cook until fragrant, about 30 seconds. Stir in the salsa and corn and bring to a boil. Reduce the heat to a simmer, cover, and cook until the chicken is cooked through, about 5 minutes.

3. Divide the pasta among 4 plates, spoon the sauce over, sprinkle with the cilantro, and serve.

Helpful hint: Heating the cumin brings out its toasty flavor and fragrance. Other spices, such as coriander and curry powder, benefit from this treatment, too.

FAT: 5G/10%
CALORIES: 447
SATURATED FAT: 0.9G
CARBOHYDRATE: 63G
PROTEIN: 36G
CHOLESTEROL: 66MG
SODIUM: 959MG

Mixing sweet spices (like cinnamon, nutmeg, and cloves) with savory flavors (like onion, peppers, and garlic) has a long culinary history in Italy. This Italian-inspired sauce is made with ground turkey and spiked with orange zest, fennel seeds, and a number of sweet and savory spices.

TURKEY SAUCE WITH ORANGE AND SWEET SPICES

SERVES: 4
WORKING TIME: 20 MINUTES
TOTAL TIME: 40 MINUTES

1 tablespoon olive oil

1 onion, diced

2 cloves garlic, minced

¾ pound lean ground turkey

1 teaspoon fennel seeds, crushed
(see tip)

¾ teaspoon grated orange zest

½ teaspoon cinnamon

⅛ teaspoon nutmeg

⅛ teaspoon ground cloves

⅛ teaspoon cayenne pepper

2 cups diced fresh fennel or celery

1 red bell pepper, diced

2¼ cups reduced-sodium chicken
broth, defatted

3 tablespoons no-salt-added
tomato paste

1 tablespoon honey

½ teaspoon salt

10 ounces medium strand pasta,
such as spaghetti or linguine

1 tablespoon red wine vinegar

1. In a large nonstick skillet, heat the oil until hot but not smoking over medium heat. Add the onion and garlic and cook, stirring, until the onion begins to soften, 3 to 4 minutes. Crumble in the turkey and cook until no longer pink, about 5 minutes. Stir in the fennel seeds, orange zest, cinnamon, nutmeg, cloves, and cayenne and cook until fragrant, about 1 minute.

2. Stir the fresh fennel, bell pepper, broth, tomato paste, honey, and salt into the pan and bring to a boil. Reduce to a simmer, cover, and cook until the sauce is richly flavored and thickened, about 20 minutes.

3. Meanwhile, in a large pot of boiling water, cook the pasta until just tender. Drain well.

4. Add the vinegar to the sauce and stir to combine. Toss the sauce with the hot pasta, divide among 4 bowls, and serve.

Helpful hint: If you like, you can substitute another type of vinegar—such as white wine or cider—for the red wine vinegar.

FAT: 11G/20%
CALORIES: 485
SATURATED FAT: 2.3G
CARBOHYDRATE: 67G
PROTEIN: 28G
CHOLESTEROL: 62MG
SODIUM: 739MG

TIP

Although fennel can be purchased already ground, its flavor will be more intense if you buy the seeds and crush them with a mortar and pestle—the traditional kitchen tool for grinding spices at home. This set is marble; porcelain mortar-and-pestle sets, in a variety of sizes, are also widely available. You can use a mortar and pestle for other whole spices too—cumin, cloves, coriander, anise, and the like.

MEAT SAUCES

Left, Pasta alla Genovese. Above, Cheesy Beef, Corn, and Tomato Sauce.

BEEF STROGANOFF

SERVES: 4
WORKING TIME: 20 MINUTES
TOTAL TIME: 25 MINUTES

*B*eef Stroganoff is a speedy dish by nature. The thin strips of beef need only moments in the skillet, and the sour cream sauce is quickly stirred up in the same pan. So we've concentrated on lowering the fat content, using a little olive oil in place of lots of butter and incorporating a modest amount of reduced-fat sour cream.

8 ounces wide egg noodles

2 tablespoons flour

1 tablespoon paprika

¾ teaspoon salt

½ teaspoon freshly ground black pepper

10 ounces well-trimmed top round of beef, cut into 2 x ½-inch strips

2 teaspoons olive oil

1 leek or 2 scallions, cut into 2 x ¼-inch julienne strips

2 carrots, peeled and cut into 2 x ¼-inch julienne strips

1⅓ cups reduced-sodium chicken broth, defatted

¼ cup gherkin pickles, rinsed, drained, and thinly sliced

¼ teaspoon dried rosemary, crumbled

3 tablespoons reduced-fat sour cream

1. In a large pot of boiling water, cook the noodles until just tender. Drain well.

2. Meanwhile, on a sheet of waxed paper, combine the flour, paprika, ¼ teaspoon of the salt, and ¼ teaspoon of the pepper. Dredge the beef in the flour mixture, shaking off and reserving the excess. In a large nonstick skillet, heat the oil until hot but not smoking over medium heat. Add the beef and cook, stirring frequently, until browned, about 1 minute. With a slotted spoon, transfer the beef to a plate.

3. Add the leek, carrots, and ⅓ cup of the broth to the pan and cook until the carrots are crisp-tender, about 3 minutes. Add the pickles, stirring to coat. Add the remaining 1 cup broth, the rosemary, the remaining ½ teaspoon salt, and remaining ¼ teaspoon pepper. Bring to a boil, reduce to a simmer, and cook until the vegetables are tender, about 3 minutes.

4. In a small bowl, combine the sour cream and the reserved flour mixture. Stir into the pan along with the noodles and beef and cook until heated through and slightly thickened, about 2 minutes.

Helpful hint: To further reduce the cholesterol content of the Stroganoff, you can use yolkless egg noodles instead of the regular kind.

FAT: 9G/19%
CALORIES: 424
SATURATED FAT: 2.4G
CARBOHYDRATE: 58G
PROTEIN: 27G
CHOLESTEROL: 98MG
SODIUM: 781MG

SPAGHETTI WITH CHILI SAUCE

SERVES: 4
WORKING TIME: 25 MINUTES
TOTAL TIME: 25 MINUTES

Making chili can be an all-day project; the Tex-Mex favorite is usually slow-simmered to blend the flavors of beans, meat, and complex spices. But this praiseworthy chili dinner is ready in less than half an hour. Just toss the chili with the spaghetti, crown it with a dollop of creamy yogurt sauce, and bring it to the table with a basket of seeded semolina bread.

8 ounces spaghetti
2 teaspoons vegetable oil
½ pound lean ground beef
1 onion, coarsely chopped
3 cloves garlic, minced
1 tablespoon chili powder
Two 14½-ounce cans no-salt-added stewed tomatoes
15-ounce can red kidney beans, rinsed and drained
4½-ounce can chopped mild green chilies, drained
¼ teaspoon salt
¼ cup plain nonfat yogurt
2 tablespoons reduced-fat sour cream
¼ cup sliced scallions

1. In a large pot of boiling water, cook the spaghetti until just tender. Drain well.

2. Meanwhile, in a large nonstick skillet, heat the oil until hot but not smoking over medium heat. Add the beef, onion, and garlic and cook, stirring to break up the meat, until the meat is browned, about 5 minutes.

3. Add the chili powder to the skillet and cook until fragrant, about 1 minute. Stir in the tomatoes, kidney beans, green chilies, and salt and bring to a boil. Reduce the heat to a simmer and cook until the chili sauce is slightly thickened, about 10 minutes.

4. Meanwhile, in a small bowl, combine the yogurt, sour cream, and scallions. Transfer the chili sauce to a large bowl, add the pasta, and toss to combine. Divide the pasta mixture among 4 plates, top with a dollop of the yogurt-scallion mixture, and serve.

Helpful hint: If you like your chili hot, you can increase the amount of chili powder and substitute chopped jalapeños for the mild green chilies.

FAT: 17G/27%
CALORIES: 565
SATURATED FAT: 5.7G
CARBOHYDRATE: 77G
PROTEIN: 27G
CHOLESTEROL: 45MG
SODIUM: 577MG

ORANGE-FLAVORED BEEF NOODLES

SERVES: 4
WORKING TIME: 25 MINUTES
TOTAL TIME: 30 MINUTES

Our sauce for the thread-like angel hair pasta is a classic stir-fry—a mix of crisp-tender vegetables with a small amount of meat for flavoring. Dusting the beef with cornstarch and stirring a little cornstarch into the sauce adds body without fat. And the orange marmalade provides color, sheen, and a welcome sweetness.

½ cup reduced-sodium chicken broth, defatted

3 tablespoons reduced-sodium soy sauce

2 tablespoons orange marmalade

1 tablespoon dry sherry

3 teaspoons cornstarch

2 teaspoons rice vinegar or cider vinegar

½ pound beef top round, trimmed and cut into 2-by-¼-inch strips

2 tablespoons vegetable oil

3 cloves garlic, minced

1 tablespoon minced fresh ginger

1 tablespoon slivered orange zest

1 red bell pepper, cut into thin strips

1 green bell pepper, cut into thin strips

6 ounces snow peas, trimmed and cut lengthwise in half

1 rib celery, thinly sliced

8 ounces angel hair or capellini pasta

½ cup thinly sliced scallions

1. Start heating a large pot of water to boiling for the pasta. In a small bowl, combine the broth, soy sauce, marmalade, sherry, 1 teaspoon of the cornstarch, and vinegar; stir to blend. Set aside.

2. On a plate, spread the remaining 2 teaspoons cornstarch. Dredge the beef in the cornstarch, shaking off the excess. In a large non-stick skillet, heat 1 tablespoon of the oil until hot but not smoking over medium heat. Add the beef and cook, stirring frequently, until golden brown, about 3 minutes. With a slotted spoon, transfer the beef to a plate.

3. Add the remaining 1 tablespoon oil, the garlic, ginger, and zest to the pan and cook, stirring frequently, until fragrant, about 1 minute. Add the bell peppers, snow peas, and celery and cook, stirring frequently, until the vegetables are crisp-tender, about 4 minutes. Stir the broth mixture again and add to the pan. Bring to a boil over medium-high heat and cook, stirring constantly, until the mixture is slightly thickened, about 1 minute. Stir in the beef and cook until heated through, about 3 minutes longer.

4. Meanwhile, cook the angel hair pasta in the boiling water until just tender. Drain well. Transfer the beef mixture to a large bowl, add the pasta and scallions, and toss to combine. Spoon the pasta mixture onto 4 plates and serve.

Suggested accompaniments: Almond tea, and orange wedges for dessert.

FAT: 10G/21%
CALORIES: 430
SATURATED FAT: 1.6G
CARBOHYDRATE: 61G
PROTEIN: 23G
CHOLESTEROL: 32MG
SODIUM: 582MG

PORK AND PEPPER SAUCE

SERVES: 4
WORKING TIME: 35 MINUTES
TOTAL TIME: 35 MINUTES

B right bell pepper strips, sautéed with onion and garlic, are the highlight of this easy dinner dish. Pork tenderloin gives the sauce substance; balsamic vinegar provides a gentle tang. Accompany the pasta with a tossed salad of mixed greens. Serve the salad before, with, or—Italian style—after the main course.

10 ounces shaped pasta, such as rotini, radiatore, or cavatappi

3 tablespoons flour

½ teaspoon salt

¼ teaspoon freshly ground black pepper

10 ounces well-trimmed pork tenderloin, cut into ½-inch cubes

1 tablespoon olive oil

1 onion, quartered and thinly sliced

4 cloves garlic, slivered

1 green bell pepper, cut into 1 x ¼-inch strips

1 red bell pepper, cut into 1 x ¼-inch strips

1⅓ cups reduced-sodium chicken broth, defatted

1 tablespoon no-salt-added tomato paste

2 tablespoons balsamic vinegar

1. In a large pot of boiling water, cook the pasta until just tender. Drain well.

2. Meanwhile, on a sheet of waxed paper, combine 2 tablespoons of the flour, the salt, and black pepper. Dredge the pork in the flour mixture, shaking off and reserving the excess. In a large nonstick skillet, heat the oil until hot but not smoking over medium heat. Add the pork and cook, stirring, until golden brown all over, about 4 minutes. With a slotted spoon, transfer the pork to a plate.

3. Add the onion and garlic to the pan and cook until the onion is softened, about 7 minutes. Add the bell peppers and cook, stirring, until the bell peppers are crisp-tender, about 5 minutes.

4. Sprinkle the remaining 1 tablespoon flour and the reserved dredging mixture over the vegetables, stirring to coat. Gradually add the broth, stirring until smooth and slightly thickened, about 2 minutes. Return the pork to the pan. Add the tomato paste and vinegar and cook, stirring frequently, until the sauce is thickened, and the pork is cooked through, about 1 minute. Toss the sauce with the hot pasta, divide among 4 plates, and serve.

Helpful hint: Pork should be thoroughly cooked, but overcooking will toughen it. These small cubes of meat will cook through in 4 minutes.

FAT: 7G/14%
CALORIES: 439
SATURATED FAT: 1.5G
CARBOHYDRATE: 66G
PROTEIN: 27G
CHOLESTEROL: 46MG
SODIUM: 506MG

This will remind you of good old-fashioned spaghetti and meatballs, but without all the fat. For our meatballs, we've used lean ground meats, low-fat milk, a sprinkle of sharp Parmesan, and an egg white rather than a whole egg. If lean ground pork is not available, substitute an extra quarter pound of lean ground round.

SPAGHETTI AND LITTLE MEATBALLS

SERVES: 4
WORKING TIME: 20 MINUTES
TOTAL TIME: 25 MINUTES

1 tablespoon olive oil

1 medium onion, minced

2 cloves garlic, minced

¼ pound lean ground beef round

¼ pound lean ground pork

3 tablespoons chopped fresh parsley

½ teaspoon dried oregano

½ teaspoon salt

¼ teaspoon dried sage

¼ teaspoon freshly ground black pepper

2 slices (1 ounce each) white bread, crumbled

3 tablespoons low-fat (1%) milk

⅓ cup grated Parmesan cheese

1 egg white

14½-ounce can no-salt-added stewed tomatoes

8-ounce can no-salt-added tomato sauce

10 ounces spaghetti

1. Start heating a large pot of water to boiling for the pasta. In a large nonstick skillet, heat the oil until hot but not smoking over medium heat. Add the onion and garlic and cook, stirring frequently, until the onion begins to soften, about 5 minutes. Transfer the onion to a large bowl. Reserve the skillet.

2. Add the ground beef and pork, the parsley, oregano, salt, sage, and pepper to the onion and mix well. Stir in the bread, milk, 3 tablespoons of the Parmesan, and egg white until well combined. Shape into 32 small meatballs (see tip).

3. In the reserved skillet, combine the tomatoes and the tomato sauce, breaking the tomatoes up with the back of a spoon. Bring to a boil over medium-high heat, reduce to a simmer, and add the meatballs. Cover and cook until the meatballs are cooked through, about 7 minutes.

4. Meanwhile, cook the spaghetti in the boiling water until just tender. Drain well. Transfer the meatballs and sauce to a large bowl, add the spaghetti and the remaining Parmesan, and toss to combine. Spoon the spaghetti and meatballs onto 4 plates and serve.

Suggested accompaniments: Romaine and cherry tomato salad with an herbed buttermilk dressing, and pears poached in apricot nectar with grated lemon zest for dessert.

FAT: 15G/25%
CALORIES: 547
SATURATED FAT: 4.8G
CARBOHYDRATE: 76G
PROTEIN: 27G
CHOLESTEROL: 44MG
SODIUM: 570MG

TIP

Keeping the meatballs small distributes the meat more evenly throughout each serving, creating the sensation of richness in every bite. Lightly dampen your hands, pull off a piece of meat mixture about the size of a walnut, and gently roll into balls with your fingertips or the palms of your hands. Place on a clean plate.

SPICY LINGUINE WITH BEEF AND BROCCOLI

SERVES: 4
WORKING TIME: 25 MINUTES
TOTAL TIME: 30 MINUTES

Juicy strips of beef are deliciously joined with vegetables to create this robust topping for pasta. Our sauce is beef broth based, lightly thickened with cornstarch, and then spiked with chili sauce, pepper flakes, and a little cinnamon. When shopping, remember that cuts of beef containing the words "round" or "loin" are among the leanest choices.

3 teaspoons cornstarch
½ pound beef top round, trimmed and cut into 2-by-¼-inch strips
2 tablespoons vegetable oil
1 carrot, thinly sliced
1 red bell pepper, cut into 1-inch squares
4 cloves garlic, slivered
⅔ cup reduced-sodium beef broth, defatted
2 tablespoons chili sauce
1 teaspoon ground ginger
½ teaspoon red pepper flakes
½ teaspoon salt
¼ teaspoon cinnamon
¼ teaspoon freshly ground black pepper
3 cups small broccoli florets
8 ounces linguine

1. Start heating a large pot of water to boiling for the pasta. On a plate, spread 2 teaspoons of the cornstarch. Dredge the beef in the cornstarch, shaking off the excess. In a large nonstick skillet, heat the oil until hot but not smoking over medium heat. Add the beef and cook, stirring frequently, until golden brown, about 3 minutes. With a slotted spoon, transfer the beef to a plate.

2. Add the carrot to the pan and cook until beginning to soften, about 2 minutes. Add the bell pepper and garlic and cook, stirring frequently, until the bell pepper is crisp-tender, about 3 minutes. Add the broth, chili sauce, ginger, pepper flakes, salt, cinnamon, and black pepper and bring to a boil over medium-high heat. Add the broccoli, cover, and cook until the broccoli is crisp-tender, about 3 minutes longer.

3. In a cup, combine the remaining 1 teaspoon cornstarch and 1 tablespoon of water, stir to blend, and stir into the broccoli mixture. Stir in the beef. Return to a boil and cook, uncovered, stirring constantly, until the sauce is slightly thickened, about 1 minute longer.

4. Meanwhile, cook the linguine in the boiling water until just tender. Drain well. Transfer the beef mixture to a large bowl, add the linguine, and toss to combine. Spoon the linguine mixture into 4 shallow bowls and serve.

Suggested accompaniment: Lemon sherbet garnished with toasted coconut.

FAT: 10G/22%
CALORIES: 412
SATURATED FAT: 1.6G
CARBOHYDRATE: 57G
PROTEIN: 25G
CHOLESTEROL: 32MG
SODIUM: 557MG

RIGATONI WITH TOMATOES, MUSHROOMS, AND SAUSAGE

SERVES: 4
WORKING TIME: 30 MINUTES
TOTAL TIME: 35 MINUTES

1 teaspoon olive oil

¼ pound sweet Italian pork sausage, casings removed

1 medium red onion, finely chopped

½ pound mushrooms, cut into quarters

14½-ounce can no-salt-added stewed tomatoes

8-ounce can no-salt-added tomato sauce

½ teaspoon fennel seeds

½ teaspoon dried oregano

½ teaspoon salt

2 tablespoons chopped fresh parsley

10 ounces rigatoni pasta

1. Start heating a large pot of water to boiling for the pasta. In a large nonstick skillet, heat the oil until hot but not smoking over medium heat. Add the sausage and cook, stirring frequently to crumble, until no longer pink, about 4 minutes. With a slotted spoon, remove the sausage to a plate.

2. Add the onion to the pan and cook, stirring frequently, until the onion has softened, about 7 minutes. Add the mushrooms and cook, stirring frequently, until the mushrooms release their juices and are tender, about 5 minutes.

3. Stir in the tomatoes, breaking them up with the back of a spoon. Add the tomato sauce, ¼ cup of water, fennel seeds, oregano, salt, and sausage. Bring to a boil over high heat, reduce to a simmer, cover, and cook until the sauce is slightly thickened and the sausage is cooked through, about 5 minutes longer. Stir in the parsley.

4. Meanwhile, cook the rigatoni in the boiling water until just tender. Drain well. Transfer the sauce to a large bowl, add the rigatoni, and toss to combine. Spoon the rigatoni mixture into 4 shallow bowls and serve.

Suggested accompaniments: Cold steamed broccoli with a balsamic vinaigrette, and gingersnaps with fresh pineapple wedges for dessert.

FAT: 14G/27%
CALORIES: 471
SATURATED FAT: 4.5G
CARBOHYDRATE: 71G
PROTEIN: 16G
CHOLESTEROL: 19MG
SODIUM: 505MG

Here we've transformed a quarter pound of flavor-packed Italian sausage into a deeply satisfying pasta sauce that serves four. We did it by adding a generous amount of mushrooms and then tossing the sauce with rigatoni, a hearty pasta shape. To prepare mushrooms, wipe them clean with a damp cloth or rinse lightly, then pat dry with paper towels.

CHEESE TORTELLINI WITH PROSCIUTTO AND PEAS

SERVES: 4
WORKING TIME: 20 MINUTES
TOTAL TIME: 50 MINUTES

*K*eep a package of fresh cheese tortellini on hand and you'll be ready to make this great meal on short notice.

1 teaspoon olive oil
1 onion, coarsely chopped
2 cloves garlic, minced
2 cups sliced mushrooms
¼ teaspoon red pepper flakes
Two 16-ounce cans no-salt-added tomatoes, drained and chopped
⅓ cup dry red wine
⅓ cup chopped fresh basil
¼ cup plus 2 tablespoons finely chopped prosciutto or Canadian bacon (2 ounces)
2 cups frozen peas, thawed
15-ounce package fresh cheese tortellini

1. In a large nonstick saucepan, heat the oil until hot but not smoking over medium heat. Add the onion and cook until softened, about 5 minutes. Add the garlic, mushrooms, and red pepper flakes and cook, stirring, until the mushrooms are tender, about 5 minutes.

2. Add the tomatoes and wine, bring to simmer, and cook until slightly thickened, about 15 minutes. Stir in the basil, prosciutto, and peas and cook until the peas are warmed through, about 2 minutes.

3. Meanwhile, in a large pot of boiling water, cook the tortellini until just tender. Drain well. Toss the tortellini with the sauce, divide among 4 bowls, and serve.

Helpful hint: If you have a hinged egg slicer, you can use it to slice mushrooms quickly. Buy large mushrooms and place them stemmed-side up in the slicer.

FAT: 12G/21%
CALORIES: 508
SATURATED FAT: 3.9G
CARBOHYDRATE: 77G
PROTEIN: 25G
CHOLESTEROL: 55MG
SODIUM: 736MG

STIR-FRIED BEEF WITH GREEN PEPPER SAUCE

SERVES: 4
WORKING TIME: 15 MINUTES
TOTAL TIME: 30 MINUTES

8 ounces linguine

2 green bell peppers, quartered lengthwise and seeded

3 cloves garlic, peeled

½ cup packed fresh parsley leaves

½ cup frozen peas, thawed

1 slice (1 ounce) firm-textured white bread

2 tablespoons capers, rinsed and drained

⅔ cup reduced-sodium chicken broth, defatted

2 tablespoons flour

½ teaspoon salt

10 ounces well-trimmed beef sirloin, cut into 2 x ¼-inch strips

1 tablespoon olive oil

1 red bell pepper, cut into strips

1. In a large pot of boiling water, cook the linguine until just tender. Drain well.

2. Meanwhile, preheat the broiler. Place the green bell peppers, cut-sides down, on the broiler rack. Broil the peppers 4 inches from the heat for about 10 minutes, or until the skin is blackened. When cool enough to handle, peel the peppers. Transfer the green bell peppers to a food processor. Add the garlic, parsley, peas, bread, and capers and process until well combined. Add the broth and process until smooth, about 1 minute.

3. On a sheet of waxed paper, combine the flour and salt. Dredge the beef in the flour mixture, shaking off the excess. In a large nonstick skillet, heat the oil until hot but not smoking over medium-high heat. Add the beef and cook, stirring frequently, until no longer pink, about 1 minute. Stir in the red bell pepper strips and the green pepper sauce and cook just until heated through, about 3 minutes. Toss with the pasta, divide among 4 bowls, and serve.

Helpful hint: To make it easier to peel the broiled peppers, transfer them directly from the oven to a bowl; cover and let stand for a few minutes to steam. This helps loosen the skins.

FAT: 8G/18%
CALORIES: 408
SATURATED FAT: 1.7G
CARBOHYDRATE: 57G
PROTEIN: 26G
CHOLESTEROL: 43MG
SODIUM: 668MG

This thick puréed sauce, made with roasted bell peppers, green peas, garlic, and capers, is practically fat-free.

PAPRIKASH SAUCE

SERVES: 4
WORKING TIME: 35 MINUTES
TOTAL TIME: 35 MINUTES

Paprika is one of the defining ingredients of Hungarian cuisine. Dishes called "paprikash" (which may be made with poultry, meat, or fish) are lavished with a velvety paprika sauce made with sour cream. Such dishes are traditionally served over dumplings, rice, or egg noodles. Offer a green salad or a steamed green vegetable on the side.

10 ounces wide egg noodles
2 teaspoons olive oil
4 scallions, thinly sliced
3 cloves garlic, minced
½ pound mushrooms, thinly sliced
1 cup jarred roasted red peppers, rinsed and drained
2 tablespoons no-salt-added tomato paste
2 teaspoons paprika
10 ounces well-trimmed top round of beef, cut into chunks
½ cup plain nonfat yogurt
3 tablespoons reduced-fat sour cream
2 tablespoons flour
¾ teaspoon salt

1. In a large pot of boiling water, cook the pasta until just tender. Drain well.

2. Meanwhile, in a large nonstick skillet, heat the oil until hot but not smoking over medium heat. Add the scallions and garlic and cook, stirring frequently, until the scallions are tender, about 2 minutes. Add the mushrooms and cook, stirring frequently, until the mushrooms are slightly softened, about 5 minutes.

3. In a food processor, combine the roasted red peppers, tomato paste, and paprika and process to a smooth purée. Transfer the purée to a small bowl and set aside. In the same processor bowl, process the beef until coarsely chopped.

4. Crumble the ground beef into the skillet and cook until no longer pink, about 4 minutes. Add the pepper purée and cook until the sauce is heated through, about 3 minutes. In a small bowl, combine the yogurt, sour cream, flour, and salt. Stir the yogurt mixture and ⅓ cup of water into the skillet and cook, stirring constantly, until the sauce is slightly thickened and no floury taste remains, about 2 minutes. Toss with the hot pasta, divide among 4 plates, and serve.

Helpful hint: Stirring flour into the yogurt-sour cream mixture helps keep the sauce from "breaking." Stirring gently (not vigorously) helps, too.

FAT: 10G/19%
CALORIES: 473
SATURATED FAT: 2.6G
CARBOHYDRATE: 65G
PROTEIN: 31G
CHOLESTEROL: 112MG
SODIUM: 574MG

PENNE BOLOGNESE

SERVES: 4
WORKING TIME: 25 MINUTES
TOTAL TIME: 45 MINUTES

Our streamlined version of the classic Bolognese meat sauce captures all the hearty goodness of the long-simmering version, but takes just one-quarter of the time to prepare. Low-fat milk adds creaminess but little extra fat. The penne pasta stands up well to this thick red sauce, but you could substitute another sturdy shape, such as rigatoni or ziti.

2 teaspoons olive oil
1 large onion, minced
1 carrot, minced
1 rib celery, minced
½ pound lean ground beef
½ cup dry white wine
⅓ cup no-salt-added tomato paste
1⅔ cups low-fat (1%) milk
¾ teaspoon salt
½ teaspoon freshly ground black pepper
½ teaspoon dried oregano
12 ounces penne pasta
¼ cup chopped fresh parsley (optional)
3 tablespoons grated Parmesan or Romano cheese

1. In a large nonstick skillet, heat the oil until hot but not smoking over medium heat. Add the onion and cook, stirring frequently, until softened, about 7 minutes. Stir in the carrot, celery, and ⅓ cup of water and cook until the vegetables are tender and the liquid has evaporated, about 5 minutes.

2. Start heating a large pot of water to boiling for the pasta. Add the ground beef to the vegetable mixture and cook, stirring frequently, until the beef is no longer pink, about 4 minutes. Add the wine and cook until the liquid has evaporated, about 5 minutes. Stir in the tomato paste, ⅔ cup of the milk, the salt, pepper, and oregano. Reduce to a simmer and cook, stirring frequently, until the milk has been absorbed, about 3 minutes. Continue to cook until the sauce is creamy and thickened, gradually adding the remaining 1 cup milk until completely absorbed, about 20 minutes longer.

3. Meanwhile, cook the penne in the boiling water until just tender. Drain well. Transfer the sauce to a large bowl, add the penne, parsley, and Parmesan, and toss to combine. Spoon the penne mixture into 4 shallow bowls and serve.

Suggested accompaniments: Shredded Belgian endive with cooked frozen artichoke hearts tossed with a nonfat Italian dressing, and raspberry granita for dessert.

FAT: 18G/27%
CALORIES: 596
SATURATED FAT: 6.6G
CARBOHYDRATE: 80G
PROTEIN: 28G
CHOLESTEROL: 50MG
SODIUM: 610MG

Thai-Style Beef and Peanut Sauce

Serves: 4
Working time: 30 minutes
Total time: 30 minutes

The savory peanut sauce of Thailand, commonly served with skewers of grilled meat, is a lively blend of peanut butter, chilies, coconut milk, lime juice, and a bit of fish sauce. Our version, sweetened and smoothed with honey (without the fish sauce and coconut milk), richly coats fettuccine, beef, bell pepper, and baby corn. Serve glasses of mixed tropical fruit juice as a cooling accompaniment.

10 ounces fettuccine
2 tablespoons flour
¼ teaspoon salt
½ pound well-trimmed sirloin, cut into 2 x ¼-inch strips
2 teaspoons vegetable oil
1 red bell pepper, cut into ¼-inch-wide strips
3 cloves garlic, minced
¼ cup chili sauce
2 tablespoons reduced-sodium soy sauce
2 tablespoons honey
2 tablespoons creamy peanut butter
3 tablespoons fresh lime juice
1 cup canned baby corn, rinsed, drained, and cut into 1-inch lengths
¼ cup chopped fresh basil

1. In a large pot of boiling water, cook the pasta until just tender. Drain well.

2. Meanwhile, on a sheet of waxed paper, combine the flour and salt. Dredge the beef in the flour mixture, shaking off the excess. In a large nonstick skillet, heat the oil until hot but not smoking over medium heat. Add the beef and cook, stirring, until lightly browned, about 2 minutes. Add the bell pepper and garlic and cook, stirring frequently, until the pepper is crisp-tender, about 3 minutes.

3. In a small bowl, stir together the chili sauce, soy sauce, ⅓ cup of water, the honey, peanut butter, and lime juice. Add the mixture to the skillet along with the corn and basil and bring to a simmer. Toss the sauce with the hot pasta and serve.

Helpful hint: You'll need 2 medium limes to yield 3 tablespoons of juice.

Fat: 13g/23%
Calories: 515
Saturated Fat: 2.5g
Carbohydrate: 75g
Protein: 27g
Cholesterol: 102mg
Sodium: 764mg

PORK PICCATA SAUCE

SERVES: 4
WORKING TIME: 30 MINUTES
TOTAL TIME: 30 MINUTES

10 ounces shaped pasta, such as gemelli, rotini, or radiatore

2 tablespoons flour

½ teaspoon salt

¼ teaspoon freshly ground black pepper

10 ounces well-trimmed pork tenderloin, cut into 2 x ½-inch strips

1 tablespoon olive oil

1 red onion, finely chopped

6 cloves garlic, minced

1 cup reduced-sodium chicken broth, defatted

1 teaspoon grated lemon zest

2 tablespoons fresh lemon juice

¼ cup pimiento-stuffed green olives, coarsely chopped

1 tablespoon capers, rinsed and drained

¼ cup chopped fresh parsley

1. In a large pot of boiling water, cook the pasta until just tender. Drain well.

2. Meanwhile, on a sheet of waxed paper, combine the flour, salt, and pepper. Dredge the pork in the flour mixture, shaking off and reserving the excess. In a large nonstick skillet, heat the oil until hot but not smoking over medium heat. Add the pork and cook, stirring frequently, until lightly browned, about 2 minutes. Add the onion and garlic and cook, stirring frequently, until the onion is crisp-tender, about 5 minutes. Sprinkle the reserved flour over, stirring to combine.

3. Gradually add the broth to the pan, stirring constantly, until well combined. Add the lemon zest, lemon juice, olives, and capers. Cook, stirring constantly, until the sauce is slightly thickened, about 3 minutes. Add the parsley, toss with the hot pasta, divide among 4 plates, and serve.

Helpful hint: If you squeeze a large lemon, you're likely to get more juice than the 2 tablespoons called for here. Use the extra juice in a salad dressing to serve with this meal, or add it to orange or grape juice for an extra-refreshing beverage.

Veal piccata, a fixture on Italian restaurant menus, can also be made with thin cuts of poultry or pork. We've cut the pork tenderloin in strips so it can be tossed with pasta; the familiar lemon-garlic sauce remains the same. Gemelli—the word means "twins"—are double pasta tubes, twisted or scrolled together.

FAT: 8G/17%
CALORIES: 433
SATURATED FAT: 1.6G
CARBOHYDRATE: 63G
PROTEIN: 26G
CHOLESTEROL: 46MG
SODIUM: 720MG

BEEF AND VEGETABLE STIR-FRY

SERVES: 4
WORKING TIME: 25 MINUTES
TOTAL TIME: 25 MINUTES

Rather than serving this stir-fry over rice, we've tossed the beef and vegetables—asparagus, carrots, and bell pepper—with freshly cooked fettuccine for a delightfully colorful dish. Chicken broth, lightly thickened with cornstarch and seasoned with sesame oil and ground ginger, forms a glossy, delicate sauce. Quick and simple to prepare, this stir-fry is great for casual entertaining.

8 ounces fettuccine

2 tablespoons flour

¾ teaspoon salt

¼ teaspoon freshly ground black pepper

½ pound well-trimmed top round of beef, cut into 2 x ½-inch strips

1 tablespoon olive oil

1 onion, halved and thinly sliced

2 carrots, halved lengthwise and thinly sliced

1 red bell pepper, cut into 2 x ½-inch strips

¾ pound asparagus, tough ends trimmed, cut into 2-inch lengths

1¼ cups reduced-sodium chicken broth, defatted

1¼ teaspoons cornstarch

1 teaspoon dark Oriental sesame oil

¾ teaspoon ground ginger

1. In a large pot of boiling water, cook the pasta until just tender. Drain well. Meanwhile, on a sheet of waxed paper, combine the flour, ¼ teaspoon of the salt, and the black pepper. Dredge the beef in the flour mixture, shaking off the excess. In a large non-stick skillet, heat the olive oil until hot but not smoking over medium-high heat. Add the beef and cook, stirring frequently, until lightly browned, about 1 minute. With a slotted spoon, transfer the beef to a plate.

2. Add the onion to the skillet, reduce the heat to medium, and cook, stirring frequently, until softened, about 5 minutes. Add the carrots and bell pepper and cook, stirring frequently, until the carrots are crisp-tender, about 3 minutes. Add the asparagus and ¼ cup of the broth and cook, stirring, until the asparagus are crisp-tender, about 3 minutes.

3. In a small bowl, combine the cornstarch, the remaining 1 cup broth, the sesame oil, ginger, and the remaining ½ teaspoon salt, whisking to blend. Stir into the skillet, bring to a boil, and return the beef to the pan. Cook, stirring, until slightly thickened, about 1 minute. Toss with the hot pasta and serve.

Helpful hint: The vegetables can be cut up in advance, wrapped separately, and refrigerated.

FAT: 9G/20%
CALORIES: 403
SATURATED FAT: 1.8G
CARBOHYDRATE: 55G
PROTEIN: 25G
CHOLESTEROL: 86MG
SODIUM: 645MG

Naples is the home of pizzaiola sauce, a simple tomato sauce of the sort used on pizza. This particular version is seasoned with basil rather than the usual oregano. The strips of beef and red bell pepper harmonize nicely with long pasta strands. Although we call for long fusilli, any strand pasta will work well. For a burst of color, try the sauce with spinach linguine.

BEEF PIZZAIOLA SAUCE

SERVES: 4
WORKING TIME: 35 MINUTES
TOTAL TIME: 35 MINUTES

10 ounces medium strand pasta, such as long fusilli, linguine, or spaghetti

2 tablespoons flour

½ teaspoon salt

½ pound well-trimmed sirloin, cut into 2 x ¼-inch strips (see tip)

1 tablespoon olive oil

1 onion, halved and thinly sliced

1 red bell pepper, cut into ¼-inch-wide strips

Half of a 10-ounce package Italian flat green beans, thawed and halved crosswise

4 cloves garlic, minced

½ pound plum tomatoes, coarsely chopped

8-ounce can no-salt-added tomato sauce

½ cup chopped fresh basil

1. In a large pot of boiling water, cook the pasta until just tender. Drain well.

2. Meanwhile, on a sheet of waxed paper, combine the flour and salt. Dredge the beef in the flour mixture, shaking off and reserving the excess. In a large nonstick skillet, heat the oil until hot but not smoking over medium heat. Add the beef and cook, stirring frequently, until lightly browned, about 2 minutes.

3. Add the onion, bell pepper, green beans, and garlic to the pan and cook, stirring frequently, until the pepper is tender, about 5 minutes. Sprinkle the reserved flour mixture over, stirring to coat. Add the tomatoes, tomato sauce, and basil and cook until the sauce is slightly thickened, about 4 minutes. Toss with the hot pasta, divide among 4 plates, and serve.

Helpful hint: If you can't get Italian flat green beans, use regular frozen green beans.

FAT: 8G/16%
CALORIES: 458
SATURATED FAT: 1.5G
CARBOHYDRATE: 73G
PROTEIN: 25G
CHOLESTEROL: 35MG
SODIUM: 332MG

TIP

To cut the meat, first chill the steak in the freezer for about 15 minutes to firm it. Then, with a long, sharp knife, cut the steak in half horizontally, using a careful sawing motion. Separate the two pieces of meat and cut each piece crosswise into 2 x ¼-inch strips.

LINGUINE WITH BEEF AND CARAMELIZED ONIONS

SERVES: 4
WORKING TIME: 30 MINUTES
TOTAL TIME: 40 MINUTES

Diced sirloin makes a most luxurious meat sauce in this traditional dish, and sherry adds a subtle, graceful note.

1 tablespoon olive oil

1½ tablespoons finely chopped pancetta or Canadian bacon

3 large onions, coarsely chopped

3 cloves garlic, minced

1 large carrot, finely chopped

10 ounces linguine

¼ cup dry sherry

1 cup reduced-sodium chicken broth, defatted

¾ teaspoon salt

½ teaspoon dried oregano

¼ teaspoon freshly ground black pepper

6 ounces well-trimmed sirloin, cut into ¼-inch dice

2 tablespoons flour

2 tablespoons grated Parmesan cheese

1. Bring a large pot of boiling water to a boil for the pasta. In a large nonstick skillet, heat the oil until hot but not smoking over medium heat. Add the pancetta and cook until lightly crisped, about 1 minute. Add the onions and garlic and cook, stirring frequently, until the onions are golden brown, about 10 minutes. Add the carrot and cook, stirring frequently, until the carrot is tender, about 5 minutes.

2. Meanwhile, in a large pot of boiling water, cook the linguine until tender. Drain well.

3. Add the sherry to the skillet, increase the heat to high, and cook until the sherry has evaporated, about 2 minutes. Stir in the broth, salt, oregano, and pepper and reduce the heat to medium. Add the meat, stirring to coat. Sprinkle the flour on top, stirring until the meat is well coated. Cook, stirring frequently, until the sauce is slightly thickened and the meat is cooked through, about 3 minutes. Transfer to a large bowl, add the linguine, and toss well to combine. Add the Parmesan, toss again, divide the mixture among 4 bowls, and serve.

Helpful hint: Sherry comes in varying degrees of sweetness: Choose a dry sherry for use in savory dishes such as this one—Manzanilla and fino are among the best.

FAT: 8G/15%
CALORIES: 482
SATURATED FAT: 1.9G
CARBOHYDRATE: 75G
PROTEIN: 23G
CHOLESTEROL: 30MG
SODIUM: 712MG

STIR-FRIED BEEF WITH TOMATO-PESTO SAUCE

SERVES: 4
WORKING TIME: 40 MINUTES
TOTAL TIME: 40 MINUTES

12 ounces bow-tie pasta

1 cup packed fresh basil leaves

½ cup packed fresh parsley leaves

3 cloves garlic, peeled

2 teaspoons cornstarch

1 cup reduced-sodium chicken broth, defatted

3 tablespoons pine nuts, toasted

1 teaspoon salt

¼ teaspoon hot pepper sauce

1 teaspoon olive oil

¾ pound well-trimmed top round of beef, cut into 2-by-¼-inch strips

2 cups cherry tomatoes, halved

2 tablespoons grated Parmesan cheese

1. In a large pot of boiling water, cook the pasta until just tender. Drain well.

2. Meanwhile, in a food processor or blender, combine the basil, parsley, 1 clove of the garlic, the cornstarch, broth, pine nuts, salt, and hot pepper sauce and process to a smooth purée.

3. In a large nonstick skillet or wok, heat the oil until hot but not smoking over medium heat. Add the beef and stir-fry until still slightly pink in the center. With a slotted spoon, transfer the beef to a plate.

4. Mince the remaining 2 cloves garlic and add them to the skillet along with the tomatoes. Stir-fry for 1 minute and add the basil purée. Bring to simmer, stirring, and cook until heated through and slightly thickened. Return the beef to the pan, stirring to combine. Combine the beef mixture with the pasta. Divide the beef and pasta among 4 bowls, sprinkle with the Parmesan, and serve.

Helpful hint: To toast the pine nuts, place them in a small, dry skillet and cook over medium heat, stirring and shaking the pan, for 3 minutes, or until golden.

FAT: 12G/20%
CALORIES: 532
SATURATED FAT: 2.9G
CARBOHYDRATE: 71G
PROTEIN: 37G
CHOLESTEROL: 131MG
SODIUM: 840MG

This bow tie and beef dish, lightly perfumed with basil, is a nice change from pasta with plain tomato sauce.

PENNE ALL'ARRABBIATA

SERVES: 4
WORKING TIME: 25 MINUTES
TOTAL TIME: 30 MINUTES

2 tablespoons olive oil

3 ounces Canadian bacon, diced

1 large red onion, diced

3 cloves garlic, minced

1½ pounds tomatoes

½ teaspoon dried rosemary

½ teaspoon salt

¼ to ½ teaspoon red pepper flakes

12 ounces penne pasta

3 tablespoons chopped fresh parsley

1. Start heating a large pot of water to boiling for the tomatoes and the pasta. In a large nonstick skillet, heat the oil until hot but not smoking over medium heat. Add the bacon and cook until lightly crisped, about 5 minutes. With a slotted spoon, transfer the bacon to a plate.

2. Add the onion and garlic to the pan and cook, stirring frequently, until the onion has softened, about 7 minutes. Meanwhile, blanch the tomatoes in the boiling water for 10 seconds. Reserve the boiling water for the pasta and, with a slotted spoon, transfer the tomatoes to a cutting board.

3. Using a paring knife, peel the tomatoes. Cut each tomato in half, and squeeze through a sieve set over a bowl to catch the juices. Discard the seeds. Coarsely chop the tomatoes and add to the onion mixture. Stir in the tomato juices, rosemary, salt, pepper flakes, and bacon and cook, stirring occasionally, until the sauce is slightly thickened, about 7 minutes longer.

4. Meanwhile, cook the penne in the reserved boiling water until just tender. Transfer the sauce to a large bowl, add the penne and parsley, and toss to combine. Spoon the penne mixture into 4 shallow bowls and serve.

Suggested accompaniments: Spinach salad with mushrooms and a red wine vinaigrette. For dessert, ripe fresh peaches or nectarines.

FAT: 10G/19%
CALORIES: 467
SATURATED FAT: 1.7G
CARBOHYDRATE: 77G
PROTEIN: 18G
CHOLESTEROL: 11MG
SODIUM: 600MG

The trademark of an "arrabbiata" sauce is the dominance of hot peppers, either fresh or dried. To tame the fiery flavor, we've added Canadian bacon and a dose of parsley to this great-tasting dish. If good-quality fresh tomatoes are unavailable, substitute a large can (twenty-eight ounces) of plum tomatoes. Rigatoni or rotini can be used instead of the penne.

Curry
and linguine didn't
exactly grow up next
door to one another,
but they get along very
well indeed. This
fusion of Indian and
Italian ingredients is
an unquestionable
success: The curry-
chutney sauce gilds the
pasta and lends vivid
flavor to the pork,
peppers, and peas.

LINGUINE WITH PORK AND CURRY

SERVES: 4
WORKING TIME: 25 MINUTES
TOTAL TIME: 25 MINUTES

8 ounces linguine

1 tablespoon vegetable oil

½ pound well-trimmed
pork tenderloin, cut into thin
slices (see tip)

1 red or green bell pepper, cut
into thin strips

1 onion, coarsely chopped

1 clove garlic, minced

2 teaspoons curry powder

1 cup reduced-sodium chicken
broth, defatted

10-ounce package frozen peas
and carrots, thawed

¼ cup mango chutney

1 teaspoon cornstarch mixed
with 1 tablespoon water

1. In a large pot of boiling water, cook the linguine until just tender. Drain well.

2. Meanwhile, in a large nonstick skillet, heat 2 teaspoons of the oil until hot but not smoking over medium heat. Add the pork and cook, stirring, until the pork is cooked through, about 6 minutes. With a slotted spoon, transfer the pork to a plate.

3. Add the remaining 1 teaspoon oil to the skillet. Add the bell pepper, onion, and garlic and cook, stirring, until the pepper and onion are crisp-tender, about 5 minutes. Stir in the curry powder and cook until fragrant, about 30 seconds. Stir in the broth, peas and carrots, chutney, and cornstarch mixture. Return the pork to the pan. Bring to a boil and cook, stirring, until the mixture is slightly thickened and the peas and carrots are warmed through, about 2 minutes. Transfer the mixture to a large bowl, add the drained pasta, and toss to combine. Divide the pasta mixture among 4 bowls and serve.

Helpful hint: Although chutney can be made with all sorts of fruits and vegetables, mango chutney is most familiar to Americans. Traditionally served with curries, chutney is also delicious as a condiment with cold meats or cheese. Mango chutney often contains large chunks of mango; for even flavoring, you may need to chop the chutney before using it in this dish.

FAT: 7G/15%
CALORIES: 428
SATURATED FAT: 1.3G
CARBOHYDRATE: 69G
PROTEIN: 23G
CHOLESTEROL: 37MG
SODIUM: 428MG

TIP

Pork tenderloin is a lean, boneless cut that takes the form of a tapered cylinder. When cut crosswise, it forms neat, uniform slices.

BEEF AND MACARONI SKILLET DINNER

SERVES: 4
WORKING TIME: 35 MINUTES
TOTAL TIME: 35 MINUTES

Those prepackaged meals-in-a-skillet mixes sure are tempting when you're short on time. But they don't compare with the fresh onions, peppers, scallions, and sharp Cheddar found here. And do you really want additives and preservatives on your dinner plate? It's well worth a few extra minutes to stir up this deliciously satisfying meal from scratch.

8 ounces ditalini pasta
2 teaspoons olive oil
1 onion, finely chopped
3 cloves garlic, minced
1 red bell pepper, cut into ½-inch squares
1 green bell pepper, cut into ½-inch squares
½ pound well-trimmed top round of beef, cut into chunks
2 teaspoons chili powder
1 teaspoon salt
14½-ounce can no-salt-added stewed tomatoes, chopped with their juices
3 tablespoons no-salt-added tomato paste
½ cup shredded Cheddar cheese (2 ounces)
1 scallion, thinly sliced

1. In a large pot of boiling water, cook the pasta until just tender. Drain well.

2. Meanwhile, in a large nonstick skillet, heat the oil until hot but not smoking over medium heat. Add the onion and garlic and cook, stirring frequently, until the onion is softened, about 5 minutes. Add the bell peppers and cook, stirring frequently, until crisp-tender, about 4 minutes.

3. In a food processor, process the beef until finely ground, about 30 seconds. Add to the skillet along with the chili powder and salt and cook, stirring frequently, until the beef is no longer pink, about 4 minutes. Stir in the tomatoes and tomato paste and bring to a boil. Reduce to a simmer and cook, stirring occasionally, until the flavors have blended, about 5 minutes.

4. Stir the drained ditalini into the skillet and cook until heated through, about 3 minutes. Sprinkle the Cheddar and scallion over and heat without stirring until the cheese has just melted, about 1 minute.

Helpful hint: Elbow macaroni or small pasta shells can be substituted for the ditalini, if you like.

FAT: 10G/21%
CALORIES: 431
SATURATED FAT: 4.1G
CARBOHYDRATE: 59G
PROTEIN: 26G
CHOLESTEROL: 47MG
SODIUM: 713MG

FETTUCCINE ALLA CARBONARA

SERVES: 4
WORKING TIME: 20 MINUTES
TOTAL TIME: 25 MINUTES

We've retained the rich texture of the classic carbonara sauce, but have used a few tricks to create a scrumptious slimmed-down version with only one-fifth the fat. Instead of the usual pancetta bacon, we've used leaner Canadian bacon. And we've replaced the standard cream and egg yolks with low-fat cottage cheese and light sour cream.

⅔ cup low-fat (1%) cottage cheese

1 tablespoon olive oil

¼ pound Canadian bacon, diced

1 large onion, finely chopped

3 cloves garlic, minced

½ cup reduced-sodium beef broth, defatted

¼ teaspoon freshly ground black pepper

2 tablespoons light sour cream

2 tablespoons grated Parmesan cheese

12 ounces fettuccine

¼ cup chopped fresh parsley

1. Start heating a large pot of water to boiling for the pasta. In a blender or food processor, purée the cottage cheese until smooth, about 1 minute. Set aside. In a large nonstick skillet, heat the oil until hot but not smoking over medium heat. Add the bacon and cook until lightly crisped, about 5 minutes. With a slotted spoon, transfer the bacon to a plate.

2. Add the onion and garlic to the pan and cook, stirring frequently, until the onion has softened, about 7 minutes. Add the broth and pepper and cook until heated through, about 1 minute. Reduce the heat to low. Whisk in the cottage cheese purée until well combined. Whisk in the sour cream, Parmesan, and bacon and cook just until the mixture is heated through, about 1 minute longer.

3. Meanwhile, cook the fettuccine in the boiling water until just tender. Transfer the sauce to a large bowl, add the fettuccine and parsley, and toss to combine. Spoon the fettuccine mixture onto 4 plates and serve.

Suggested accompaniments: Mulled cider, and a red leaf lettuce salad with slivers of roasted red bell pepper. For dessert, chilled green and red seedless grapes.

FAT: 11G/21%
CALORIES: 478
SATURATED FAT: 3G
CARBOHYDRATE: 69G
PROTEIN: 25G
CHOLESTEROL: 101MG
SODIUM: 700MG

BEEF AND BROCCOLI LO MEIN

SERVES: 4
WORKING TIME: 30 MINUTES
TOTAL TIME: 30 MINUTES

For the many and varied dishes that come under the heading of lo mein, Chinese cooks toss freshly cooked egg noodles with a sizzling stir-fry. We've substituted vermicelli (very thin spaghetti) for the Chinese noodles. The stir-fry is a mixture of beef and vegetables in a rich, savory sauce flavored with molasses, rice vinegar, and hot pepper sauce.

12 ounces vermicelli pasta

1 pound broccoli

¾ cup reduced-sodium chicken broth, defatted

3 tablespoons reduced-sodium soy sauce

1 tablespoon rice vinegar

1 tablespoon light molasses

½ teaspoon hot pepper sauce

2 teaspoons olive oil

2 cloves garlic, finely chopped

1 tablespoon chopped fresh ginger

¾ pound well-trimmed sirloin, cut into 2-by-¼-inch strips

3 plum tomatoes, halved, seeded, and cut into ¾-inch cubes

7-ounce jar baby corn, rinsed and drained

1 tablespoon cornstarch mixed with 2 tablespoons water

1. In a large pot of boiling water, cook the pasta until just tender. Drain well.

2. Meanwhile, cut the florets off the broccoli and set aside. Peel the broccoli stems and cut into ¼-inch-thick slices. In a small bowl, combine the broth, soy sauce, vinegar, molasses, and hot pepper sauce.

3. In a large nonstick skillet or wok, heat the oil until hot but not smoking over medium heat. Add the broccoli stems and stir-fry for 1 minute. Add the florets and stir-fry for 2 minutes. Add the garlic, ginger, and beef and stir-fry until the beef is no longer pink, about 1 minute. Add the tomatoes, broth mixture, and baby corn and bring to a boil. Stir in the cornstarch mixture and cook, stirring constantly, until slightly thickened, about 1 minute. Toss with the vermicelli and serve.

Helpful hint: Peeling the broccoli stems eliminates the tough outer layer, so they cook more quickly. It's easiest to do with a swivel-bladed vegetable peeler.

FAT: 8G/14%
CALORIES: 518
SATURATED FAT: 1.8G
CARBOHYDRATE: 78G
PROTEIN: 33G
CHOLESTEROL: 52MG
SODIUM: 673MG

BEEF AND MUSHROOM RAGÙ

SERVES: 4
WORKING TIME: 25 MINUTES
TOTAL TIME: 40 MINUTES

The Italian word ragù simply means a stew (think of ragoût). In culinary parlance, however, it denotes a rich, slow-cooked meat sauce. The ragùs of Bologna and Naples are quite famous: The Bolognese version is rich with butter and cream, while the Neapolitan sauce is made with red wine. Ours is an adaptation of the latter, with the addition of mushrooms.

1 tablespoon olive oil
1 onion, finely chopped
1 rib celery, finely chopped
1 carrot, finely chopped
¼ pound fresh shiitake or button mushrooms, trimmed and coarsely chopped
2 cloves garlic, minced
10 ounces medium tube pasta, such as ziti or penne
10 ounces well-trimmed top round of beef, cut into chunks
⅓ cup Marsala or dry red wine
1 cup reduced-sodium beef broth, defatted
2 cups no-salt-added canned tomatoes, chopped with their juices
¼ teaspoon salt
⅛ teaspoon red pepper flakes

1. In a large nonstick skillet, heat the oil until hot but not smoking over medium heat. Add the onion, celery, carrot, mushrooms, and garlic and cook, stirring frequently, until the vegetables are softened, about 9 minutes.

2. In a large pot of boiling water, cook the pasta until just tender. Drain well.

3. Meanwhile, in a food processor, process the meat until finely ground, about 1 minute. Add the meat to the skillet and cook until no longer pink, about 3 minutes. Add the Marsala, increase the heat to high, and cook until almost evaporated, about 2 minutes. Add the broth, tomatoes, salt, and red pepper flakes and bring to a boil. Reduce to a simmer, cover, and cook until the sauce is rich and flavorful, about 15 minutes. Divide the pasta among 4 bowls, spoon the sauce over, and serve.

Helpful hint: This sauce will freeze well. You can even package it in 4 individual portions and thaw it in the microwave as needed.

FAT: 7G/14%
CALORIES: 456
SATURATED FAT: 1.5G
CARBOHYDRATE: 68G
PROTEIN: 29G
CHOLESTEROL: 40MG
SODIUM: 369MG

SOUTHWESTERN CHILI SAUCE

SERVES: 4
WORKING TIME: 30 MINUTES
TOTAL TIME: 30 MINUTES

This hearty pork-and-bean sauce is based on traditional chili, but it's served over pasta for a healthier, high-carbohydrate meal. Tenderloin is the leanest pork cut, and there's no waste whatsoever. And because the meat is cut into small pieces, it cooks in minutes. Serve a green salad dressed with a lime-juice vinaigrette alongside.

10 ounces medium tube pasta, such as penne or ziti

1 tablespoon olive oil

1 onion, finely chopped

3 cloves garlic, minced

1 green bell pepper, cut into ½-inch squares

½ pound well-trimmed pork tenderloin, cut into ½-inch chunks

2 teaspoons chili powder

1 teaspoon ground cumin

½ cup reduced-sodium chicken broth, defatted

8-ounce can no-salt-added tomato sauce

16-ounce can black beans, rinsed and drained

1 pickled jalapeño, seeded and finely chopped

3 tablespoons reduced-fat sour cream

1. In a large pot of boiling water, cook the pasta until just tender. Drain well.

2. Meanwhile, in a large nonstick skillet, heat the oil until hot but not smoking over medium heat. Add the onion and garlic and cook, stirring frequently, until the onion is lightly browned, about 5 minutes. Add the bell pepper and cook, stirring frequently, until the pepper is crisp-tender, about 4 minutes.

3. Add the pork to the pan, sprinkle with the chili powder and cumin, and cook, stirring frequently, until the pork is almost cooked through, about 4 minutes. Stir in the broth and tomato sauce and bring to a boil. Add the beans and the jalapeño and cook until heated through, about 3 minutes. Toss with the hot pasta. Divide among 4 bowls, top with a dollop of the sour cream, and serve.

Helpful hints: As always, when using chili powder, take your family's tastes into consideration. If they don't appreciate hot food, use less chili powder than the recipe calls for. Also, check the label on the jar of chili powder you are using; some chili powders are hot while others are mild. The hot variety is often labeled "Hot Mexican Chili Powder."

FAT: 9G/16%
CALORIES: 495
SATURATED FAT: 2.1G
CARBOHYDRATE: 75G
PROTEIN: 28G
CHOLESTEROL: 41MG
SODIUM: 375MG

Water chestnuts, snow peas, and red pepper provide crunch, while the subtle sweetness of whole wheat linguine plays well against this gingery sauce. Compared to regular green cabbage, Napa cabbage has longer, crisper, and milder flavored leaves. If unavailable, you may substitute three or four ribs of thinly sliced celery.

PORK AND LINGUINE STIR-FRY

SERVES: 4
WORKING TIME: 25 MINUTES
TOTAL TIME: 30 MINUTES

1 cup reduced-sodium chicken broth, defatted

2½ tablespoons reduced-sodium soy sauce

2 tablespoons rice vinegar or cider vinegar

4 teaspoons cornstarch

6 ounces pork loin, trimmed and cut into 2-by-¼-inch strips

1 tablespoon plus 2 teaspoons peanut oil

1 red bell pepper, cut into thin strips

2 cups ¼-inch-wide shredded Napa cabbage (see tip)

4 cloves garlic, minced

⅓ cup chopped scallions

2 tablespoons minced fresh ginger

½ pound snow peas, trimmed and cut in half lengthwise

½ cup sliced water chestnuts, rinsed and drained

3 tablespoons chopped fresh cilantro or parsley

10 ounces whole wheat linguine

1. Start heating a large pot of water to boiling for the pasta. In a small bowl, combine the broth, soy sauce, and vinegar and stir to blend. Set aside. On a plate, spread 2 teaspoons of the cornstarch. Dredge the pork in the cornstarch, shaking off excess. In a large nonstick skillet, heat the oil until hot but not smoking over medium heat. Add the pork and cook, stirring frequently, until golden brown, about 3 minutes. With a slotted spoon, transfer the pork to a plate.

2. Add the bell pepper to the pan and cook for 1 minute. Add the cabbage and cook, stirring frequently, until crisp-tender, about 3 minutes. Add the garlic, scallions, and ginger and cook until fragrant, about 1 minute. Add the snow peas and water chestnuts and cook until the snow peas are crisp-tender, about 2 minutes. Add the broth mixture. Bring to a boil over medium-high heat.

3. In a cup, combine the remaining 2 teaspoons cornstarch and 1 tablespoon of water, stir to blend, and stir into the vegetable mixture. Cook, stirring constantly, until slightly thickened, about 1 minute. Add the pork, reduce the heat to medium-low, and cook until cooked through, about 1 minute longer. Stir in the cilantro.

4. Meanwhile, cook the linguine in the boiling water until just tender. Drain well. Transfer the sauce to a large bowl, add the linguine, and toss to combine. Spoon the pasta mixture onto 4 plates and serve.

Suggested accompaniment: Mandarin oranges served over vanilla ice milk.

FAT: 9G/19%
CALORIES: 437
SATURATED FAT: 1.9G
CARBOHYDRATE: 69G
PROTEIN: 24G
CHOLESTEROL: 27MG
SODIUM: 578MG

TIP

To shred Napa cabbage, first remove each leaf individually. Stack three to four leaves at a time and, with a large chef's knife, trim off and discard the tough ends. Then cut the stacked leaves crosswise into thin shreds about ¼ inch wide.

CHUNKY TOMATO AND MEATBALL SAUCE

SERVES: 4
WORKING TIME: 30 MINUTES
TOTAL TIME: 30 MINUTES

These juicy meatballs are made with a blend of beef and pork, but for a change, you can use one or the other instead of both.

10 ounces medium strand pasta, such as spaghetti or linguine

5 ounces well-trimmed pork tenderloin, cut into chunks

5 ounces well-trimmed top round of beef, cut into chunks

¼ cup evaporated low-fat or skimmed milk

1 slice (1 ounce) firm-textured white sandwich bread, torn into small pieces

6 tablespoons grated Parmesan cheese

3 tablespoons raisins

1 egg white

½ teaspoon dried marjoram or oregano

¼ teaspoon hot pepper sauce

1 tablespoon olive oil

¼ cup flour

2 cups no-salt-added canned tomatoes, chopped with their juices

1. In a large pot of boiling water, cook the pasta until just tender. Drain well.

2. In a food processor, combine the pork and beef and process until coarsely chopped and well combined, about 30 seconds. Transfer to a medium bowl and add the evaporated milk, bread, 3 tablespoons of the Parmesan, the raisins, egg white, marjoram, and hot pepper sauce, mixing to combine well. Shape the mixture into 24 small meatballs.

3. In a large nonstick skillet, heat the oil until hot but not smoking over medium heat. Dredge the meatballs in the flour, shaking off the excess. Add the meatballs to the pan and cook, turning them as they color, until golden brown, about 3 minutes.

4. Add the tomatoes and bring to a boil. Reduce to a simmer, cover, and cook until the meatballs are cooked through, about 5 minutes. Toss the sauce with the hot pasta. Divide among 4 plates, sprinkle the remaining 3 tablespoons Parmesan over, and serve.

Helpful hint: Whenever you're making meatballs or ground-beef patties, handle the mixture lightly so the finished product will be juicy and tender. It's a good idea to mix the ingredients with two forks, tossing them gently to combine.

FAT: 10G/17%
CALORIES: 524
SATURATED FAT: 3G
CARBOHYDRATE: 75G
PROTEIN: 32G
CHOLESTEROL: 52MG
SODIUM: 274MG

SMOTHERED BEEF AND ONION SAUCE

SERVES: 4
WORKING TIME: 35 MINUTES
TOTAL TIME: 35 MINUTES

½ pound all-purpose potatoes, peeled and cut into ½-inch cubes

10 ounces shaped pasta, such as small shells, ruote (wagon wheels), or radiatore

1 tablespoon olive oil

2 onions, finely chopped

3 cloves garlic, minced

1 green bell pepper, cut into ½-inch squares

10 ounces well-trimmed sirloin, cut into ½-inch cubes

¾ cup reduced-sodium beef broth, defatted

¾ teaspoon salt

¾ teaspoon dried oregano

3 tablespoons grated Parmesan cheese

1. In a large pot of boiling water, cook the potatoes until firm-tender, about 4 minutes. With a slotted spoon or sieve, transfer the potatoes to a bowl; set aside. In the same pot, cook the pasta until just tender. Drain well.

2. Meanwhile, in a large nonstick skillet, heat the oil until hot but not smoking over medium heat. Add the onions and garlic and cook, stirring frequently, until the onions are soft and lightly golden, about 10 minutes. Add the bell pepper and potatoes and cook, stirring frequently, until the pepper is crisp-tender, about 4 minutes.

3. Add the beef to the pan, stirring to combine. Add the broth, salt, and oregano and cook until the meat and potatoes are cooked through, about 4 minutes. Remove ½ cup of the vegetables, transfer to a food processor, and process to a smooth purée. Return to the skillet and heat gently until the sauce is slightly thickened, about 1 minute. Toss the sauce with the Parmesan and the hot pasta, divide among 4 plates, and serve.

Helpful hint: Instead of transferring the vegetables to a food processor, you can use a hand blender right in the pot. Run the blender in 1 or 2 on/off pulses to purée about ½ cup of the vegetables, while leaving the sauce chunky.

T his sauce is cleverly thickened by puréeing some of the vegetables rather than by adding butter or cream.

FAT: 9G/17%
CALORIES: 480
SATURATED FAT: 2.4G
CARBOHYDRATE: 70G
PROTEIN: 28G
CHOLESTEROL: 46MG
SODIUM: 651MG

CURRIED LAMB SAUCE

SERVES: 4
WORKING TIME: 20 MINUTES
TOTAL TIME: 30 MINUTES

Lamb and curry are a classic combination; the richness of the meat and the complex spicing of the seasoning are a natural match. Tangy morsels of dried apricot add interest to this short-cut curry, which is served over fettuccine rather than the traditional rice. As a common sense time-saver, the potatoes and pasta are cooked—one after the other—in a single pot.

½ pound all-purpose potatoes, peeled and cut into ½-inch cubes

10 ounces fettuccine

½ pound well-trimmed boneless lamb shoulder, cut into large chunks

2 teaspoons olive oil

4 scallions, thinly sliced

3 cloves garlic, minced

2 teaspoons curry powder

1 teaspoon ground ginger

1 teaspoon salt

Two 8-ounce cans no-salt-added tomato sauce

½ cup dried apricots, coarsely chopped

1 cup frozen peas

1. In a large pot of boiling water, cook the potatoes until firm-tender, about 4 minutes. With a slotted spoon or sieve, transfer the potatoes to a bowl and set aside. In the same pot, cook the pasta until just tender. Drain well.

2. Meanwhile, in a food processor, process the lamb until finely ground, about 30 seconds. In a large nonstick skillet, heat the oil until hot but not smoking over medium heat. Add the scallions and garlic and cook, stirring frequently, until the scallions are tender, about 2 minutes. Add the lamb and cook, stirring frequently, until no longer pink, about 2 minutes. Add the curry powder, ginger, and salt, stirring to coat.

3. Stir the tomato sauce, apricots, and ½ cup of water into the pan and bring to a boil. Reduce to a simmer, add the potatoes, cover, and cook until the sauce is flavorful, about 4 minutes. Add the peas and cook until just heated through. Toss with the hot pasta, divide among 4 plates, and serve.

Helpful hint: After removing the potatoes, be sure the water is still at a rolling boil before adding the pasta (otherwise the strands of fettuccine may stick together).

FAT: 10G/17%
CALORIES: 525
SATURATED FAT: 2.3G
CARBOHYDRATE: 84G
PROTEIN: 26G
CHOLESTEROL: 105MG
SODIUM: 677MG

A
cream sauce flavored
with delicate dill,
sharp mustard, and
tart lemon is typical of
Swedish cuisine. Such
a sauce might grace
anything from cured
salmon to a pot roast.
We've created a
lightened version of a
creamy Scandinavian-
style sauce by using
nonfat yogurt and
reduced-fat sour cream,
and incorporated it
into this beef stir-fry
served over noodles.

SWEDISH-STYLE BEEF STIR-FRY

SERVES: 4
WORKING TIME: 35 MINUTES
TOTAL TIME: 35 MINUTES

8 ounces wide egg noodles

1 tablespoon vegetable oil

½ pound well-trimmed sirloin, cut into 2-by-⅛-inch strips

2 cups sliced leeks, white and tender green parts only

2 carrots, thinly sliced

1 cup frozen peas, thawed

1 cup sliced scallions

¾ cup reduced-sodium chicken broth, defatted

½ teaspoon salt

¼ teaspoon freshly ground black pepper

2 teaspoons cornstarch

2 teaspoons Dijon mustard

1 teaspoon grated lemon zest

¼ cup reduced-fat sour cream

¼ cup plain nonfat yogurt

¼ cup snipped fresh dill (see tip)

1. In a large pot of boiling water, cook the noodles until just tender. Drain well.

2. Meanwhile, in a large nonstick skillet or wok, heat 2 teaspoons of the oil until hot but not smoking over medium-high heat. Add the beef and stir-fry until browned, 3 to 4 minutes. With a slotted spoon, transfer the beef to a plate.

3. Add the remaining 1 teaspoon oil to the skillet. Add the leeks and carrots and stir-fry until the vegetables are beginning to brown, about 2 minutes. Add the peas, scallions, broth, salt, and pepper. Bring to a boil, reduce to a simmer, and cook until the carrots are tender, 3 to 4 minutes.

4. In a small bowl, combine the cornstarch, 2 tablespoons of water, the mustard, lemon zest, sour cream, and yogurt. Add to the skillet and cook, stirring constantly, until the mixture is slightly thickened, about 1 minute. Return the beef to the skillet along with the dill and cook until heated through, about 1 minute. Combine with the noodles and serve.

Helpful hint: You can substitute an additional 1 cup sliced scallions for the leeks, if you like. Add them with the other scallions in step 3.

TIP

After rinsing and drying fresh dill, use kitchen shears to snip the feathery fronds directly into a measuring cup, avoiding the stems, until you have the amount the recipe calls for.

FAT: 11G/22%
CALORIES: 449
SATURATED FAT: 2.9G
CARBOHYDRATE: 62G
PROTEIN: 26G
CHOLESTEROL: 94MG
SODIUM: 587MG

STRAW AND HAY WITH HAM, MUSHROOMS, AND PEAS

SERVES: 4
WORKING TIME: 20 MINUTES
TOTAL TIME: 25 MINUTES

2 tablespoons olive oil

5 ounces baked ham, diced

4 shallots or 1 medium onion, minced

6 ounces mushrooms, thinly sliced

1 tablespoon flour

1 cup evaporated skimmed milk

½ teaspoon dried rosemary

¼ teaspoon salt

¼ teaspoon freshly ground black pepper

½ cup frozen peas

1 tablespoon light sour cream

6 ounces fresh fettuccine

6 ounces fresh spinach fettuccine

2 tablespoons chopped fresh parsley

1. Start heating a large pot of water to boiling for the pasta. In a large nonstick skillet, heat the oil until hot but not smoking over medium heat. Add the ham and cook, stirring frequently, until lightly browned, about 4 minutes. With a slotted spoon, transfer the ham to a plate.

2. Add the shallots to the pan and cook, stirring frequently, until softened, about 4 minutes. Add the mushrooms and cook, stirring frequently, until tender, about 4 minutes. Stir in the flour and cook until the liquid has been absorbed, about 3 minutes. Stir in the evaporated milk, rosemary, salt, pepper, and ham and cook, stirring occasionally, until the mixture is slightly thickened, about 4 minutes. Add the peas and cook until the peas are heated through, about 2 minutes longer. Remove from the heat and stir in the sour cream.

3. Meanwhile, cook the fettuccine in the boiling water until just tender. Drain well. Transfer the ham mixture to a large bowl, add the fettuccine and parsley, and toss to combine. Spoon the fettuccine mixture into 4 shallow bowls and serve.

Suggested accompaniments: Sliced red onion and romaine lettuce salad with a reduced-fat poppy seed dressing, and chocolate biscotti and espresso afterward.

FAT: 15G/29%
CALORIES: 469
SATURATED FAT: 2.3G
CARBOHYDRATE: 57G
PROTEIN: 27G
CHOLESTEROL: 129MG
SODIUM: 826MG

Two colors of fettuccine, green and yellow, are the "straw and hay" in this well-known ham and pea combination, traditionally made with heavy cream. We've substituted evaporated skimmed milk and a spoonful of light sour cream for extra richness. Thin ribbons of fresh fettuccine cook very quickly—in about two minutes—so time the sauce accordingly.

PASTA ALLA GENOVESE

SERVES: 4
WORKING TIME: 25 MINUTES
TOTAL TIME: 45 MINUTES

*L*iberal use of herbs and onion are two of the culinary hallmarks of Genovese cooking. Our delectable sauce is enriched with sherry, thickened with a little flour, and flavored with a surprise ingredient—a touch of grated orange zest that wonderfully complements the beef. Although we've used egg noodles, this sauce would also be good over bow ties or other small pasta shapes.

1 tablespoon olive oil

1 large onion, cut into large dice

1 carrot, halved lengthwise and thinly sliced

1 red bell pepper, cut into thin strips

2 teaspoons slivered orange zest

1 tablespoon flour

½ pound beef top round, trimmed and cut into 2-by-¼-inch strips

⅓ cup dry sherry

¾ cup reduced-sodium beef broth, defatted

½ teaspoon dried rosemary

½ teaspoon salt

¼ teaspoon freshly ground black pepper

2 tablespoons chopped fresh parsley

12 ounces wide egg noodles

¼ cup grated Parmesan cheese

1. Start heating a large pot of water to boiling for the pasta. In a large nonstick skillet, heat the oil until hot but not smoking over medium heat. Add the onion and cook, stirring frequently, until the onion begins to color, about 5 minutes. Stir in ⅓ cup of water and cook until the onion is golden brown and very tender, about 10 minutes. Stir in the carrot, bell pepper, and zest and cook until the vegetables are tender, about 4 minutes.

2. On a plate, spread the flour. Dredge the beef in the flour, shaking off the excess. Add the beef to the pan and cook, stirring frequently, until lightly browned, about 5 minutes. Add the sherry and cook until almost all the liquid has evaporated, about 4 minutes. Stir in the broth, rosemary, salt, and black pepper and cook until the beef is tender and the sauce is slightly thickened, about 5 minutes longer. Stir in the parsley.

3. Meanwhile, cook the noodles in the boiling water until just tender. Drain well. Transfer the beef mixture to a large bowl, add the noodles and Parmesan, and toss to combine. Spoon the noodle mixture onto 4 plates and serve.

Suggested accompaniments: Red wine, crusty peasant bread, and grapefruit sections broiled with a touch of brown sugar and vanilla for dessert.

FAT: 11G/18%
CALORIES: 539
SATURATED FAT: 2.8G
CARBOHYDRATE: 76G
PROTEIN: 29G
CHOLESTEROL: 117MG
SODIUM: 550MG

VEGETABLE-BEEF SAUCE WITH PARMESAN

SERVES: 4
WORKING TIME: 40 MINUTES
TOTAL TIME: 40 MINUTES

Italian pastas have wonderfully literal names. Ditalini, Italian for "little thimbles," are short, straight tubes that may be either smooth or ridged. The broth-based sherry sauce used here doesn't overpower the small pasta, and the other ingredients in the dish—green peas, cubes of beef, carrot, and onion—are suitably sized to match the ditalini.

2 tablespoons flour

½ teaspoon salt

¼ teaspoon freshly ground black pepper

½ pound well-trimmed top round of beef, cut into ½-inch cubes

4 teaspoons olive oil

10 ounces small tube pasta, such as ditalini or elbow macaroni

1 onion, cut into ½-inch cubes

1 carrot, quartered lengthwise and thinly sliced

¼ cup dry sherry or white wine

1 cup reduced-sodium chicken broth, defatted

¾ teaspoon dried oregano

1 cup frozen peas

¼ cup grated Parmesan cheese

1. On a sheet of waxed paper, combine the flour, ¼ teaspoon of the salt, and the pepper. Add the beef and toss to coat, shaking off the excess. In a large nonstick skillet, heat 1 tablespoon of the oil until hot but not smoking over medium heat. Add the beef and cook until lightly browned, about 4 minutes. With a slotted spoon, transfer the beef to a plate.

2. In a large pot of boiling water, cook the pasta until just tender. Drain well.

3. Meanwhile, add the remaining 1 teaspoon oil and the onion to the skillet and cook, stirring frequently, until the onion is softened, about 7 minutes. Add the carrot and cook, stirring frequently, until the carrot is tender, about 5 minutes. Add the sherry, bring to a boil, and cook until almost evaporated, about 1 minute. Add the broth, oregano, and the remaining ¼ teaspoon salt. Bring to a boil and cook until the sauce is reduced by one-fourth, about 5 minutes. Reduce to a simmer, add the peas, and cook until the peas are heated through, about 3 minutes.

4. Transfer ½ cup of the vegetables to a food processor and process to a smooth purée. Stir the purée back into the sauce, return the beef to the pan, and cook until heated through, about 2 minutes. Toss the sauce with the hot pasta, sprinkle the Parmesan over, and serve.

FAT: 9G/17%
CALORIES: 471
SATURATED FAT: 2.4G
CARBOHYDRATE: 67G
PROTEIN: 28G
CHOLESTEROL: 36MG
SODIUM: 591MG

GROUND PORK SAUCE WITH ALMONDS

SERVES: 4
WORKING TIME: 35 MINUTES
TOTAL TIME: 35 MINUTES

The trio of green olives, golden raisins, and sliced almonds lends special interest to this lightly creamy, garlic-scented meat sauce.

10 ounces fettuccine

10 ounces well-trimmed pork tenderloin, cut into chunks

¼ cup evaporated skimmed or low-fat milk

1 tablespoon olive oil

1 red onion, finely chopped

4 cloves garlic, minced

½ cup dry red wine

14½-ounce can no-salt-added stewed tomatoes, chopped with their juices

¼ cup no-salt-added tomato paste

¼ cup golden raisins

¼ cup pimiento-stuffed green olives, coarsely chopped

½ teaspoon dried rosemary, crumbled

½ teaspoon salt

2 tablespoons sliced almonds

1. In a large pot of boiling water, cook the pasta until just tender. Drain well.

2. Meanwhile, in a food processor, process the pork and evaporated milk until the pork is finely ground. In a large nonstick skillet, heat the oil until hot but not smoking over medium heat. Add the onion and garlic and cook, stirring frequently, until the onion is softened, about 7 minutes. Add the pork mixture and cook, stirring frequently, until the pork is no longer pink, about 4 minutes.

3. Add the wine to the pan and cook, stirring frequently, until almost evaporated, about 3 minutes. Stir in the tomatoes, the tomato paste, raisins, olives, rosemary, and salt. Simmer, stirring frequently, until the sauce is thickened and richly flavored, about 5 minutes. Stir in the almonds and toss with the hot pasta. Divide among 4 plates and serve.

Helpful hint: Although we call for golden raisins, dark raisins would be fine in this recipe.

FAT: 12G/21%
CALORIES: 517
SATURATED FAT: 2.2G
CARBOHYDRATE: 75G
PROTEIN: 30G
CHOLESTEROL: 114MG
SODIUM: 583MG

ZITI WITH SPICY PORK AND TOMATO SAUCE

SERVES: 4
WORKING TIME: 25 MINUTES
TOTAL TIME: 25 MINUTES

12 ounces ziti pasta

2 teaspoons olive oil

3 cloves garlic, minced

¾ cup chopped celery

1 teaspoon fennel seeds

6 ounces well-trimmed pork tenderloin, cut into ¼-inch-thick slivers

¾ cup reduced-sodium chicken broth, defatted

¼ cup dry white wine

1 tablespoon cornstarch mixed with 1 tablespoon water

1 pound plum tomatoes, diced

¼ cup golden raisins

½ teaspoon hot pepper sauce

1 teaspoon salt

¾ teaspoon dried oregano

½ teaspoon paprika

2 tablespoons grated Parmesan cheese

1. In a large pot of boiling water, cook the ziti until just tender. Drain well.

2. Meanwhile, in a large saucepan, heat the oil until hot but not smoking over medium heat. Add the garlic, celery, and fennel seeds and cook until the celery is softened, about 8 minutes. Add the pork to the pan and cook until the pork is no longer pink, about 1 minute.

3. In a small bowl, combine the broth, wine, and cornstarch mixture. Add the broth-cornstarch mixture, the tomatoes, raisins, hot pepper sauce, salt, oregano, and paprika to the saucepan. Bring to a boil and cook until the pork is cooked through and the sauce is slightly thickened, about 1 minute.

4. Add the cooked ziti to the saucepan, tossing to coat well with the sauce. Divide the pasta among 4 plates, sprinkle with the Parmesan, and serve.

Helpful hint: If you're fond of fennel, substitute it for the celery; the fennel seeds will further accentuate its flavor.

*S*atisfy winter appetites with this hearty and well-seasoned "unbaked" ziti—it's made in a skillet on the stovetop.

FAT: 6G/11%
CALORIES: 480
SATURATED FAT: 1.5G
CARBOHYDRATE: 80G
PROTEIN: 23G
CHOLESTEROL: 30MG
SODIUM: 794MG

HAM AND RICOTTA CHEESE SAUCE

SERVES: 4
WORKING TIME: 25 MINUTES
TOTAL TIME: 30 MINUTES

We've combined green and plain fettuccine for a dish reminiscent of the classic "paglia e fieno" (straw and hay). Of course, you could use regular fettuccine alone, or spinach pasta alone, or even add rosy tomato fettuccine to echo the colors of the ham and tomatoes. Don't be deceived by the super-creamy richness of the sauce: It's made from reduced-fat cheeses.

10 ounces fettuccine, mixed colors if desired

2 teaspoons olive oil

5 ounces smoked ham, such as Black Forest or Virginia, finely slivered

⅔ cup reduced-sodium chicken broth, defatted

10-ounce package frozen chopped broccoli, thawed and drained

⅓ cup chopped fresh basil

½ teaspoon freshly ground black pepper

¾ cup low-fat (1%) cottage cheese

½ cup part-skim ricotta cheese

2 tablespoons reduced-fat cream cheese (Neufchâtel)

1 tablespoon flour

1 cup cherry tomatoes, quartered

1. In a large pot of boiling water, cook the pasta until just tender. Drain well.

2. In a large nonstick skillet, heat the oil until hot but not smoking over medium heat. Add the ham and cook, stirring occasionally, until lightly crisped, about 2 minutes. Add the broth, broccoli, basil, and pepper and bring to a boil. Reduce to a simmer and cook until the broccoli is tender, about 4 minutes.

3. In a food processor, combine the cottage cheese, ricotta, cream cheese, and flour and process to a smooth purée, about 1 minute. Add the cheese mixture to the skillet, stirring, until well combined. Add the tomatoes and cook until the sauce is thickened and the tomatoes are heated through, about 3 minutes. Toss the sauce with the hot pasta, divide among 4 plates, and serve.

Helpful hint: Black Forest ham is cured and smoked; it has an intense flavor and a dense texture. This ham is sold at most deli counters.

FAT: 11G/21%
CALORIES: 464
SATURATED FAT: 4.2G
CARBOHYDRATE: 61G
PROTEIN: 29G
CHOLESTEROL: 99MG
SODIUM: 883MG

SHELLS WITH PORK TENDERLOIN AND EGGPLANT

SERVES: 4
WORKING TIME: 25 MINUTES
TOTAL TIME: 30 MINUTES

Here the choice of the pasta shape makes all the difference—shells are the perfect partner for the halved cherry tomatoes and other chunky ingredients. We keep the fat low by using a small amount of lean pork tenderloin per serving and, for extra meatiness, adding kidney beans and eggplant chunks, all deliciously flavored with a Moroccan blend of spices.

1 tablespoon flour

½ pound pork tenderloin, trimmed and cut into ½-inch chunks

2 tablespoons olive oil

1 tablespoon mild chili powder

½ pound eggplant, peeled and cut into ½-inch chunks (about 2½ cups)

3 cloves garlic, minced

¾ teaspoon ground ginger

¾ teaspoon salt

¼ teaspoon allspice

¼ teaspoon freshly ground black pepper

2 cups cherry tomatoes, halved

1 cup canned red kidney beans, rinsed and drained

3 tablespoons chopped fresh parsley

2 tablespoons balsamic vinegar

10 ounces medium pasta shells

1. Start heating a large pot of water to boiling for the pasta. On a plate, spread the flour. Dredge the pork in the flour, shaking off the excess. In a large nonstick skillet, heat 1 tablespoon of the oil until hot but not smoking over medium heat. Stir in the chili powder and cook, stirring constantly, until fragrant, about 30 seconds. Add the pork and cook, stirring frequently, until lightly browned, about 1 minute. With a slotted spoon, transfer the pork to a plate.

2. Add the remaining 1 tablespoon oil, the eggplant, garlic, ginger, salt, allspice, and pepper to the pan and cook, stirring frequently, until the mixture is fragrant, about 3 minutes. Add 1 cup of water, increase the heat to medium-high, and cook, stirring frequently, until the eggplant is almost tender, about 3 minutes. Add the tomatoes, beans, and pork and cook until the tomatoes are softened and the pork is cooked through, about 4 minutes longer. Stir in the parsley and vinegar.

3. Meanwhile, cook the pasta shells in the boiling water until just tender. Drain well. Transfer the pork mixture to a large bowl, add the shells, and toss to combine. Spoon the pasta mixture into 4 shallow bowls and serve.

Suggested accompaniments: Sliced radish, celery, and scallion salad with a lemon dressing. For dessert, fresh or canned figs drizzled with honey.

FAT: 12G/22%
CALORIES: 492
SATURATED FAT: 2.2G
CARBOHYDRATE: 70G
PROTEIN: 26G
CHOLESTEROL: 37MG
SODIUM: 559MG

CHEESY BEEF, CORN, AND TOMATO SAUCE

SERVES: 4
WORKING TIME: 30 MINUTES
TOTAL TIME: 30 MINUTES

There's a Tex-Mex twang to this family-pleasing main dish. A toss of beef, corn, and penne, united by a chunky tomato sauce, is topped with chili-flecked jack cheese. The sauce owes much of its flavor to the lacy-leaved herb, cilantro. The seeds of the plant, also known as coriander, have a peppery, citrusy taste quite different from that of the leaves. Both go into the sauce.

10 ounces medium tube pasta, such as penne rigate, penne, or ziti

3 tablespoons flour

¾ teaspoon salt

10 ounces well-trimmed top round of beef, cut into ½-inch cubes

1 tablespoon olive oil

6 scallions, thinly sliced

¾ cup reduced-sodium chicken broth, defatted

1½ cups canned no-salt-added tomatoes, chopped with their juices

¾ teaspoon ground coriander

1 cup frozen corn kernels

½ cup chopped fresh cilantro or basil

¾ cup shredded jalapeño jack cheese (3 ounces)

1. In a large pot of boiling water, cook the pasta until just tender. Drain well.

2. Meanwhile, on a sheet of waxed paper, combine the flour and salt. Dredge the beef in the flour mixture, shaking off and reserving the excess. In a large nonstick skillet, heat the oil until hot but not smoking over medium heat. Add the beef and cook, stirring frequently, until lightly browned, about 4 minutes. Add the scallions and cook, stirring frequently, until the scallions are tender, about 2 minutes. Sprinkle the reserved flour mixture over the scallions, stirring to coat.

3. Add the broth to the pan and bring to a boil. Stir in the tomatoes, coriander, corn, and cilantro and cook until the sauce is slightly thickened and the meat is cooked through, about 4 minutes. Toss the sauce with the hot pasta. Divide among 4 plates, sprinkle the cheese over, and serve.

Helpful hint: If you like your sauce spicy, a few pinches of chili powder or a few drops of hot pepper sauce would add a nice kick.

FAT: 14G/23%
CALORIES: 551
SATURATED FAT: 5.2G
CARBOHYDRATE: 72G
PROTEIN: 34G
CHOLESTEROL: 63MG
SODIUM: 719MG

Yellow squash and zucchini keep this pasta dish light, as do the meatballs made with ground turkey, lean beef, and a splash of low-fat milk for moistness. When shopping, choose squash that are on the small side because they will be sweeter. You may replace the turkey with ground chicken, and the beef with pork.

SKILLET SPAGHETTI AND MEATBALLS

SERVES: 4
WORKING TIME: 20 MINUTES
TOTAL TIME: 40 MINUTES

¼ pound lean ground beef

¼ pound ground turkey

¼ cup grated Parmesan cheese

2 tablespoons fine plain dried bread crumbs

2 tablespoons low-fat (1%) milk

1 egg white

½ teaspoon dried thyme

½ teaspoon dried sage

¼ teaspoon salt

2 tablespoons flour

2 teaspoons olive oil

14½-ounce can no-salt-added stewed tomatoes, chopped with their juices

2 strips orange zest, each about 3 inches long (see tip)

¾ cup orange juice, preferably fresh

6 ounces thin spaghetti, broken into thirds

1 cup thinly sliced zucchini

1 cup thinly sliced yellow summer squash

1. In a medium bowl, combine the beef, turkey, Parmesan, bread crumbs, milk, egg white, ¼ teaspoon of the thyme, ¼ teaspoon of the sage, and the salt. Mix until well combined and form into 16 meatballs.

2. On a sheet of waxed paper, spread the flour. Dredge the meatballs in the flour, shaking off the excess. In a large nonstick skillet, heat the oil until hot but not smoking over medium heat. Add the meatballs, in batches if necessary, and cook until lightly browned, about 3 minutes.

3. Stir in the tomatoes with their juices, 1¼ cups of water, the orange zest, orange juice, remaining ¼ teaspoon thyme, and remaining ¼ teaspoon sage until well combined. Bring to a boil, reduce to a simmer, cover, and cook until the meatballs are almost cooked through, about 5 minutes.

4. Increase the heat to medium, return to a boil, and stir in the spaghetti, zucchini, and yellow squash. Cover again and cook, stirring occasionally, until the spaghetti is tender and the meatballs are cooked through, about 15 minutes longer. Divide the spaghetti and meatballs among 4 bowls and serve.

Suggested accompaniments: Garlic toasts and, for dessert, a fresh fruit salad garnished with sweetened whipped evaporated skimmed milk.

FAT: 13G/28%
CALORIES: 411
SATURATED FAT: 4.4G
CARBOHYDRATE: 52G
PROTEIN: 21G
CHOLESTEROL: 46MG
SODIUM: 344MG

TIP

To remove a strip of zest from the orange, use a swivel-bladed vegetable peeler to cut off a piece of the outer colored rind, avoiding the bitter white pith attached to the underside. The zest contains the intensely flavored oil found in the skin.

MACARONI WITH CABBAGE AND HAM

SERVES: 4
WORKING TIME: 20 MINUTES
TOTAL TIME: 30 MINUTES

V*ery Eastern European in flavor, this deceptively hearty combination is a cold-weather special. Just enough baked ham is mixed with cabbage and apple (natural flavor partners), and then accented with fresh dill and cider vinegar. Finally, light sour cream adds a touch of richness. For a pasta substitute, you may use wide egg noodles.*

2 teaspoons olive oil
6 ounces baked ham, diced
1 large onion, diced
4 cups diced green cabbage
1 Granny Smith apple, peeled, cored, and coarsely chopped
3 tablespoons cider vinegar
¼ teaspoon freshly ground black pepper
½ cup chopped fresh dill
⅓ cup light sour cream
10 ounces elbow macaroni

1. Start heating a large pot of water to boiling for the pasta. In a large nonstick skillet, heat the oil until hot but not smoking over medium heat. Add the ham and cook, stirring frequently, until lightly crisped, about 5 minutes. With a slotted spoon, transfer the ham to a plate.

2. Add the onion to the pan and cook, stirring frequently, until the onion is lightly golden, about 8 minutes. Stir in the cabbage, apple, vinegar, and pepper. Cover and cook, stirring occasionally, until the cabbage has wilted and the apple is tender, about 10 minutes. Stir in the dill and ham and cook, uncovered, until heated through, about 3 minutes longer. Remove from the heat and stir in the sour cream.

3. Meanwhile, cook the macaroni in the boiling water until just tender. Drain well. Transfer the cabbage mixture to a large bowl, add the macaroni, and toss to combine. Spoon the macaroni mixture onto 4 plates and serve.

Suggested accompaniments: Shredded celery root with a reduced-fat mustard dressing and, for dessert, fresh cherries steeped in brandy.

FAT: 10G/19%
CALORIES: 462
SATURATED FAT: 3.1G
CARBOHYDRATE: 71G
PROTEIN: 22G
CHOLESTEROL: 32MG
SODIUM: 659MG

STIR-FRIED BEEF AND VEGETABLES WITH ORZO

SERVES: 4
WORKING TIME: 25 MINUTES
TOTAL TIME: 35 MINUTES

1¼ cups orzo

2 tablespoons flour

10 ounces lean bottom round of beef, cut into 1½-by-¼-inch strips

2 teaspoons dark Oriental sesame oil

½ pound mushrooms, quartered

1 carrot, cut into matchsticks

3 cloves garlic, minced

1 tablespoon minced fresh ginger

3 cups diced Napa cabbage

1 cup halved cherry tomatoes

½ cup reduced-sodium beef broth, defatted

2 tablespoons reduced-sodium soy sauce

¼ teaspoon firmly packed brown sugar

¼ teaspoon red pepper flakes

2 teaspoons cornstarch

1. In a large saucepan of boiling water, cook the orzo until just tender. Drain well and set aside.

2. Meanwhile, on a sheet of waxed paper, spread the flour. Dredge the beef in the flour, shaking off the excess. In a large nonstick wok or skillet, heat the oil until hot but not smoking over medium heat. Add the beef and cook, stirring frequently, until browned, about 4 minutes. With a slotted spoon, transfer the beef to a plate and set aside.

3. Add the mushrooms, carrot, garlic, and ginger to the pan, stirring to coat. Cook, stirring frequently, until the carrot is crisp-tender, about 4 minutes. Stir in the cabbage, cherry tomatoes, broth, soy sauce, brown sugar, and red pepper flakes. Increase the heat to medium-high and bring to a boil.

4. In a cup, combine the cornstarch and 1 tablespoon of water, stir to blend, and stir into the boiling vegetable mixture along with the orzo. Cook, stirring constantly, until the mixture is slightly thickened, about 2 minutes. Return the beef to the pan and cook until the beef is heated through, about 1 minute longer.

Suggested accompaniment: Peach halves drizzled with honey and broiled, then dusted with toasted chopped macadamia nuts.

Here orzo, a rice-shaped pasta often found in Greek cooking, absorbs the Asian flavors of the nutty dark sesame oil and fragrant ginger— fusion cooking at its best. If Napa cabbage, mild-tasting with light green crinkly leaves, is unavailable, substitute romaine lettuce. And for an even deeper flavor, replace the regular button mushrooms with fresh shiitakes.

FAT: 8G/17%
CALORIES: 422
SATURATED FAT: 1.9G
CARBOHYDRATE: 61G
PROTEIN: 27G
CHOLESTEROL: 42MG
SODIUM: 442MG

PORK AND BEAN SAUCE

SERVES: 4
WORKING TIME: 35 MINUTES
TOTAL TIME: 35 MINUTES

10 ounces shaped pasta, such as fusilli bucati, rotini, or radiatore

3 tablespoons flour

½ teaspoon salt

¼ teaspoon freshly ground black pepper

½ pound well-trimmed pork tenderloin, cut into ½-inch cubes

2 teaspoons olive oil

3 tablespoons coarsely chopped Canadian bacon (1 ounce)

1 onion, finely chopped

1 green bell pepper, cut into ½-inch squares

Two 8-ounce cans no-salt-added tomato sauce

2 tablespoons firmly packed light brown sugar

1 teaspoon grated orange zest

¼ cup orange juice

10-ounce can pinto beans, rinsed and drained

1. In a large pot of boiling water, cook the pasta until just tender. Drain well.

2. Meanwhile, on a sheet of waxed paper, combine the flour, salt, and black pepper. Dredge the pork in the flour mixture, shaking off and reserving the excess.

3. In a large nonstick skillet, heat the oil until hot but not smoking over medium heat. Add the Canadian bacon and cook until lightly crisped, about 2 minutes. Add the pork and cook, stirring, until the pork is no longer pink, about 4 minutes. Stir in the onion and bell pepper and cook, stirring frequently, until the onion is crisp-tender, about 5 minutes.

4. Sprinkle the reserved flour mixture into the skillet and stir until well coated. Add the tomato sauce, brown sugar, orange zest, and orange juice and bring to a boil. Reduce to a simmer, stir in the beans, and cook until the sauce is slightly thickened, the beans are heated through, and no floury taste remains, about 2 minutes. Toss the sauce with the hot pasta, divide among 4 bowls, and serve.

Helpful hint: The thick pasta twists shown here are fusilli bucati, which are hollow in the middle. Regular rotini would work just as well.

FAT: 7G/12%
CALORIES: 517
SATURATED FAT: 1.3G
CARBOHYDRATE: 86G
PROTEIN: 28G
CHOLESTEROL: 40MG
SODIUM: 550MG

Two kinds of pork—both used in sensible quantities for a low-fat dish—make for a highly flavorful, satisfying pasta sauce. Freshly ground lean pork tenderloin is the real "meat" of the dish, while bits of Canadian bacon bring a smoky savor to the pasta and pinto beans. Hot biscuits or dinner rolls would round out the meal nicely.

SWEDISH PASTA SAUCE

SERVES: 4
WORKING TIME: 30 MINUTES
TOTAL TIME: 30 MINUTES

Cubed beets are the basis of a classic Swedish salad; the dilled sour cream sauce is also a Scandinavian inspiration.

10 ounces fettuccine

3 tablespoons flour

½ teaspoon salt

¼ teaspoon freshly ground black pepper

½ pound well-trimmed sirloin, cut into 2 x ¼-inch strips

1 tablespoon olive oil

6 scallions, thinly sliced

1½ cups cubed canned beets (½-inch cubes)

1 cup reduced-sodium beef broth

1 tablespoon Dijon mustard

2 tablespoons reduced-fat sour cream

⅓ cup snipped fresh dill

1. In a large pot of boiling water, cook the pasta until just tender. Drain well.

2. Meanwhile, on a sheet of waxed paper, combine the flour, salt, and pepper. Dredge the beef in the flour mixture, shaking off and reserving the excess. In a large nonstick skillet, heat the oil until hot but not smoking over medium heat. Add the beef and cook, stirring frequently, until lightly browned, about 2 minutes. Add the scallions and cook, stirring frequently, until the scallions are softened, about 2 minutes.

3. Add the beets to the pan, stirring to combine. In a small bowl, combine the broth and the reserved flour mixture. Stir into the skillet along with the mustard and bring to a boil. Reduce to a simmer and cook, stirring, just until the sauce is slightly thickened and no floury taste remains, about 2 minutes. Remove from the heat, stir in the sour cream and dill, and toss with the hot pasta. Divide among 4 plates and serve.

Helpful hint: Place a sheet of foil or plastic wrap over the cutting board when cubing the beets; their juice can leave indelible stains.

FAT: 10G/20%
CALORIES: 445
SATURATED FAT: 2.5G
CARBOHYDRATE: 63G
PROTEIN: 25G
CHOLESTEROL: 104MG
SODIUM: 729MG

BEEF STEW WITH APPLES AND GINGER

SERVES: 4
WORKING TIME: 25 MINUTES
TOTAL TIME: 40 MINUTES

8 ounces wide egg noodles

2 tablespoons flour

¾ teaspoon salt

½ teaspoon freshly ground black pepper

¼ teaspoon ground ginger

10 ounces well-trimmed beef sirloin, cut into ½-inch chunks

1 tablespoon olive oil

2 onions, cut into ½-inch chunks

3 cloves garlic, minced

2 sweet apples, such as McIntosh, Cortland, or Delicious, peeled, cored, and cut into ½-inch chunks

2 cups reduced-sodium chicken broth, defatted

2 ounces gingersnap cookies, crumbled

3 tablespoons cider vinegar

1 teaspoon chopped fresh parsley (optional)

1. In a large pot of boiling water, cook the noodles until just tender. Drain well.

2. Meanwhile, on a sheet of waxed paper, combine the flour, ¼ teaspoon of the salt, ¼ teaspoon of the pepper, and the ginger. Dredge the beef in the flour mixture, shaking off the excess. In a large nonstick skillet or Dutch oven, heat the oil until hot but not smoking over medium heat. Add the beef and cook, stirring frequently, until browned, about 4 minutes. With a slotted spoon, transfer the beef to a plate.

3. Add the onions and garlic to the pan and cook, stirring frequently, until the onions are tender, about 7 minutes. Add the apples and cook, stirring frequently, until lightly golden, about 3 minutes. Add the broth, gingersnaps, vinegar, the remaining ½ teaspoon salt, remaining ¼ teaspoon pepper, and ½ cup of water and bring to a boil.

4. Return the beef to the pan, reduce to a simmer, cover, and cook until the beef is tender, about 15 minutes. Toss the stew with the noodles, divide among 4 plates, sprinkle the parsley over, and serve.

Helpful hint: For a change, serve the stew over rice or mashed potatoes.

FAT: 11G/20%
CALORIES: 493
SATURATED FAT: 2.3G
CARBOHYDRATE: 73G
PROTEIN: 27G
CHOLESTEROL: 97MG
SODIUM: 841MG

Here's something new: a beef stew with the autumnal spiciness of baked apples. It's tossed with wide noodles.

The food processor does most of the work here, chopping the beef and simultaneously combining it with cream cheese and seasonings. After just a few minutes of cooking, you have a beautifully creamy sauce. As an accompaniment, brush whole-grain Italian bread with a mixture of olive oil, garlic, and parsley and toast it under the broiler.

CREAMED SPINACH SAUCE WITH GROUND BEEF

SERVES: 4
WORKING TIME: 30 MINUTES
TOTAL TIME: 30 MINUTES

10 ounces medium tube pasta,
such as penne or ziti

½ pound well-trimmed top
round of beef, cut into chunks

1 tablespoon reduced-fat cream
cheese (Neufchâtel)

2 teaspoons paprika

½ teaspoon salt

⅛ teaspoon ground allspice

1 tablespoon olive oil

2 onions, finely chopped

4 cloves garlic, minced

2 tablespoons flour

1½ cups low-fat (1%) milk

10-ounce package frozen
chopped spinach, thawed and
squeezed dry (see tip)

¼ cup grated Parmesan cheese

1. In a large pot of boiling water, cook the pasta until just tender. Drain well.

2. Meanwhile, in a food processor, combine the beef, cream cheese, paprika, salt, and allspice and process until finely chopped. In a large nonstick skillet, heat the oil until hot but not smoking over medium heat. Add the onions and garlic and cook, stirring frequently, until the onions are golden brown, about 5 minutes. Add the beef mixture to the skillet and cook, stirring frequently, until the beef is no longer pink, about 4 minutes.

3. Sprinkle the flour over the beef mixture, stirring, until well combined. Gradually add the milk and cook, stirring frequently, until slightly thickened, about 4 minutes. Add the spinach and cook, stirring frequently, until the spinach is heated through and the sauce is well blended, about 3 minutes. Add the Parmesan and stir to combine. Divide the pasta among 4 plates, spoon the sauce over, and serve.

Helpful hint: To thaw the spinach in the microwave, remove all of the packaging, place the frozen spinach in a microwave-safe container, and microwave on high power for 2 to 3 minutes.

TIP

To prepare frozen spinach, thaw according to package directions, and then squeeze out excess liquid (this keeps the sauce from becoming watery). Work over a bowl as you squeeze the spinach, one handful at a time.

FAT: 10G/18%
CALORIES: 506
SATURATED FAT: 3.3G
CARBOHYDRATE: 73G
PROTEIN: 31G
CHOLESTEROL: 42MG
SODIUM: 522MG

STIR-FRIED BEEF WITH GREEN BEANS AND PECANS

SERVES: 4
WORKING TIME: 25 MINUTES
TOTAL TIME: 25 MINUTES

There's an innovative all-American twist to this Chinese-style dish. Instead of walnuts (which have been prized in China since ancient times), we've accented the dish with toasty-sweet pecans, which are native to this country. The chopped nuts echo the satisfying crunchiness of the water chestnuts and crisp-tender green beans.

8 ounces linguine

½ pound green beans, cut into 1-inch lengths

½ pound well-trimmed beef sirloin, cut into 2 x ½-inch strips

4 teaspoons cornstarch

1 tablespoon olive oil

3 tablespoons reduced-sodium soy sauce

2 cloves garlic, minced

2 tablespoons chopped fresh ginger

8-ounce can sliced water chestnuts, drained

¾ cup reduced-sodium chicken broth, defatted

¼ teaspoon salt

¼ teaspoon red pepper flakes

2 tablespoons coarsely chopped pecans (½ ounce)

1. In a large pot of boiling water, cook the pasta until just tender. Add the green beans during the last 3 minutes of cooking time. Drain well.

2. Meanwhile, dredge the beef in 3 teaspoons of the cornstarch. In a large nonstick skillet, heat the oil until hot but not smoking over medium-high heat. Add the beef and cook, stirring frequently, until lightly browned and cooked through, about 1 minute. With a slotted spoon, transfer the beef to a plate.

3. In a medium bowl, combine the soy sauce, garlic, ginger, and the remaining 1 teaspoon cornstarch; set aside. Add the linguine, green beans, and water chestnuts to the pan and cook, stirring frequently, until heated through, about 4 minutes. Return the beef to the pan along with the broth, salt, red pepper flakes, and the reserved soy sauce mixture and cook, stirring frequently, until slightly thickened, about 2 minutes. Stir in the pecans, divide among 4 plates, and serve.

Helpful hint: For extra flavor, toast the pecans: Spread them in a small baking pan and bake in a 350° oven for 8 to 10 minutes, shaking the pan occasionally to keep the nuts from scorching. As soon as the pecans are toasted, immediately tip them onto a plate to cool.

FAT: 9G/20%
CALORIES: 397
SATURATED FAT: 1.7G
CARBOHYDRATE: 56G
PROTEIN: 22G
CHOLESTEROL: 35MG
SODIUM: 735MG

Yes, minestrone is a soup; but it's also the ideal inspiration for this pasta sauce. What the two have in common is a bounty of vegetables and a finishing flourish of Parmesan. If you have a rotary cheese grater, bring it—along with a pepper mill—to the table for customized seasoning. Or, place the grated cheese in a bowl and pass it around with the pasta.

MINESTRONE SAUCE WITH BACON

SERVES: 4
WORKING TIME: 35 MINUTES
TOTAL TIME: 35 MINUTES

10 ounces shaped pasta, such as medium shells, ruote (wagon wheels), or radiatore

2 teaspoons olive oil

¾ cup diced Canadian bacon (¼ pound)

2 ribs celery, halved lengthwise and thinly sliced

2 carrots, halved lengthwise and thinly sliced

3 cloves garlic, minced

6 ounces cabbage, cut into ½-inch chunks (see tip)

10-ounce package frozen chopped spinach, thawed and squeezed dry

2 cups no-salt-added canned tomatoes, coarsely chopped

⅔ cup reduced-sodium chicken broth, defatted

½ teaspoon dried marjoram or oregano

1½ teaspoons cornstarch mixed with 1 tablespoon water

½ cup grated Parmesan cheese

1. In a large pot of boiling water, cook the pasta until just tender. Drain well.

2. Meanwhile, in a large nonstick skillet, heat the oil until hot but not smoking over medium heat. Add the Canadian bacon and cook, stirring, until lightly crisped, about 2 minutes. Add the celery, carrots, and garlic and cook, stirring frequently, until the celery and carrots are crisp-tender, about 5 minutes.

3. Add the cabbage and spinach and cook, stirring frequently, until the cabbage is wilted, about 5 minutes. Add the tomatoes, broth, and marjoram and cook, stirring frequently, until the flavors are blended, about 5 minutes. Bring to a boil, stir in the cornstarch mixture, and cook, stirring constantly, until the sauce is slightly thickened, about 1 minute. Toss the sauce with the hot pasta, divide among 4 bowls, sprinkle the Parmesan over, and serve.

Helpful hint: You can cut up the celery, carrots, and cabbage up to 12 hours ahead of time; bag the celery and carrots together and the cabbage separately, and refrigerate until needed.

FAT: 9G/18%
CALORIES: 453
SATURATED FAT: 3.1G
CARBOHYDRATE: 70G
PROTEIN: 24G
CHOLESTEROL: 22MG
SODIUM: 791MG

TIP

To cut a head of cabbage into chunks, first quarter the head lengthwise. Cut each quarter into 1-inch-wide wedges, then cut the wedges crosswise into ½-inch chunks.

LAMB AND WHITE BEAN SAUCE

SERVES: 4
WORKING TIME: 25 MINUTES
TOTAL TIME: 25 MINUTES

With their natural meatiness, beans can double the heartiness of any pasta sauce. Here, we've used cannellini (white kidney beans), along with cubes of lamb. Some of the beans are mashed as they cook, so that they thicken the sauce with their starch. The seasonings include dried tarragon and rosemary, as well as a last-minute toss of fresh parsley for a bright green note.

10 ounces medium tube pasta, such as cavatappi, ziti, or penne

2 teaspoons olive oil

½ pound well-trimmed boneless lamb shoulder, cut into ½-inch cubes

6 scallions, thinly sliced

3 cloves garlic, minced

¾ teaspoon dried tarragon

½ teaspoon dried rosemary, crumbled

½ teaspoon salt

1 cup reduced-sodium chicken broth, defatted

2 tablespoons no-salt-added tomato paste

1 cup canned white kidney beans (cannellini), rinsed and drained

¼ cup chopped fresh parsley

1. In a large pot of boiling water, cook the pasta until just tender. Drain well.

2. Meanwhile, in a large nonstick skillet, heat the oil until hot but not smoking over medium heat. Add the lamb and cook, stirring frequently, until no longer pink, about 3 minutes. Add the scallions, garlic, tarragon, rosemary, and salt and cook, stirring frequently, until the scallions are tender, about 3 minutes.

3. Add the broth, tomato paste, and beans to the pan and bring to a boil. Reduce to a simmer and cook, stirring frequently and mashing some of the beans against the side of the skillet, until the sauce is slightly thickened, about 5 minutes. Add the parsley, toss with the hot pasta, and serve.

Helpful hint: Cavatappi, shown here, are hollow ridged pasta twists. The literal translation of the name is "corkscrews." You're more likely to find cavatappi in an imported brand of pasta than a domestic one.

FAT: 8G/16%
CALORIES: 438
SATURATED FAT: 1.9G
CARBOHYDRATE: 65G
PROTEIN: 26G
CHOLESTEROL: 38MG
SODIUM: 556MG

SEAFOOD SAUCES

Left, Fettuccine with Shrimp and Lemon Cream Sauce.
Above, Szechuan-Style Scallop Sauce.

FUSILLI WITH TUNA AND PINE NUTS

SERVES: 4
WORKING TIME: 30 MINUTES
TOTAL TIME: 35 MINUTES

The effect this dish will have on your taste buds can be best described as "fireworks." Not because it's super-hot (although the red pepper flakes do pack a punch), but because of the wide variety of flavors—tuna, garlic, pine nuts, capers, basil, oregano, parsley, and lemon. Serve it with a simple salad of tender leaf lettuces (to give your palate a rest from all the excitement).

12 ounces fusilli pasta
1 teaspoon olive oil
1 red bell pepper, diced
4 scallions, finely chopped
3 cloves garlic, minced
¾ teaspoon dried basil
½ teaspoon dried oregano
Two 8-ounce bottles clam juice
¼ cup dry white wine
½ teaspoon red pepper flakes
1 teaspoon anchovy paste
2 teaspoons cornstarch mixed
with 1 tablespoon water
2 tablespoons pine nuts, toasted
2 tablespoons capers, rinsed
and drained
6-ounce can water-packed tuna,
drained and flaked
¼ cup chopped fresh parsley
2 tablespoons fresh lemon juice

1. In a large pot of boiling water, cook the fusilli until just tender. Drain well.

2. Meanwhile, in a large nonstick saucepan, heat the oil until hot but not smoking over medium heat. Add the bell pepper and cook until crisp-tender, about 4 minutes. Add the scallions, garlic, basil, and oregano and cook until warmed through, about 3 minutes.

3. Add the clam juice, wine, red pepper flakes, and anchovy paste. Bring to a simmer and cook for 4 minutes to reduce slightly. Stir in the cornstarch mixture and cook, stirring, until slightly thickened, about 2 minutes.

4. Remove the pan from the heat and stir in the pine nuts, capers, tuna, parsley, and lemon juice. Add the pasta, toss well, and let stand for 5 minutes to absorb the liquid. Divide the mixture among 4 bowls and serve.

Helpful hint: To toast the pine nuts, spread them out on a small baking pan and cook them in a 350° oven for 8 to 10 minutes; shake the pan occasionally to keep the nuts from scorching, and turn them out of the pan as soon as they're done.

FAT: 5G/10%
CALORIES: 437
SATURATED FAT: .8G
CARBOHYDRATE: 70G
PROTEIN: 25G
CHOLESTEROL: 17MG
SODIUM: 570MG

SALMON AND LEMON-DILL SAUCE

SERVES: 4
WORKING TIME: 25 MINUTES
TOTAL TIME: 30 MINUTES

10 ounces medium strand pasta, such as long fusilli, linguine, or spaghetti

2 teaspoons olive oil

2 scallions, thinly sliced

1 yellow summer squash, quartered lengthwise and thinly sliced

¼ pound smoked salmon, coarsely chopped

6 ounces skinless salmon fillet, any visible bones removed, cut into ½-inch chunks

1 cup reduced-sodium chicken broth, defatted

½ cup snipped fresh dill

1 teaspoon grated lemon zest

1 tablespoon fresh lemon juice

½ teaspoon salt

¼ cup plain nonfat yogurt

2 tablespoons reduced-fat sour cream

2 tablespoons flour

1. In a large pot of boiling water, cook the pasta until just tender. Drain well.

2. Meanwhile, in a large nonstick skillet, heat the oil until hot but not smoking over medium heat. Add the scallions and squash and cook, stirring frequently, until the squash is crisp-tender, about 4 minutes.

3. Add the smoked salmon and fresh salmon to the pan, stirring to coat. Add the broth, dill, lemon zest, lemon juice, and salt and bring to a boil. Reduce to a simmer and cook until the fresh salmon is just opaque, about 3 minutes. In a small bowl, combine the yogurt, sour cream, and flour. Add the yogurt mixture to the skillet and cook, stirring constantly, until the sauce is thickened, about 2 minutes. Divide the pasta among 4 bowls, spoon the sauce over, and serve.

Helpful hint: There are many types of smoked salmon to choose from and quite a range of prices, too. Cold-smoked Nova Scotia salmon (called "Nova") is a reasonably priced option; imported Scottish smoked salmon is considerably more expensive.

FAT: 9G/19%
CALORIES: 431
SATURATED FAT: 1.7G
CARBOHYDRATE: 61G
PROTEIN: 26G
CHOLESTEROL: 33MG
SODIUM: 680MG

This is really a double-salmon sauce, blessed with the dual richness of smoked and fresh salmon. The smoked variety—chopped to serve as a seasoning—brings intense smoky flavor to the dish; the fresh—cut into bite-size chunks—makes the pasta a satisfying meal. The creamy yogurt sauce, made with fresh lemon and dill, is a classic complement to both types of salmon.

This dish has it all—a rich tomato cream sauce, the distinctive flavor and bite of fresh shrimp, and a hint of warmth from the garlic and ginger. Serve it piping hot for best results. Select fresh shrimp with firm, shiny shells, translucent flesh, and a sweet smell. If good-quality shrimp can't be had, substitute scallops or chunks of red snapper.

MACARONI WITH SHRIMP AND TOMATO CREAM

SERVES: 4
WORKING TIME: 20 MINUTES
TOTAL TIME: 25 MINUTES

12 ounces elbow macaroni

2 tablespoons flour

1½ cups low-fat (1%) milk

8-ounce can no-salt-added tomato sauce

2 tablespoons no-salt-added tomato paste

1 teaspoon salt

½ teaspoon dried thyme

¼ teaspoon freshly ground black pepper

¼ teaspoon ground ginger

½ cup frozen peas

2 tablespoons light sour cream

1 tablespoon olive oil

2 cloves garlic, minced

1 pound large shrimp, shelled and deveined (see tip)

3 tablespoons chopped fresh parsley (optional)

2 tablespoons snipped fresh chives (optional)

2 plum tomatoes, coarsely chopped

1. Heat a large pot of water to boiling, and cook the macaroni until just tender. Drain well.

2. Meanwhile, place the flour in a medium saucepan over medium heat, and gradually whisk in the milk. Bring to a boil and cook, whisking constantly, until the mixture is slightly thickened, about 4 minutes. Whisk in the tomato sauce, tomato paste, salt, thyme, pepper, and ginger. Stir in the peas and cook until the peas are just heated through, about 2 minutes. Remove from the heat and whisk in the sour cream.

3. In a large nonstick skillet, heat the oil until hot but not smoking over medium heat. Add the garlic and cook, stirring frequently, until tender, about 2 minutes. Add the shrimp and cook, stirring frequently, until the shrimp are almost opaque, about 3 minutes. Stir in the tomato mixture, parsley, and chives, reduce to a simmer, and cook until the shrimp are just opaque, about 1 minute longer.

4. Transfer the shrimp mixture to a large bowl, add the pasta and tomatoes, and toss to combine. Spoon the macaroni mixture into 4 shallow bowls and serve.

Suggested accompaniments: Shredded carrot salad with a reduced-fat horseradish dressing. For dessert, nonfat frozen lemon yogurt.

FAT: 9G/15%
CALORIES: 558
SATURATED FAT: 2.1G
CARBOHYDRATE: 82G
PROTEIN: 36G
CHOLESTEROL: 146MG
SODIUM: 779MG

TIP

To shell fresh shrimp, pull apart the shell at the belly of the shrimp with your fingers, splitting the shell, and remove. Leave the tail portion attached, if desired, for a garnish. To devein, with the point of a sharp knife, score the shrimp along the back, and remove the dark vein.

SCALLOPS WITH ASIAN VEGETABLES AND NOODLES

SERVES: 4
WORKING TIME: 30 MINUTES
TOTAL TIME: 30 MINUTES

While it may look complicated, this Asian-inspired pasta-and-seafood dish is a snap to prepare: You can make the marinade and begin stir-frying while the pasta is cooking. The finished dish is filled with subtle variations of taste and texture— the smoky bacon sets off the sweet scallops, while the tender linguine is a foil for the crisp vegetables.

8 ounces linguine

½ cup reduced-sodium chicken broth, defatted

3 tablespoons reduced-sodium soy sauce

3 tablespoons dry sherry

1½ teaspoons cornstarch

1 teaspoon dark Oriental sesame oil

½ teaspoon ground ginger

1 pound bay scallops or quartered sea scallops

1 tablespoon vegetable oil

3 tablespoons slivered Canadian bacon (1 ounce)

¼ teaspoon red pepper flakes

1 red bell pepper, slivered

6 ounces snow peas, strings removed

1½ cups bean sprouts

1. In a large pot of boiling water, cook the linguine until just tender. Drain well.

2. Meanwhile, in a small bowl, combine the broth, soy sauce, sherry, cornstarch, sesame oil, and ginger. Add the scallops, tossing to coat.

3. In a large nonstick skillet or wok, heat the vegetable oil until hot but not smoking over medium heat. Add the Canadian bacon and red pepper flakes and stir-fry until the bacon is lightly crisped, about 2 minutes. Add the bell pepper and stir-fry until crisp-tender, about 3 minutes.

4. Reserving the marinade, add the scallops to the pan along with the linguine, snow peas, and bean sprouts and cook, stirring, until the scallops are cooked through and the linguine is piping hot, about 4 minutes. Stir the marinade to recombine, pour into the skillet and cook, stirring, until slightly thickened, about 1 minute.

Helpful hint: There's quite a variety of sprouts on the market these days, from threadlike radish and alfalfa sprouts to the familiar thick, crunchy bean sprouts. Use a mixture, if you like.

FAT: 7G/15%
CALORIES: 425
SATURATED FAT: 1G
CARBOHYDRATE: 55G
PROTEIN: 31G
CHOLESTEROL: 41MG
SODIUM: 823MG

LEMON CREAM WITH SPINACH AND COD

SERVES: 4
WORKING TIME: 30 MINUTES
TOTAL TIME: 30 MINUTES

*C*reamed spinach, accented with lemon zest, turns into a substantial pasta topping here, with the addition of chunks of cod. Frozen chopped spinach eliminates the chore of washing and stemming the spinach. And instead of butter and heavy cream, we've created a sauce using evaporated skimmed milk, part-skim ricotta cheese, and reduced-fat sour cream.

10 ounces medium strand pasta, such as perciatelli, linguine, or spaghetti

½ cup evaporated skimmed milk

¼ cup part-skim ricotta cheese

3 tablespoons reduced-fat sour cream

2 tablespoons flour

½ teaspoon salt

¼ teaspoon freshly ground black pepper

1 tablespoon olive oil

1 onion, finely chopped

10-ounce package frozen chopped spinach, thawed and squeezed dry

1 cup reduced-sodium chicken broth, defatted

1 tablespoon grated lemon zest

10 ounces skinless cod fillets, any visible bones removed, cut into large chunks

1. In a large pot of boiling water, cook the pasta until just tender. Drain well. In a food processor, combine the evaporated milk, ricotta, sour cream, flour, salt, and pepper and process to a smooth purée, about 1 minute; set aside.

2. Meanwhile, in a large nonstick skillet, heat the oil until hot but not smoking over medium heat. Add the onion and cook, stirring frequently, until softened, about 7 minutes. Add the spinach, broth, and lemon zest and bring to a boil. Add the cod, stirring to coat.

3. Add the milk mixture to the skillet and cook, stirring occasionally, until the sauce is thickened and the cod is just opaque, about 4 minutes. Divide the pasta among 4 bowls, spoon the sauce over, and serve.

Helpful hint: If you like, grate a little extra lemon zest to sprinkle over each pasta portion.

FAT: 8G/15%
CALORIES: 468
SATURATED FAT: 2.3G
CARBOHYDRATE: 68G
PROTEIN: 30G
CHOLESTEROL: 40MG
SODIUM: 573MG

SHRIMP AND FRESH SALSA SAUCE

SERVES: 4
WORKING TIME: 20 MINUTES
TOTAL TIME: 20 MINUTES

10 ounces shaped pasta, such as orecchiette or farfalle (bow ties)

1 tablespoon olive oil

4 scallions, thinly sliced

3 cloves garlic, minced

1 teaspoon minced pickled jalapeño

¾ pound medium shrimp, shelled, deveined, and halved lengthwise

¾ pound tomatoes, coarsely chopped

½ cup chopped fresh cilantro or basil

2 tablespoons no-salt-added tomato paste

1 tablespoon red wine vinegar

½ teaspoon salt

¾ cup frozen corn kernels

1. In a large pot of boiling water, cook the pasta until just tender. Drain well.

2. Meanwhile, in a large nonstick skillet, heat the oil until hot but not smoking over medium heat. Add the scallions, garlic, and jalapeño and cook, stirring frequently, until the scallions are softened, about 2 minutes.

3. Add the shrimp to the pan, stirring to coat. Add the tomatoes, cilantro, tomato paste, vinegar, and salt and bring to a boil. Reduce to a simmer, stir in the corn, and cook, stirring occasionally, until the sauce is thickened and the shrimp are just opaque, about 3 minutes. Spoon the sauce over the hot pasta and serve.

Helpful hint: This dish is best when made with juicy vine-ripened tomatoes, but the fact is you can't always get them. If necessary, substitute 1½ cups canned no-salt-added tomatoes.

Shrimp cook in so little time that they are a perfect starting point for quick and easy meals. Here, the shrimp cook right in the sauce, a tangy mixture of tomatoes and corn that's brightened with garlic, jalapeño, and red wine vinegar. Be sure not to overcook this—that would toughen the shrimp and lessen the textural "bite" of the corn and fresh tomatoes.

FAT: 6G/13%
CALORIES: 427
SATURATED FAT: 0.9G
CARBOHYDRATE: 68G
PROTEIN: 26G
CHOLESTEROL: 105MG
SODIUM: 409MG

TUNA AND CREAMY MUSHROOM SAUCE

SERVES: 4
WORKING TIME: 30 MINUTES
TOTAL TIME: 35 MINUTES

This lively stovetop version of the old tuna-noodle casserole, packed with flavorful fresh ingredients, is sure to please.

10 ounces shaped pasta, such as small shells, ruote (wagon wheels), or radiatore

2 teaspoons olive oil

3 tablespoons coarsely chopped Canadian bacon (1 ounce)

3 cloves garlic, minced

6 ounces mushrooms, halved and thinly sliced

2 tablespoons flour

1 cup reduced-sodium chicken broth, defatted

½ cup evaporated skimmed milk

½ teaspoon salt

½ teaspoon freshly ground black pepper

Two 6-ounce cans water-packed tuna, drained and flaked

⅓ cup grated Parmesan cheese

¼ cup chopped fresh parsley

1. In a large pot of boiling water, cook the pasta until just tender. Drain well.

2. Meanwhile, in a large nonstick skillet, heat the oil until hot but not smoking over medium heat. Add the Canadian bacon and cook until lightly crisped, about 2 minutes. Add the garlic and cook, stirring occasionally, until the garlic is softened, about 2 minutes.

3. Add the mushrooms to the pan and cook, stirring frequently, until the mushrooms are tender, about 5 minutes. Sprinkle the flour over the vegetables and cook, stirring to coat, for 1 minute. Gradually stir in the broth, evaporated milk, salt, and pepper. Bring to a boil, reduce to a simmer, and cook until the sauce is slightly thickened and no floury taste remains, about 3 minutes. Add the tuna and cook until heated through, about 3 minutes. Stir in the Parmesan and parsley.

4. Divide the pasta among 4 bowls, spoon the sauce over, and serve.

Helpful hint: Read labels carefully when buying canned tuna. Some national brands of water-packed solid white tuna have as much as 5 grams of fat in 2 ounces. Look for a brand with no more than 1 gram of fat in 2 ounces.

FAT: 7G/13%
CALORIES: 482
SATURATED FAT: 2G
CARBOHYDRATE: 63G
PROTEIN: 40G
CHOLESTEROL: 42MG
SODIUM: 951MG

SNAPPER, ASPARAGUS, AND ALMOND SAUCE

SERVES: 4
WORKING TIME: 25 MINUTES
TOTAL TIME: 25 MINUTES

10 ounces fettuccine

1 tablespoon olive oil

4 scallions, thinly sliced

1 pound asparagus, tough ends trimmed, cut on the diagonal into 1-inch lengths

¾ pound skinless red snapper fillets, any visible bones removed, cut into 1-inch chunks

¾ cup reduced-sodium chicken broth, defatted

2 teaspoons Dijon mustard

½ teaspoon salt

¼ teaspoon freshly ground black pepper

2 tablespoons reduced-fat cream cheese (Neufchâtel)

1 tablespoon fresh lemon juice

2 tablespoons slivered almonds, toasted

1. In a large pot of boiling water, cook the pasta until just tender. Drain well.

2. Meanwhile, in a large nonstick skillet, heat the oil until hot but not smoking over medium heat. Add the scallions and cook, stirring frequently, until tender, about 2 minutes. Add the asparagus, stirring to coat. Add the snapper, broth, mustard, salt, and pepper and bring to a boil. Reduce to a simmer and cook, stirring occasionally, until the fish is almost cooked through, about 4 minutes.

3. Add the cream cheese and lemon juice to the pan and cook, stirring, until the sauce is thickened and the fish is opaque, about 2 minutes. Stir in the almonds. Divide the pasta among 4 bowls, spoon the sauce over, and serve.

Helpful hint: To toast the almonds, place them in a small, ungreased skillet and cook over medium-high heat for 3 to 4 minutes, shaking the pan occasionally, until golden. Immediately tip them out of the pan onto a plate so they do not burn or scorch.

FAT: 11G/22%
CALORIES: 459
SATURATED FAT: 2.4G
CARBOHYDRATE: 57G
PROTEIN: 33G
CHOLESTEROL: 103MG
SODIUM: 550MG

For dinner-party fare in under 30 minutes, try this sophisticated sauce. Serve a raspberry sorbet for dessert.

Lime
juice, soy sauce, and
the combination of
fresh mint and basil
give this distinctive
pasta sauce its true
Thai flavor. Crisp-
tender vegetables,
including snow peas
and bamboo shoots,
provide a crunchy
contrast to the delicate
crabmeat. Spaghetti
is a suitable stand-in
for traditional Thai
rice noodles.

THAI CRAB SAUCE

SERVES: 4
WORKING TIME: 30 MINUTES
TOTAL TIME: 30 MINUTES

10 ounces medium strand pasta, such as spaghetti or linguine

1 tablespoon olive oil

6 scallions, thinly sliced

4 cloves garlic, minced

1 red bell pepper, cut into ¼-inch-wide strips

¼ pound snow peas, trimmed and cut into thin slivers

8-ounce can sliced bamboo shoots, drained

½ pound lump crabmeat, picked over to remove any cartilage (see tip)

½ cup reduced-sodium chicken broth, defatted

3 tablespoons reduced-sodium soy sauce

3 tablespoons fresh lime juice

2 tablespoons firmly packed dark brown sugar

¼ teaspoon salt

1 teaspoon cornstarch

⅓ cup chopped fresh basil

⅓ cup chopped fresh mint

1. In a large pot of boiling water, cook the pasta until just tender. Drain well.

2. Meanwhile, in a large nonstick skillet, heat the oil until hot but not smoking over medium heat. Add the scallions and garlic and cook, stirring occasionally, until the scallions are tender, about 3 minutes. Add the bell pepper and cook until crisp-tender, about 2 minutes. Add the snow peas and bamboo shoots, stirring to combine. Add the crab and cook, stirring, until heated through, about 5 minutes.

3. In a small bowl, combine the broth, soy sauce, lime juice, brown sugar, and salt. Add the cornstarch and stir until well combined. Pour the mixture into the skillet along with the basil and mint and bring to a boil. Cook, stirring constantly, until the sauce is thickened, about 1 minute. Divide the pasta among 4 plates, spoon the sauce over, and serve.

Helpful hint: Frozen snow peas may be used if fresh are unavailable.

FAT: 6G/13%
CALORIES: 431
SATURATED FAT: 0.8G
CARBOHYDRATE: 71G
PROTEIN: 24G
CHOLESTEROL: 57MG
SODIUM: 830MG

TIP

Lump crabmeat consists of large chunks of meat from the body (rather than the claws) of the crab. Before using lump crabmeat, whether fresh or canned, look it over carefully and remove any bits of cartilage or shell that may have remained in the meat. Don't over-handle the crabmeat or the "lumps" will fall apart.

ROTINI WITH FLOUNDER AND SUN-DRIED TOMATO PESTO

SERVES: 4
WORKING TIME: 15 MINUTES
TOTAL TIME: 20 MINUTES

The savory pesto that deliciously coats the pasta and sautéed flounder in this dish is remarkably low in fat with no loss of flavor. Feel free to try this recipe with cod, scrod, haddock, or grouper instead of flounder. When buying fish, be sure it smells clean and sweet—never fishy.

8 ounces rotini pasta

½ cup sun-dried (not oil-packed) tomato halves

2 cloves garlic, peeled

1 tablespoon pine nuts

1 tablespoon grated Parmesan cheese

1 tablespoon olive oil

¼ teaspoon salt

¼ cup low-fat (1%) milk

¼ cup flour

¾ pound skinned flounder fillets, any visible bones removed, cut into 1-inch pieces

⅓ cup reduced-sodium chicken broth, defatted

2 teaspoons fresh lemon juice

3 tablespoons chopped fresh parsley (optional)

1. Heat a large pot of water to boiling, and cook the rotini until just tender. Drain well. Meanwhile, in a medium saucepan, bring 1 cup of water to a boil over medium-high heat. Add the tomatoes and cook until slightly softened, about 3 minutes. Add the garlic and cook until the tomatoes are tender, about 2 minutes longer. Transfer the mixture to a blender or food processor. Add the pine nuts, Parmesan, 1 teaspoon of the oil, and salt and purée until smooth, about 1 minute. Set aside.

2. Place the milk in a shallow bowl. Spread the flour on a plate. Dip the flounder into the milk, then dredge in the flour, shaking off the excess. In a large nonstick skillet, heat the remaining 2 teaspoons oil until hot but not smoking over medium heat. Add the flounder and cook until golden, about 1 minute per side. With a slotted spatula, transfer the flounder to a plate.

3. Add the broth and lemon juice to the pan and cook, scraping up any brown bits, until slightly reduced, about 1 minute. Swirl in the tomato pesto. Add the flounder and cook until just heated through, about 1 minute longer. Transfer the flounder mixture to a large bowl, add the rotini, and toss gently to combine. Spoon the pasta mixture into 4 shallow bowls, sprinkle with the parsley, and serve.

Suggested accompaniments: Green beans in a red wine vinaigrette. Follow with fruit salad topped with nonfat vanilla yogurt and sunflower seeds.

FAT: 7G/16%
CALORIES: 400
SATURATED FAT: 1.4G
CARBOHYDRATE: 56G
PROTEIN: 27G
CHOLESTEROL: 42MG
SODIUM: 304MG

SHELLS WITH CREAMY SALMON AND DILL SAUCE

SERVES: 4
WORKING TIME: 30 MINUTES
TOTAL TIME: 30 MINUTES

12 ounces small pasta shells

2 shallots or scallions, finely chopped

8-ounce bottle clam juice

½ cup dry white wine

¾ teaspoon dried thyme

½ teaspoon dried dillweed

½ pound salmon, cut into ¾-inch pieces

1½ cups peeled, seeded, and sliced cucumber

3 tablespoons flour

¼ cup plain low-fat yogurt

½ cup reduced-fat sour cream

1½ teaspoons Worcestershire sauce

¾ teaspoon salt

¼ teaspoon freshly ground black pepper

1. In a large pot of boiling water, cook the pasta shells until just tender. Drain well.

2. Meanwhile, in a large saucepan, combine the shallots, clam juice, wine, thyme, and dillweed and bring to a boil over medium heat. Reduce the heat to a simmer, add the salmon and cucumber, cover, and cook until the salmon is just opaque, about 3 minutes. With a slotted spoon, transfer the salmon and cucumber to a plate.

3. In a small bowl, combine the flour and yogurt until blended. Stir the yogurt mixture into the saucepan and cook, stirring, until slightly thickened, about 2 minutes. Stir in the sour cream.

4. Transfer the mixture to a large bowl and stir in the Worcestershire sauce, salt, and pepper. Add the pasta and toss to combine. Add the salmon and cucumber, tossing gently to combine. Divide the pasta mixture among 4 bowls and serve.

Helpful hint: To seed a cucumber, halve the cucumber lengthwise and scoop out the seeds with the tip of a small spoon.

FAT: 9G/16%
CALORIES: 512
SATURATED FAT: 2.9G
CARBOHYDRATE: 74G
PROTEIN: 26G
CHOLESTEROL: 42MG
SODIUM: 624MG

Many an elegant dinner party has salmon with dilled cucumber sauce as its centerpiece. In this more casual guise, chunks of salmon and sliced cucumber are simmered in a dilled broth, then combined with pasta and a creamy sauce. By using flour mixed with low-fat yogurt, we add creamy richness to the sauce while stabilizing the yogurt, preventing it from separating during cooking.

PASTA SHELLS WITH SCALLOPS AND BASIL

SERVES: 4
WORKING TIME: 15 MINUTES
TOTAL TIME: 20 MINUTES

This scallop dish, with a tomato and orange juice sauce, is quick and simple—and simply delicious. Dredging the scallops in cornstarch not only lightly colors the scallops during sautéing but also thickens the sauce. Bay scallops, shelled shrimp, or chunks of red snapper, sea bass, or swordfish are all tasty substitutes for the sea scallops.

10 ounces medium pasta shells

2 tablespoons cornstarch

1 pound sea scallops, halved crosswise if very large

2 tablespoons olive oil

2 cloves garlic, minced

½ cup sliced scallions

¾ pound tomatoes, coarsely chopped

3 tablespoons chopped fresh basil

3 tablespoons orange juice

1 teaspoon grated orange zest

¾ teaspoon salt

1. Heat a large pot of water to boiling, and cook the pasta shells until just tender. Drain well.

2. Meanwhile, spread the cornstarch on a plate. Dredge the scallops in the cornstarch, shaking off the excess. In a large nonstick skillet, heat the oil until hot but not smoking over medium heat. Add the scallops and cook, stirring frequently, until lightly golden, about 2 minutes. Add the garlic and scallions and cook, stirring frequently, until the garlic is tender, about 2 minutes. With a slotted spoon, transfer the scallop mixture to a plate.

3. Add the tomatoes, basil, orange juice, zest, and salt to the pan and cook until the mixture is slightly thickened, about 4 minutes. Stir in the scallop mixture and cook until the scallops are just opaque, about 1 minute longer. Transfer the scallop mixture to a large bowl, add the pasta shells, and toss to combine. Spoon the pasta mixture into 4 shallow bowls and serve.

Suggested accompaniments: Rye flat bread, and a salad of watercress, red leaf lettuce, and sliced cucumber with cider vinegar vinaigrette. For dessert, sliced fresh strawberries sprinkled with orange liqueur.

FAT: 9G/17%
CALORIES: 470
SATURATED FAT: 1.2G
CARBOHYDRATE: 66G
PROTEIN: 29G
CHOLESTEROL: 37MG
SODIUM: 610MG

SHRIMP AND RADIATORE ROMESCO

SERVES: 4
WORKING TIME: 20 MINUTES
TOTAL TIME: 25 MINUTES

Almonds, garlic, and roasted red peppers (we've used jarred for convenience) figure prominently in this classic and very rich Spanish sauce.

1 tablespoon plus 2 teaspoons olive oil

2 tablespoons whole almonds, with skins

2 cloves garlic, peeled and crushed

1 slice (1 ounce) white bread, crumbled

12-ounce jar roasted red peppers, rinsed and drained

⅓ cup reduced-sodium chicken broth, defatted

2 tablespoons no-salt-added tomato paste

2 teaspoons red wine vinegar

¾ teaspoon salt

¼ teaspoon red pepper flakes

1 yellow or red bell pepper, diced

1 pound medium shrimp, shelled and deveined

¼ cup snipped fresh dill

10 ounces radiatore pasta, preferably 5 ounces each of spinach radiatore and regular radiatore

1. Start heating a large pot of water to boiling for the pasta. In a large nonstick skillet, heat 1 tablespoon of the oil until hot but not smoking over medium heat. Add the almonds, garlic, and bread and cook, stirring constantly, until the bread is lightly browned, about 4 minutes.

2. Transfer the almond mixture to a blender or food processor. Wipe the skillet clean. Add the roasted peppers, ⅔ cup of water, the broth, tomato paste, vinegar, salt, and pepper flakes to the almond mixture. Purée the mixture until almost smooth, about 1 minute.

3. In the same skillet, heat the remaining 2 teaspoons oil until hot but not smoking over medium heat. Stir in the bell pepper and cook until almost tender, about 4 minutes. Add the shrimp and cook, stirring frequently, until almost opaque, about 4 minutes. Stir in the almond purée and dill and cook, stirring frequently, until the shrimp are just opaque, 2 to 3 minutes longer.

4. Meanwhile, cook the radiatore in the boiling water until just tender. Drain well. Transfer the radiatore to a large bowl, add the shrimp mixture, and toss to combine. Spoon the pasta mixture into 4 shallow bowls and serve.

Suggested accompaniment: For dessert, gingersnaps and nut-flavored coffee.

FAT: 10G/19%
CALORIES: 481
SATURATED FAT: 1.4G
CARBOHYDRATE: 66G
PROTEIN: 31G
CHOLESTEROL: 140MG
SODIUM: 674MG

ROTINI WITH COD, POTATOES, AND ONION

SERVES: 4
WORKING TIME: 20 MINUTES
TOTAL TIME: 40 MINUTES

¾ pound small red potatoes, cut into ½-inch chunks

1 pound tomatoes

1 tablespoon olive oil

1 large onion, diced

3 cloves garlic, minced

1 tablespoon minced fresh ginger

3 tablespoons brandy or reduced-sodium chicken broth, defatted

½ cup bottled clam juice

½ teaspoon hot pepper sauce

½ teaspoon dried thyme

½ teaspoon salt

¾ pound skinned cod fillets, any visible bones removed, cut into 2-inch chunks

¼ cup chopped, pitted oil-cured black olives

3 tablespoons chopped fresh parsley

10 ounces tricolor rotini pasta

1. In a large pot of boiling water, cook the potatoes until almost tender, about 5 minutes. Reserve the boiling water for the tomatoes and, with a slotted spoon, transfer the potatoes to a plate. Blanch the tomatoes in the reserved boiling water for 10 seconds. Reserve the boiling water for the pasta and, with a slotted spoon, transfer the tomatoes to a cutting board. Peel the tomatoes and coarsely chop. Set aside.

2. In a large nonstick skillet, heat the oil until hot but not smoking over medium heat. Add the onion, garlic, and ginger and cook, stirring frequently, until the onion has softened, about 7 minutes. Add the potatoes, stirring to coat. Add the brandy and cook until the liquid has evaporated, about 2 minutes. Stir in the tomatoes, clam juice, hot pepper sauce, thyme, and salt. Bring to a boil over medium-high heat and cook, stirring occasionally, until the sauce is slightly thickened, about 5 minutes. Reduce to a simmer, add the cod and olives, and cook until the cod is just opaque, about 5 minutes longer. Stir in the parsley.

3. Meanwhile, cook the rotini in the reserved boiling water until just tender. Transfer the cod mixture to a large bowl, add the rotini, and toss gently to combine. Spoon the pasta mixture into 4 shallow bowls and serve.

Suggested accompaniments: Crusty peasant bread and steamed broccoli.

FAT: 9G/15%
CALORIES: 536
SATURATED FAT: 1.1G
CARBOHYDRATE: 80G
PROTEIN: 28G
CHOLESTEROL: 37MG
SODIUM: 746MG

T his Mediterranean-inspired dish, as chunky as a stew, is a marriage of wonderfully complementary flavors.

SOLE WITH BASIL AND TOMATO SAUCE

SERVES: 4
WORKING TIME: 30 MINUTES
TOTAL TIME: 35 MINUTES

*ole
and flounder, along
with their larger kin,
halibut and turbot,
enjoy widespread
popularity, perhaps
because of their mild,
sweet, "unfishy" flavor.
This quality also
makes these fish a
versatile ingredient.
For a simple but
delicious main dish,
we've cut the fillets into
chunks and simmered
them in a tomato-
vegetable sauce finished
with a generous
quantity of fresh basil.

1 tablespoon olive oil

1 onion, finely chopped

10 ounces medium strand pasta, such as linguine or spaghetti

2 carrots, quartered lengthwise and thinly sliced

2 ribs celery, quartered lengthwise and thinly sliced

½ cup dry white wine

2 cups canned no-salt-added tomatoes, chopped with their juices

1 cup bottled clam juice or reduced-sodium chicken broth, defatted

½ teaspoon salt

¾ pound sole or flounder fillets, any visible bones removed, cut into large chunks

½ cup chopped fresh basil

1½ teaspoons cornstarch mixed with 1 tablespoon water

1. In a large nonstick skillet, heat the oil until hot but not smoking over medium heat. Add the onion and cook, stirring frequently, until the onion is tender, about 7 minutes.

2. In a large pot of boiling water, cook the pasta until just tender. Drain well.

3. Meanwhile, add the carrots and celery to the skillet and cook, stirring frequently, until the carrots are crisp-tender, about 5 minutes. Add the wine, increase the heat to high, and cook until the wine is almost evaporated, about 4 minutes. Add the tomatoes, clam juice, and salt and cook, stirring occasionally, until the sauce is slightly reduced, about 4 minutes.

4. Add the sole and basil to the pan, cover, and cook until the fish is almost cooked through and the sauce is flavorful, about 3 minutes. Add the cornstarch mixture and cook, stirring constantly, until the sauce is thickened and the fish is opaque, about 1 minute. Divide the pasta among 4 bowls, spoon the sauce over, and serve.

Helpful hint: East Coast sole varieties you can use in this recipe include gray sole, winter flounder, and summer flounder; on the West Coast, petrale sole and so-called Dover sole are two options.

FAT: 6G/12%
CALORIES: 460
SATURATED FAT: 0.9G
CARBOHYDRATE: 69G
PROTEIN: 28G
CHOLESTEROL: 41MG
SODIUM: 526MG

SHRIMP LO MEIN

SERVES: 4
WORKING TIME: 20 MINUTES
TOTAL TIME: 25 MINUTES

A feast for the eye as well as the palate, this dish is a great alternative to classic lo mein. We've replaced the usual fat-laden fried noodles with fettuccine and used lots of vegetables for crunch. The shrimp are briefly marinated in a sherry-sesame oil blend, which would take to scallops just as readily. Baby corn can be purchased in the Oriental foods section of supermarkets.

2 tablespoons reduced-sodium soy sauce

2 tablespoons dry sherry

2 teaspoons Oriental sesame oil

1 teaspoon cornstarch

¾ pound medium shrimp, shelled and deveined

1 tablespoon vegetable oil

3 tablespoons minced fresh ginger

3 scallions, minced

2 carrots, diced

1 large leek, halved lengthwise and cut into 2-inch julienne

½ cup sliced water chestnuts, rinsed and drained

½ cup bottled or canned baby corn (optional)

½ cup frozen peas

¼ cup chili sauce

⅔ cup reduced-sodium chicken broth, defatted

8 ounces fettuccine

1. Start heating a large pot of water to boiling for the pasta. In a medium bowl, combine the soy sauce, sherry, sesame oil, and cornstarch. Add the shrimp, toss to coat, and set aside.

2. In a large nonstick skillet, heat the vegetable oil until hot but not smoking over medium heat. Add the ginger and scallions and cook, stirring frequently, until fragrant, about 1 minute. Stir in the carrots and leek and cook, stirring frequently, until the vegetables are almost tender, about 3 minutes.

3. Add the shrimp with their marinade to the pan and cook, stirring constantly, until the shrimp are almost opaque, about 2 minutes. Stir in the water chestnuts, baby corn, peas, and chili sauce. Add the broth, increase the heat to high, and cook, stirring constantly, until the shrimp are just opaque and the vegetables are heated through, about 1 minute.

4. Meanwhile, cook the fettuccine in the boiling water until just tender. Drain well. Transfer the shrimp mixture to the pasta pot, add the fettuccine, and cook over low heat just until the fettuccine is well coated, about 1 minute longer. Spoon the shrimp lo mein into 4 shallow bowls and serve.

Suggested accompaniments: Shredded Napa cabbage with a rice vinegar dressing, and fresh plums for dessert.

FAT: 10G/18%
CALORIES: 469
SATURATED FAT: 1.5G
CARBOHYDRATE: 67G
PROTEIN: 27G
CHOLESTEROL: 159MG
SODIUM: 801MG

FETTUCCINE WITH FRESH SALMON

SERVES: 4
WORKING TIME: 15 MINUTES
TOTAL TIME: 25 MINUTES

1 cup reduced-sodium chicken broth, defatted

⅓ cup dry white wine

¾ pound skinned salmon fillets, any visible bones removed, cut into ½-inch-thick slices

4 scallions, minced

1 red bell pepper, diced

1 tablespoon no-salt-added tomato paste

1 tablespoon fresh lemon juice

¼ cup snipped fresh dill

1½ teaspoons cornstarch

¼ cup light sour cream

5 ounces fresh fettuccine

5 ounces fresh spinach fettuccine

1. Start heating a large pot of water to boiling for the pasta. In a large skillet, combine the broth and wine and bring to a boil over high heat. Reduce to a simmer, add the salmon, cover, and cook until the salmon is just opaque, about 4 minutes. With a slotted spoon, transfer the salmon to a plate.

2. Add the scallions and bell pepper to the pan and simmer, uncovered, until the bell pepper is tender, about 3 minutes. Stir in the tomato paste and lemon juice and simmer until the flavors are blended, about 1 minute. Stir in the dill.

3. In a cup, combine the cornstarch and 1 tablespoon of water and stir to blend. Bring the broth mixture to a boil over medium-high heat, stir in the cornstarch mixture, and cook, stirring constantly, until the mixture is slightly thickened, about 1 minute. Reduce to a simmer, add the salmon, and cook until the salmon is just heated through, about 30 seconds. Remove from the heat and stir in the sour cream.

4. Meanwhile, cook the fettuccine in the boiling water until just tender. Drain well. Transfer the fettuccine to a large bowl, add the salmon mixture, and toss gently to combine. Spoon the pasta mixture into 4 shallow bowls and serve.

Suggested accompaniment: Leafy green salad with red onion, cucumber, and cherry tomatoes with a reduced-fat herb vinaigrette.

FAT: 10G/21%
CALORIES: 419
SATURATED FAT: 2.3G
CARBOHYDRATE: 50G
PROTEIN: 29G
CHOLESTEROL: 111MG
SODIUM: 242MG

We've used the classically complementary flavors of salmon and fresh dill, highlighted with a luscious sour cream sauce, lightly thickened with cornstarch. You may use all one color fettuccine and any strongly flavored, firm-textured fish, such as swordfish, tuna, or shark instead of the salmon.

GARLICKY COD SAUCE

SERVES: 4
WORKING TIME: 25 MINUTES
TOTAL TIME: 25 MINUTES

This aromatic sauce will delight garlic lovers in particular, but it's likely to be well received by everyone else, too: The garlic is sautéed, then simmered, so it lacks the cutting pungency of raw garlic. Reduced-fat mayonnaise creates a creamy texture that's a wonderful foil for the sauce's rich flavor. Serve a salad of tender greens and sweet red onions alongside the pasta.

10 ounces shaped pasta, such as farfalle (bow ties) or orecchiette

2 teaspoons olive oil

4 scallions, thinly sliced

8 cloves garlic, minced

2 red bell peppers, cut into ½-inch squares

10 ounces skinless cod fillets, any visible bones removed, cut into ½-inch chunks

1 cup bottled clam juice or reduced-sodium chicken broth, defatted

¼ teaspoon salt

1 cup frozen peas

3 tablespoons reduced-fat mayonnaise

⅓ cup chopped fresh parsley

1. In a large pot of boiling water, cook the pasta until just tender. Drain well.

2. Meanwhile, in a large nonstick skillet, heat the oil until hot but not smoking over medium heat. Add the scallions and garlic and cook, stirring frequently, until the scallions are tender, about 2 minutes. Add the bell peppers and cook, stirring frequently, until the bell peppers are crisp-tender, about 4 minutes. Add the cod and cook, stirring occasionally, until well coated, about 2 minutes.

3. Add the clam juice and salt to the pan and bring to a boil. Reduce to a simmer and stir in the peas, mayonnaise, and parsley. Cook, stirring occasionally, until the sauce is thickened and the fish is just opaque, about 5 minutes. Divide the pasta among 4 bowls, spoon the sauce over, and serve.

Helpful hint: For a head start, cut up the scallions, garlic, and bell peppers ahead of time and refrigerate until needed. Be sure to seal the scallions and garlic well before storing them.

FAT: 6G/13%
CALORIES: 425
SATURATED FAT: 0.9G
CARBOHYDRATE: 66G
PROTEIN: 25G
CHOLESTEROL: 31MG
SODIUM: 444MG

CHILI SHRIMP SAUCE

SERVES: 4
WORKING TIME: 15 MINUTES
TOTAL TIME: 20 MINUTES

Chili is a longtime favorite for casual buffets and parties. This chili-inspired sauce, ready in a fraction of the time, is just the ticket for hungry groups. You can double the recipe as long as you possess a pot big enough to cook pasta for eight at one time. All you need to complete the meal is a great big salad and some warm rolls or bread sticks.

10 ounces small tube pasta, such as elbow macaroni or ditalini

1 tablespoon olive oil

4 scallions, thinly sliced

5 cloves garlic, minced

2 cups no-salt-added canned tomatoes, chopped with their juices

¼ cup chili sauce

½ teaspoon salt

½ teaspoon dried oregano

¾ pound medium shrimp, shelled, deveined, and cut into thirds

1. In a large pot of boiling water, cook the pasta until just tender. Drain well.

2. Meanwhile, in a large nonstick skillet, heat the oil until hot but not smoking over medium heat. Add the scallions and garlic and cook, stirring frequently, until the scallions are softened, about 2 minutes.

3. Add the tomatoes, chili sauce, and salt to the pan and bring to a boil. Stir in the oregano and shrimp, reduce to a simmer, cover, and cook until the shrimp are just opaque, about 3 minutes. Spoon the sauce over the hot pasta and serve.

Helpful hint: A sprinkling of a chopped fresh herb, such as parsley, basil, or oregano, would add extra visual appeal (and bright flavor) to the pasta.

FAT: 6G/13%
CALORIES: 419
SATURATED FAT: 0.9G
CARBOHYDRATE: 65G
PROTEIN: 25G
CHOLESTEROL: 105MG
SODIUM: 628MG

FETTUCCINE WITH TUNA AND CANNELLINI

SERVES: 4
WORKING TIME: 25 MINUTES
TOTAL TIME: 30 MINUTES

America's favorite fish, canned tuna, is much more than a sandwich filling; it makes fine dinner fare, too. Here, tuna is paired with cannellini (white kidney beans) to make a substantial pasta sauce. Light tuna is more flavorful (and cheaper) than solid white. To keep the meal light, be sure to buy fish that's packed in water, not oil.

8 ounces fettuccine
1 tablespoon vegetable oil
1 onion, coarsely chopped
2 ribs celery, coarsely chopped
1 cup shredded carrot
1 clove garlic, minced
13¾-ounce can reduced-sodium chicken broth, defatted
19-ounce can white kidney beans (cannellini), rinsed and drained
1 teaspoon dried rosemary
¼ teaspoon freshly ground black pepper
6½-ounce can water-packed tuna, drained and flaked
1 medium tomato, diced
2 tablespoons slivered Calamata or other brine-cured black olives

1. In a large pot of boiling water, cook the fettuccine until just tender. Drain well.

2. Meanwhile, in a large saucepan, heat the oil until hot but not smoking over medium-high heat. Add the onion, celery, carrot, and garlic and cook, stirring, until the vegetables are crisp-tender, about 5 minutes. Stir in the broth, beans, rosemary, and pepper and cook until the sauce is slightly thickened, about 6 minutes. Stir in the tuna and cook until the tuna is warmed through, about 1 minute.

3. Transfer the mixture to a large bowl, add the pasta, tomato, and olives and toss to combine.

Helpful hint: You can chop the onion and celery, shred the carrot, and mince the garlic up to 4 hours in advance; since they will all be added to the pan at once, you can combine them in a single container and refrigerate until needed.

FAT: 8G/16%
CALORIES: 455
SATURATED FAT: 1.2G
CARBOHYDRATE: 66G
PROTEIN: 30G
CHOLESTEROL: 71MG
SODIUM: 710MG

VERACRUZ SNAPPER SAUCE

SERVES: 4
WORKING TIME: 25 MINUTES
TOTAL TIME: 30 MINUTES

This vibrant pasta dinner is an adaptation of a classic Mexican recipe. The interplay of jalapeños and citrus is irresistible.

10 ounces medium strand pasta, such as spaghetti or linguine

1 tablespoon olive oil

1 red onion, halved and thinly sliced

4 cloves garlic, minced

2 pickled jalapeños, finely chopped

Two 8-ounce cans no-salt-added tomato sauce

½ teaspoon grated orange zest

½ cup orange juice

¾ teaspoon salt

½ teaspoon dried oregano

¾ pound skinless red snapper fillets, any visible bones removed, cut into 1-inch chunks

1 tablespoon fresh lime juice

⅓ cup chopped fresh cilantro (optional)

1. In a large pot of boiling water, cook the pasta until just tender. Drain well.

2. Meanwhile, in a large nonstick skillet, heat the oil until hot but not smoking over medium heat. Add the onion, garlic, and jalapeños and cook, stirring frequently, until the onion is tender, about 7 minutes.

3. Add the tomato sauce, orange zest, orange juice, salt, and oregano to the pan and bring to a boil. Reduce to a simmer and cook, stirring occasionally, until the flavors have blended, about 4 minutes. Add the snapper and simmer until the fish is just opaque, about 4 minutes. Stir in the lime juice and cilantro. Divide the pasta among 4 bowls, spoon the sauce over, and serve.

Helpful hint: Other types of fish that will work well in this sauce include flounder, cod, haddock, and rockfish.

FAT: 6G/12%
CALORIES: 457
SATURATED FAT: 0.9G
CARBOHYDRATE: 71G
PROTEIN: 29G
CHOLESTEROL: 32MG
SODIUM: 611MG

FARFALLE WITH CODFISH AND SPICY TOMATO SAUCE

SERVES: 4
WORKING TIME: 30 MINUTES
TOTAL TIME: 40 MINUTES

2 tablespoons flour

1 pound cod fillets, cut into 8 chunks

1 tablespoon olive oil

10 ounces farfalle pasta

1 large yellow or red bell pepper, diced

2 cloves garlic, minced

½ cup Marsala wine

3 tomatoes, coarsely chopped

2 tablespoons no-salt-added tomato paste

¼ cup chopped fresh mint

¾ teaspoon salt

¼ to ½ teaspoon hot pepper sauce

1 teaspoon cornstarch mixed with 1 tablespoon water

1. Start heating a large pot of water to boiling for the pasta. Place the flour on a sheet of waxed paper and dredge the cod in the flour, shaking off the excess. In a large nonstick skillet, heat the oil until hot but not smoking over medium heat. Cook the cod until golden brown and lightly crisped, about 3 minutes per side. With a slotted spatula, transfer the cod to a plate.

2. Cook the farfalle in the boiling water until just tender. Drain well. Meanwhile, add the bell pepper and garlic to the skillet and cook, stirring frequently, until the pepper is tender, about 4 minutes. Stir in the Marsala and cook until slightly reduced, about 2 minutes. Add the tomatoes, tomato paste, mint, salt, and hot pepper sauce and bring to a boil. Reduce to a simmer and cook, uncovered, until the sauce is richly flavored, about 7 minutes.

3. Return the sauce to a boil, stir in the cornstarch mixture, and cook, stirring, until slightly thickened, about 1 minute. Transfer the sauce to a large bowl and add the pasta and cod, tossing gently to combine. Spoon into 4 pasta bowls and serve.

Helpful hint: Marsala is a fortified wine made from Sicilian grapes and sweetened with concentrated grape juice. The driest Marsala is labeled "virgine." Dry sherry may be substituted, if necessary.

FAT: 6G/11%
CALORIES: 485
SATURATED FAT: .8G
CARBOHYDRATE: 68G
PROTEIN: 31G
CHOLESTEROL: 49MG
SODIUM: 508MG

I*n this dish, juicy nuggets of codfish are paired with pasta "butterflies" in an aromatic Marsala sauce.*

DITALINI WITH SALMON, BELL PEPPERS, AND FRESH DILL

SERVES: 4
WORKING TIME: 20 MINUTES
TOTAL TIME: 30 MINUTES

Ditalini, the tiny tube pasta, is a smart choice to soak up this flavorful sauce, enlivened with vinegar, dill, and tomato-vegetable juice. As a pasta alternative, rotini or elbow macaroni would also work well. For other variations, use all red or all green bell peppers, and substitute two cans of water-packed tuna for the salmon.

1 tablespoon olive oil

1 medium red onion, diced

3 bell peppers, preferably 1 each of red, green, and yellow, diced

2 tablespoons red wine vinegar

1 tomato, diced

1 cup reduced-sodium tomato-vegetable juice

½ teaspoon dried tarragon

¼ teaspoon salt

1 teaspoon cornstarch

15-ounce can sockeye salmon, drained and flaked

1 scallion, sliced

¼ cup snipped fresh dill

8 ounces ditalini pasta

1. Start heating a large pot of water to boiling for the pasta. In a large nonstick skillet, heat the oil until hot but not smoking over medium heat. Add the onion and cook, stirring frequently, until softened, about 7 minutes. Stir in the bell peppers, cover, and cook, stirring frequently, until the peppers are softened, about 5 minutes. Stir in the vinegar until well combined. Stir in the tomato, tomato-vegetable juice, tarragon, and salt and cook, uncovered, until the flavors are blended, about 5 minutes.

2. In a cup, combine the cornstarch and 1 tablespoon of water, stir to blend, and stir into the bell pepper mixture. Bring to a boil over medium-high heat and cook, stirring constantly, until the mixture is slightly thickened, about 1 minute. Reduce to a simmer, add the salmon, scallion, and dill, and cook until the salmon is just heated through, about 3 minutes longer.

3. Meanwhile, cook the ditalini in the boiling water until just tender. Drain well. Transfer the salmon mixture to a large bowl, add the ditalini, and toss to combine. Spoon the pasta mixture onto 4 plates and serve.

Suggested accompaniments: Soft garlic bread sticks, followed by sliced fresh peaches poached in Riesling spiked with cinnamon, vanilla, and ginger.

FAT: 11G/23%
CALORIES: 433
SATURATED FAT: 2G
CARBOHYDRATE: 56G
PROTEIN: 27G
CHOLESTEROL: 38MG
SODIUM: 695MG

FETTUCCINE WITH SHRIMP AND LEMON CREAM SAUCE

SERVES: 4
WORKING TIME: 30 MINUTES
TOTAL TIME: 35 MINUTES

There could hardly be a quicker, easier dinner-party dish—or a more welcome weekday treat for the family—than this luscious pairing of seafood and pasta. The rich-but-slim sauce gets its velvety consistency from evaporated low-fat milk and cornstarch. Any thick, long-stranded fresh pasta (such as linguine or long fusilli) will complement the sauce nicely.

2 teaspoons olive oil

1 pound medium shrimp, shelled and deveined

3 cloves garlic, minced

12 ounces fresh spinach fettuccine

2 tablespoons fresh lemon juice

¾ cup reduced-sodium chicken broth, defatted

1 cup evaporated low-fat milk

¾ teaspoon grated lemon zest

½ teaspoon salt

1½ teaspoons cornstarch mixed with 1 tablespoon water

¼ cup chopped fresh parsley

1. Start heating a large pot of water to boiling for the pasta. In a large nonstick skillet, heat the oil until hot but not smoking over medium heat. Add the shrimp and garlic and cook, stirring occasionally, until the shrimp are opaque on the outside but still translucent in the center, about 2 minutes. With a slotted spoon, transfer the shrimp to a plate. Set aside.

2. Cook the fettuccine in the boiling water until just tender. Drain well.

3. Meanwhile, add the lemon juice to the skillet, stirring to incorporate the garlic. Add the broth and cook for 1 minute to blend the flavors. Stir in the milk, lemon zest, and salt and bring to a boil. Stir in the cornstarch mixture and cook, stirring constantly, until slightly thickened, about 1 minute. Return the shrimp to the skillet and cook until opaque throughout. Add the parsley and transfer to a large bowl. Add the fettuccine, toss well, and serve.

Helpful hint: Fresh pasta cooks in much less time than dried; check it frequently to avoid overcooking.

FAT: 9G/16%
CALORIES: 510
SATURATED FAT: 1.5G
CARBOHYDRATE: 70G
PROTEIN: 36G
CHOLESTEROL: 231MG
SODIUM: 659MG

MEDITERRANEAN COD SAUCE

SERVES: 4
WORKING TIME: 30 MINUTES
TOTAL TIME: 35 MINUTES

In Italy, France, and Spain—countries that harvest abundant seafood along their Mediterranean coastlines—a favorite way to cook fish is with tomatoes, bell peppers, and herbs as we do here. Olive oil, garlic, and wine are often used as well. A basket of grissini (crisp, pencil-thin Italian bread sticks) would go well with this pasta dish.

10 ounces shaped pasta, such as rotini or radiatore

1 tablespoon olive oil

1 red bell pepper, cut into ½-inch squares

1 green bell pepper, cut into ½-inch squares

4 cloves garlic, minced

½ cup dry white wine

1 cup canned no-salt-added tomatoes, chopped with their juices

¾ cup bottled clam juice or reduced-sodium chicken broth, defatted

½ cup chopped fresh basil

⅓ cup chopped fresh parsley

½ teaspoon dried thyme

¾ teaspoon salt

¾ pound skinless cod fillets, any visible bones removed, cut into 1-inch chunks

1 teaspoon cornstarch mixed with 1 tablespoon water

1. In a large pot of boiling water, cook the pasta until just tender. Drain well.

2. Meanwhile, in a large nonstick skillet, heat the oil until hot but not smoking over medium heat. Add the bell peppers and garlic and cook, stirring frequently, until the bell peppers are tender, about 5 minutes. Add the wine, increase the heat to high, and cook until the wine is almost evaporated, about 4 minutes.

3. Add the tomatoes, clam juice, basil, parsley, thyme, and salt to the pan and bring to a boil. Reduce to a simmer and cook, stirring occasionally, until the flavors have blended, about 5 minutes. Add the cod, cover, return to a boil, and cook until the fish is almost cooked through, about 3 minutes. Stir in the cornstarch mixture and cook, stirring constantly, until the fish is opaque and the sauce is thickened, about 1 minute. Spoon the sauce over the hot pasta and serve.

Helpful hint: You can substitute 1 large fresh tomato or 3 plum tomatoes for the canned, if you like.

FAT: 5G/11%
CALORIES: 420
SATURATED FAT: 0.7G
CARBOHYDRATE: 62G
PROTEIN: 26G
CHOLESTEROL: 37MG
SODIUM: 573MG

*I*n
this Szechuan-inspired dish, capellini stand in for Chinese egg noodles. The pasta is topped with a colorful stir-fry of scallops, carrot, and snow peas. Most Chinese noodles take the form of long strands. Feel free to try the various types found in Chinese markets and specialty shops. You can use wheat noodles, as well as those made of buckwheat or rice.

SZECHUAN-STYLE SCALLOP SAUCE

SERVES: 4
WORKING TIME: 20 MINUTES
TOTAL TIME: 20 MINUTES

10 ounces fine strand pasta, such as capellini or spaghettini

4 teaspoons dark Oriental sesame oil

4 scallions, thinly sliced

3 cloves garlic, slivered

2 tablespoons slivered fresh ginger

2 tablespoons cornstarch

¾ pound bay scallops or quartered sea scallops (see tip)

¼ pound snow peas, trimmed and cut lengthwise into ¼-inch-wide strips

1 carrot, cut into 2 x ¼-inch julienne strips

1 cup reduced-sodium chicken broth, defatted

2 tablespoons chili sauce

¾ teaspoon salt

¼ teaspoon red pepper flakes

1. In a large pot of boiling water, cook the pasta until just tender. Drain well.

2. Meanwhile, in a large nonstick skillet, heat 2 teaspoons of the sesame oil until hot but not smoking over medium heat. Add the scallions, garlic, and ginger and cook, stirring frequently, until the scallions are tender, about 2 minutes.

3. Place all but 1 teaspoon of the cornstarch on a sheet of waxed paper. Dredge the scallops in the cornstarch, shaking off the excess. Add the remaining 2 teaspoons sesame oil to the skillet along with the scallops, snow peas, and carrot and cook, stirring constantly, until the scallops are just opaque and the vegetables are crisp-tender, about 2 minutes.

4. In a small bowl, combine the broth, chili sauce, salt, red pepper flakes, and the remaining 1 teaspoon cornstarch. Add the cornstarch mixture to the skillet and bring to a boil. Cook, stirring, until the sauce is slightly thickened, about 1 minute. Divide the pasta among 4 bowls, spoon the sauce over, and serve.

Helpful hint: The chili sauce used here is nothing exotic—just the familiar tomato-based sauce you'll find on the shelf near the ketchup at your supermarket.

FAT: 7G/14%
CALORIES: 436
SATURATED FAT: 0.9G
CARBOHYDRATE: 67G
PROTEIN: 26G
CHOLESTEROL: 28MG
SODIUM: 819MG

TIP

Tender, sweet bay scallops, no bigger across than a dime, may only be available seasonally. The larger sea scallops—about 1½ inches in diameter— are usually available year-round. If you can't find the smaller bay scallops, cut sea scallops into quarters to produce a reasonable facsimile.

PROVENÇAL SHRIMP SAUCE

SERVES: 4
WORKING TIME: 35 MINUTES
TOTAL TIME: 35 MINUTES

You may recognize the ingredients for ratatouille, the Provençal vegetable dish, in this recipe. But we've expanded the scenario by adding shrimp (and pasta) to the eggplant, peppers, zucchini, and tomatoes that make a basic ratatouille. Radiatore make an especially appropriate pasta choice for this dish, since their shape slightly resembles shrimp.

10 ounces shaped pasta, such as radiatore, ruote (wagon wheels), or small shells

1 tablespoon olive oil

1 onion, finely chopped

4 cloves garlic, minced

1 small eggplant (about 8 ounces), cut into ¼-inch dice

1 red or yellow bell pepper, cut into ¼-inch squares

1 zucchini, cut into ¼-inch dice

14½-ounce can no-salt-added stewed tomatoes, chopped with their juices

2 tablespoons no-salt-added tomato paste

¾ teaspoon dried tarragon

1 teaspoon salt

¾ pound medium shrimp, shelled, deveined, and halved crosswise

1. In a large pot of boiling water, cook the pasta until just tender. Drain well.

2. Meanwhile, in a large nonstick skillet, heat the oil until hot but not smoking over medium heat. Add the onion and garlic and cook, stirring occasionally, until the onion is softened, about 7 minutes. Add the eggplant, stirring to combine. Add ½ cup of water and cook, stirring frequently, until the eggplant is tender, about 7 minutes.

3. Add the bell pepper and zucchini to the pan and cook, stirring frequently, until the bell pepper is crisp-tender, about 4 minutes. Add the tomatoes, tomato paste, tarragon, and salt and bring to a boil. Add the shrimp, reduce to a simmer, and cook until the shrimp are just opaque, about 2 minutes. Spoon the sauce over the hot pasta and serve.

Helpful hint: An eggplant might look as sturdy as a winter squash, but it's actually thin skinned and quite perishable. If you won't be using the eggplant for a day or two after buying it, store it in a plastic bag in the refrigerator.

FAT: 6G/12%
CALORIES: 447
SATURATED FAT: 0.9G
CARBOHYDRATE: 73G
PROTEIN: 26G
CHOLESTEROL: 105MG
SODIUM: 687MG

MINTED SALMON SAUCE

SERVES: 4
WORKING TIME: 25 MINUTES
TOTAL TIME: 25 MINUTES

With morsels of salmon bathed in a lush cream sauce and served atop broad egg noodles, this dish suggests a sort of Stroganoff. The fresh mint, oregano, and slivered black olives, however, suggest lighter fare. For a side dish, mix up a colorful slaw of cabbage and carrots, and toss it with a citrus vinaigrette rather than a heavy mayonnaise dressing.

10 ounces wide egg noodles
1¼ cups evaporated skimmed milk
1 tablespoon flour
2 tablespoons no-salt-added tomato paste
2 teaspoons olive oil
2 cloves garlic, minced
¾ pound skinless salmon fillet, any visible bones removed, cut into 1-inch chunks
1 tablespoon reduced-fat cream cheese (Neufchâtel)
⅓ cup chopped fresh mint
½ teaspoon dried oregano
¾ teaspoon salt
¼ cup oil-cured black olives or brine-cured black olives (such as Calamata), pitted and slivered

1. In a large pot of boiling water, cook the pasta until just tender. Drain well. In a small bowl, whisk the evaporated milk into the flour. Stir in the tomato paste; set aside.

2. Meanwhile, in a large nonstick skillet, heat the oil until hot but not smoking over medium heat. Add the garlic and cook until softened, about 2 minutes. Add the salmon, stirring to coat.

3. Pour the milk mixture along with ⅓ cup of water into the skillet and bring to a simmer. Add the cream cheese, mint, oregano, and salt. Cover and cook, stirring occasionally, until the salmon is just opaque, about 4 minutes. Stir in the olives. Divide the pasta among 4 bowls, spoon the sauce over, and serve.

Helpful hint: Run your hand over the surface of the salmon to detect any tiny feather bones; if you find some, remove them with your fingers, or with tweezers or needle-nose pliers.

FAT: 14G/24%
CALORIES: 525
SATURATED FAT: 2.6G
CARBOHYDRATE: 65G
PROTEIN: 34G
CHOLESTEROL: 119MG
SODIUM: 732MG

VEGETABLE SAUCES

Left, Vegetable-Cheese Sauce. Above, Fettuccine al Pesto.

CHEESE TORTELLINI IN TOMATO CREAM SAUCE

SERVES: 4
WORKING TIME: 20 MINUTES
TOTAL TIME: 35 MINUTES

The recipe title may say cream sauce, but our rich yet trimmed-down sauce (with low-fat milk and flour) skips the heavy cream entirely. And there's a flavor surprise in the background—a touch of orange juice that lends a slight sweetness to this excellent dish. For best results, use fresh tortellini, sold in the refrigerator section of most supermarkets.

2 teaspoons olive oil
1 large onion, minced
2 cloves garlic, minced
1½ cups canned crushed tomatoes
½ teaspoon sugar
¼ teaspoon ground ginger
2 tablespoons flour
1¼ cups low-fat (1%) milk
¼ teaspoon salt
¼ teaspoon freshly ground black pepper
2 tablespoons orange juice
2 tablespoons chopped fresh parsley (optional)
1 tablespoon chopped fresh mint (optional)
1 pound cheese tortellini

1. In a large nonstick skillet, heat the oil until hot but not smoking over medium heat. Add the onion and garlic and cook, stirring frequently, until the onion is golden brown, about 10 minutes.

2. Start heating a large pot of water to boiling for the pasta. Add ½ cup of water to the onion mixture and cook until most of the liquid has evaporated, about 5 minutes. Stir in the tomatoes, sugar, and ginger and cook until the sauce is flavorful and slightly thickened, about 5 minutes. In a food processor or blender, purée the tomato mixture until smooth.

3. Place the flour in a medium saucepan over medium heat, and gradually whisk in the milk. Bring to a boil and cook, whisking constantly, until the mixture is slightly thickened, about 4 minutes. Whisk in the tomato purée, salt, and pepper and cook until the flavors are blended, about 1 minute. Whisk in the orange juice, parsley, and mint.

4. Meanwhile, cook the tortellini in the boiling water until just tender. Drain well. Place the tortellini in 4 shallow bowls, spoon the tomato cream sauce on top, and serve.

Suggested accompaniments: Watercress and Belgian endive salad with a lemon vinaigrette. Follow with plum halves broiled with a little brown sugar and sprinkled with crushed gingersnaps.

FAT: 9G/18%
CALORIES: 447
SATURATED FAT: 0.8G
CARBOHYDRATE: 69G
PROTEIN: 23G
CHOLESTEROL: 65MG
SODIUM: 829MG

PASTA AND VEGETABLES WITH LEMON SAUCE

SERVES: 4
WORKING TIME: 25 MINUTES
TOTAL TIME: 25 MINUTES

Looking like a brimming bowl of confetti, this pasta medley is as delicious and satisfying as it is colorful. A light sauce, redolent of lemon and enriched with Parmesan, fuses the varied flavors into a harmonious whole. A simple vinaigrette-dressed green salad is the perfect first course or accompaniment.

8 ounces penne pasta
1 tablespoon vegetable oil
2 zucchini or yellow summer squash, thinly sliced
1 red bell pepper, diced
1 onion, coarsely chopped
1 clove garlic, minced
19-ounce can red kidney beans, rinsed and drained
1 teaspoon dried oregano
1 teaspoon grated lemon zest
1 cup evaporated skimmed milk
1 teaspoon cornstarch
½ teaspoon salt
¼ teaspoon freshly ground black pepper
¼ cup grated Parmesan cheese

1. In a large pot of boiling water, cook the pasta until just tender. Drain well.

2. Meanwhile, in a large nonstick skillet, heat the oil until hot but not smoking over medium heat. Add the zucchini, bell pepper, onion, and garlic and cook, stirring, until the vegetables are crisp-tender, about 7 minutes. Stir in the beans, oregano, and lemon zest and cook, stirring, until warmed through, about 1 minute.

3. In a small bowl, combine the evaporated milk, cornstarch, salt, and black pepper. Stir the cornstarch mixture into the skillet. Bring to a boil and cook, stirring, until the mixture is slightly thickened, about 1 minute. Stir in the Parmesan.

4. Transfer the mixture to a large bowl, add the pasta, and toss to combine. Divide the pasta mixture among 4 bowls and serve.

Helpful hint: If you halve the zucchini lengthwise before slicing it crosswise, the slices won't roll off the cutting board—sparing your time and temper.

FAT: 7G/14%
CALORIES: 447
SATURATED FAT: 1.7G
CARBOHYDRATE: 73G
PROTEIN: 23G
CHOLESTEROL: 7MG
SODIUM: 616MG

ZITI WITH BROCCOLI AND POTATOES

SERVES: 4
WORKING TIME: 25 MINUTES
TOTAL TIME: 35 MINUTES

¾ pound all-purpose potatoes, peeled and cut into 1-inch chunks

4 cups broccoli florets

2 tablespoons olive oil

1 large onion, cut into 1-inch chunks

4 cloves garlic, slivered

¾ teaspoon salt

½ teaspoon dried sage

½ teaspoon freshly ground black pepper

¼ teaspoon dried marjoram

12 ounces ziti

⅓ cup grated Parmesan cheese

1. Start heating a large pot of water to boiling for the broccoli and the pasta. In a large saucepan, combine the potatoes with water to cover, bring to a boil, reduce to a simmer, and cover. Cook until the potatoes are tender, about 5 minutes. Drain, reserving 2 cups of the potato cooking liquid.

2. Cook the broccoli in the large pot of boiling water until crisp-tender, about 2 minutes. With a slotted spoon, transfer the broccoli to a colander to drain. Reserve the boiling water for the pasta.

3. In a large nonstick skillet, heat the oil until hot but not smoking over medium heat. Add the onion and garlic and cook, stirring frequently, until the onion has softened, about 7 minutes. Stir in the potatoes, salt, sage, pepper, and marjoram and cook until the potatoes begin to brown and form a crust, about 7 minutes. Add the broccoli and 1 cup of the reserved potato liquid and cook until the broccoli is heated through, about 2 minutes longer.

4. Meanwhile, cook the ziti in the reserved boiling water until just tender. Drain well. Transfer the ziti to a large bowl, add the broccoli mixture and the remaining 1 cup potato liquid, and toss to combine. Spoon the ziti mixture into 4 shallow bowls, sprinkle with the Parmesan, and serve.

Suggested accompaniments: For dessert, fresh peaches or nectarines and Italian roast coffee with a shot of anise-flavored liqueur.

FAT: 11G/19%
CALORIES: 517
SATURATED FAT: 2.4G
CARBOHYDRATE: 87G
PROTEIN: 20G
CHOLESTEROL: 5MG
SODIUM: 577MG

This chunky combination is designed for the heartiest of appetites. Tender broccoli florets and pieces of crusty browned potatoes and onion mingle with quill-shaped ziti, all scented with sage and marjoram. Rigatoni may be substituted for the ziti. When shopping, choose broccoli with tightly packed, deep green or purple-tinged florets and firm stalks.

FARFALLE WITH SPINACH, GARLIC, AND RICOTTA

SERVES: 4
WORKING TIME: 25 MINUTES
TOTAL TIME: 30 MINUTES

The whimsically shaped farfalle, also called bow ties, deliciously soak up the creamy spinach sauce made with part-skim ricotta in this scrumptious dish. You may substitute two (ten-ounce) packages of thawed frozen chopped spinach for the fresh—be sure to squeeze out all the liquid from the thawed spinach to avoid a watery sauce.

1 tablespoon plus 1 teaspoon olive oil

1 red bell pepper, diced

5 cloves garlic, minced

1 pound spinach, stemmed and coarsely chopped (about 8 cups)

¾ teaspoon salt

½ teaspoon freshly ground black pepper

¼ teaspoon ground nutmeg

1 cup part-skim ricotta cheese

⅓ cup low-fat (1%) milk

12 ounces farfalle (bow-tie) pasta

⅓ cup chopped fresh basil, or 1 teaspoon dried

1. Start heating a large pot of water to boiling for the pasta. In a large nonstick skillet, heat the oil until hot but not smoking over medium heat. Add the bell pepper and cook, stirring frequently, until tender, about 5 minutes. Stir in the garlic and cook, stirring frequently, until the garlic is tender, about 2 minutes.

2. Stir in the spinach, salt, black pepper, and nutmeg and cook, stirring frequently, until the spinach has wilted, about 3 minutes. Stir in the ricotta and milk and cook until the sauce is creamy and heated through, about 4 minutes longer.

3. Meanwhile, cook the farfalle in the boiling water until just tender. Drain well. Transfer the spinach sauce to a large bowl, add the farfalle and basil, and toss to combine. Spoon the pasta mixture into 4 shallow bowls and serve.

Suggested accompaniments: Sliced orange and red onion salad with a reduced-fat Italian dressing. For dessert, slices of fat-free chocolate pound cake.

FAT: 11G/20%
CALORIES: 489
SATURATED FAT: 4G
CARBOHYDRATE: 75G
PROTEIN: 22G
CHOLESTEROL: 20MG
SODIUM: 596MG

MACARONI WITH ROASTED PEPPER AND CHEESE SAUCE

SERVES: 4
WORKING TIME: 15 MINUTES
TOTAL TIME: 15 MINUTES

R*oasted red peppers (often sold in the international section of the grocery store) and two cheeses make a rich purée to toss with pasta.*

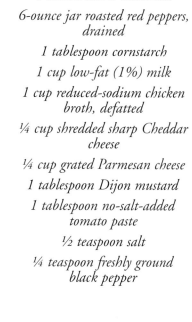

8 ounces elbow macaroni

6-ounce jar roasted red peppers, drained

1 tablespoon cornstarch

1 cup low-fat (1%) milk

1 cup reduced-sodium chicken broth, defatted

¼ cup shredded sharp Cheddar cheese

¼ cup grated Parmesan cheese

1 tablespoon Dijon mustard

1 tablespoon no-salt-added tomato paste

½ teaspoon salt

¼ teaspoon freshly ground black pepper

1. In a large pot of boiling water, cook the macaroni until just tender. Drain well.

2. Meanwhile, in a blender or food processor, purée the red peppers until smooth. Set aside. In a jar with a tight-fitting lid, combine the cornstarch and milk and shake until smooth.

3. In a medium saucepan, combine the broth and cornstarch mixture. Cook over medium heat, stirring frequently, until the mixture boils and thickens, about 4 minutes. Stir in the reserved pepper purée, the Cheddar, Parmesan, mustard, tomato paste, salt, and black pepper. Cook until the cheeses are melted, about 1 minute.

4. Transfer the mixture to a large bowl, add the pasta, and toss to combine.

Helpful hint: The longer Cheddar cheese is aged, the sharper and more flavorful it becomes. For a great macaroni dinner, look for cheese that's been aged at least 6 months; many supermarket cheeses specify on the label when they've been aged 6 months or longer.

FAT: 5G/14%
CALORIES: 322
SATURATED FAT: 3G
CARBOHYDRATE: 52G
PROTEIN: 14G
CHOLESTEROL: 14MG
SODIUM: 789MG

PASTA E FAGIOLI

SERVES: 6
WORKING TIME: 45 MINUTES
TOTAL TIME: 45 MINUTES

1 teaspoon olive oil

1 onion, chopped

2 ribs celery, diced

1 carrot, quartered lengthwise
and sliced

2 cloves garlic, minced

3 cups reduced-sodium chicken
broth, defatted

½ cup dry white wine

2 teaspoons dried rosemary

¾ teaspoon dried thyme

1 cup diced red potatoes

¼ pound green beans, cut into
1-inch pieces

½ cup ditalini pasta

19-ounce can chick-peas, rinsed
and drained

2 tablespoons chopped
prosciutto or Canadian bacon

¼ teaspoon freshly ground
black pepper

1. In a medium nonstick saucepan, heat the oil until hot but not smoking over medium heat. Add the onion, celery, and carrot and cook, stirring occasionally, until the vegetables are softened, about 5 minutes. Add the garlic and cook until fragrant, about 1 minute.

2. Add the broth, 2 cups of water, the wine, rosemary, thyme, and potatoes. Bring to a simmer and cook 5 minutes. Add the green beans and pasta and simmer, covered, until the beans are crisp-tender, about 8 minutes. Add the chick-peas, prosciutto, and pepper and cook until warmed through, about 3 minutes. Divide the mixture among 6 bowls and serve.

Helpful hints: Like all good country recipes, this one is quite amenable to the substitution of similar ingredients. Cannellini (white kidney beans) can replace the chick-peas, and tiny elbow macaroni (or even broken spaghetti) can stand in for the thimble-shaped ditalini.

For a warming yet light supper, serve this classic bean soup with wedges of Italian focaccia or with bread sticks.

FAT: 3G/15%
CALORIES: 181
SATURATED FAT: .4G
CARBOHYDRATE: 27G
PROTEIN: 9G
CHOLESTEROL: 4MG
SODIUM: 531MG

SPAGHETTI WITH FRESH MARINARA SAUCE

SERVES: 8
WORKING TIME: 30 MINUTES
TOTAL TIME: 40 MINUTES

3 tablespoons olive oil

2 large onions, minced

2 carrots, minced

3 pounds plum tomatoes (about 12)

6 cloves garlic, minced

Two 8-ounce cans no-salt-added tomato sauce

½ cup chopped fresh basil, or 1½ teaspoons dried

1 teaspoon salt

¾ teaspoon red pepper flakes

¼ teaspoon freshly ground black pepper

1½ pounds spaghetti

1 cup coarsely grated Parmesan cheese

1. In a large nonstick skillet, heat the oil until hot but not smoking over medium heat. Add the onions and cook, stirring frequently, until the onions are golden brown and very tender, about 10 minutes. Add the carrots and cook, stirring frequently, until the carrots are tender, about 7 minutes.

2. Start heating a large pot of water to boiling for the pasta. Cut each tomato in half, and squeeze through a sieve set over a bowl to catch the juices. Discard the seeds. Coarsely chop the tomatoes. Stir the garlic into the carrot mixture and cook until the garlic is tender, about 3 minutes. Add the tomatoes and their juices, the tomato sauce, basil, salt, pepper flakes, and pepper and cook, stirring occasionally, until the sauce is flavorful and thickened, about 10 minutes longer.

3. Meanwhile, cook the spaghetti in the boiling water until just tender. Drain well. Transfer the marinara sauce to a large bowl, add the spaghetti and ¾ cup of the Parmesan, and toss to combine. Spoon the spaghetti mixture onto 8 plates, sprinkle with the remaining ¼ cup Parmesan, and serve.

Suggested accompaniments: Mixed salad of romaine and red leaf lettuce with a parsley vinaigrette. For dessert, a fresh fruit cup served with wedges of lime.

The ripest plum tomatoes will create the most superb sauce imaginable—but no-salt-added canned tomatoes (about six cups) may be substituted. Here it pays to splurge on a really good aged Parmesan. If your dinner crowd only amounts to four, use just twelve ounces of pasta and half the sauce. Freeze the extra sauce for up to six months.

FAT: 10G/18%
CALORIES: 489
SATURATED FAT: 2.9G
CARBOHYDRATE: 82G
PROTEIN: 18G
CHOLESTEROL: 8MG
SODIUM: 502MG

ANGEL HAIR PASTA WITH SNOW PEAS AND SCALLIONS

SERVES: 4
WORKING TIME: 20 MINUTES
TOTAL TIME: 30 MINUTES

For this tantalizing dish, the clean taste of fresh ginger marries well with the assertiveness of garlic and scallions, and the delicate texture of the angel hair pasta is complemented by the mild crunch of the snow peas. Use frozen snow peas if fresh aren't available. Cornstarch is the key to the lightly thickened, glossy sauce.

2 tablespoons olive oil
1 red bell pepper, diced
1 cup thinly sliced scallions
4 cloves garlic, minced
1 tablespoon plus 1 teaspoon minced fresh ginger
¾ pound snow peas, trimmed and cut diagonally into 1-inch pieces
1⅓ cups reduced-sodium chicken broth, defatted
¾ teaspoon salt
¼ teaspoon freshly ground black pepper
2 teaspoons cornstarch
12 ounces angel hair or capellini pasta

1. Start heating a large pot of water to boiling for the pasta. In a large nonstick skillet, heat the oil until hot but not smoking over medium heat. Add the bell pepper and cook, stirring frequently, until tender, about 5 minutes. Add the scallions, garlic, and ginger and cook, stirring frequently, until the scallions are tender, about 4 minutes longer.

2. Stir in the snow peas and cook until the snow peas are just crisp-tender, about 1 minute. Add the broth, salt, and black pepper and bring to a boil. In a cup, combine the cornstarch and 1 tablespoon of water, stir to blend, and stir into the sauce. Cook, stirring constantly, until the sauce is slightly thickened, about 1 minute longer.

3. Meanwhile, cook the angel hair pasta in the boiling water until just tender. Drain well. Transfer the vegetable mixture to a large bowl, add the pasta, and toss to combine. Spoon the pasta mixture onto 4 plates and serve.

Suggested accompaniment: Lemon sorbet with fat-free chewy cranberry cookies.

FAT: 9G/18%
CALORIES: 443
SATURATED FAT: 1.1G
CARBOHYDRATE: 76G
PROTEIN: 15G
CHOLESTEROL: 0MG
SODIUM: 639MG

PAN-FRIED RAVIOLI WITH VEGETABLES

SERVES: 4
WORKING TIME: 20 MINUTES
TOTAL TIME: 20 MINUTES

Sautéing ravioli gives this familiar filled pasta an appetizing new texture and taste. The pan-fried ravioli, delicately browned and slightly crisped, are tossed with an Italian-style vegetable medley that includes green beans, tomatoes, and cannellini. Other small filled pastas, such as tortellini or cappelletti, can be cooked in the same way.

¾ pound fresh small cheese ravioli

1 tablespoon olive oil

2 scallions, thinly sliced

4 cloves garlic, finely chopped

10-ounce package frozen Italian flat green beans, thawed

2 tomatoes, coarsely chopped

19-ounce can white kidney beans (cannellini), rinsed and drained

½ cup raisins

1 tablespoon no-salt-added tomato paste

¼ cup chopped fresh basil

¼ teaspoon salt

¼ teaspoon freshly ground black pepper

⅛ teaspoon cayenne pepper

1. In a large pot of boiling water, cook the ravioli until just tender. Drain, reserving 1 cup of the cooking liquid. Pat the ravioli dry on paper towels.

2. In a large nonstick skillet or wok, heat the oil until hot but not smoking over medium heat. Add the ravioli to the pan and gently stir-fry until lightly crisped and golden on both sides, about 4 minutes. With a slotted spoon, transfer the ravioli to a plate.

3. Add the scallions and garlic to the skillet and stir-fry until softened, about 1 minute. Add the green beans, stirring to coat. Add the tomatoes, white kidney beans, raisins, tomato paste, basil, salt, black pepper, cayenne, and the reserved ravioli cooking liquid and bring to a boil. Cook, stirring frequently, until slightly thickened, about 3 minutes. Return the ravioli to the pan, tossing to coat well, and cook until heated through, about 1 minute.

Helpful hint: When local tomatoes are not in season, the best choice at the market may well be plum tomatoes. If you do opt for this smaller variety, use three instead of two.

FAT: 16G/29%
CALORIES: 501
SATURATED FAT: 6.5G
CARBOHYDRATE: 71G
PROTEIN: 23G
CHOLESTEROL: 75MG
SODIUM: 677MG

Most commonly used on the Italian braised veal dish called osso buco, gremolata is a tantalizing mixture of parsley, garlic, and lemon zest. Sprinkling it over cooked food adds a burst of startlingly fresh flavor. Here, the gremolata is also used to flavor the sauce as it cooks. Follow the pasta with a bowl of fruit for a heart-healthy Italian dinner.

GREEN BEAN GREMOLATA SAUCE

SERVES: 4
WORKING TIME: 30 MINUTES
TOTAL TIME: 35 MINUTES

10 ounces medium tube pasta, such as penne rigate, penne, or ziti

1 tablespoon olive oil

¾ pound green beans, cut into 1-inch pieces

1 red onion, cut into thin slivers

½ cup chopped fresh parsley

4 cloves garlic, minced

1 tablespoon grated lemon zest (see tip)

35-ounce can no-salt-added tomatoes, chopped with their juices

¼ cup chopped fresh basil

¾ teaspoon salt

¼ teaspoon freshly ground black pepper

1 teaspoon cornstarch mixed with 1 tablespoon water

1. In a large pot of boiling water, cook the pasta until just tender. Drain well.

2. Meanwhile, in a large nonstick skillet, heat the oil until hot but not smoking over medium heat. Add the green beans and onion, cover, and cook, stirring occasionally, until the beans are crisp-tender, about 10 minutes.

3. In a small bowl, combine the parsley, garlic, and lemon zest. Add half of the parsley mixture, the tomatoes, basil, salt, and pepper to the skillet and simmer until the vegetables are tender, about 5 minutes. Add the cornstarch mixture and cook, stirring constantly, until the sauce is slightly thickened, about 1 minute. Divide the pasta among 4 plates and spoon the sauce over. Sprinkle with the remaining parsley mixture and serve.

Helpful hint: Even if you don't need it at the time, grate the zest from lemons whenever you use them. Wrap the zest and freeze it for future use.

The colored outer part of citrus peel, called zest, is full of intensely flavored oils that can add a fresh zing to any dish. To remove zest, while avoiding the bitter white pith underneath, use a fine-holed grater, a citrus zester for long thin curls (pictured above, which can be chopped to approximate grating), or a vegetable peeler for wider strips that can then be thinly slivered or chopped.

FAT: 5G/11%
CALORIES: 400
SATURATED FAT: 0.7G
CARBOHYDRATE: 77G
PROTEIN: 14G
CHOLESTEROL: 0MG
SODIUM: 463MG

SPAGHETTINI WITH GARLIC AND OIL

SERVES: 4
WORKING TIME: 15 MINUTES
TOTAL TIME: 25 MINUTES

Nothing could be simpler than this classic pasta throw-together, snappily accented with a drizzle of lemon juice and a scattering of grated lemon zest. The addition of bread crumbs gives a little extra body and stretches the Parmesan, keeping the fat low. If fresh chives are unavailable, you may substitute the chopped green tops of scallions.

12 ounces spaghettini

3 tablespoons olive oil

6 cloves garlic, minced

½ cup reduced-sodium chicken broth, defatted

3 tablespoons fresh lemon juice

3 tablespoons chopped fresh parsley

3 tablespoons snipped fresh chives

1 teaspoon grated lemon zest

¾ teaspoon salt

¼ teaspoon freshly ground black pepper

2 tablespoons grated Parmesan cheese

1 tablespoon plain dried bread crumbs

1. Heat a large pot of water to boiling, and cook the spaghettini until just tender. Drain well.

2. Meanwhile, in a large nonstick skillet, heat the oil until hot but not smoking over low heat. Add the garlic and cook, stirring frequently, until tender, about 5 minutes. Stir in the broth, lemon juice, parsley, chives, lemon zest, salt, and pepper and cook until the mixture is heated through, about 1 minute.

3. Transfer the spaghettini to a large bowl, add the garlic sauce, and toss to combine. Sprinkle with the Parmesan and bread crumbs and toss again. Spoon the spaghettini mixture into 4 shallow bowls and serve.

Suggested accompaniments: Sliced fresh tomatoes drizzled with a balsamic vinaigrette, and orange wedges for dessert.

FAT: 12G/25%
CALORIES: 438
SATURATED FAT: 2G
CARBOHYDRATE: 68G
PROTEIN: 13G
CHOLESTEROL: 2MG
SODIUM: 561MG

Rigatoni with Sun-Dried Tomato Pesto

SERVES: 4
WORKING TIME: 25 MINUTES
TOTAL TIME: 45 MINUTES

Hours of simmering and stirring are not the only route to a thick, rich tomato sauce. Here, flavor-packed sun-dried tomatoes, bell peppers, onion, and garlic are sautéed and then puréed to produce a vibrant tomato "pesto." The sauce coats chunky rigatoni, broccoli florets, and slivered black olives.

½ cup sun-dried (not oil-packed) tomato halves
1 cup boiling water
1 tablespoon olive oil
1 onion, halved and thinly sliced
2 red bell peppers, thinly sliced
2 cloves garlic, thinly sliced
½ cup reduced-sodium chicken broth, defatted
1 tablespoon balsamic vinegar
½ teaspoon salt
12 ounces rigatoni pasta
2 cups small broccoli florets
⅓ cup slivered Calamata or other brine-cured black olives

1. In a small bowl, combine the sun-dried tomatoes and boiling water and let stand until the tomatoes have softened, about 20 minutes. Drain the tomatoes, reserving the soaking liquid.

2. Meanwhile, in a large nonstick skillet, heat the oil until hot but not smoking over medium heat. Add the onion and cook, stirring occasionally, until golden brown, about 8 minutes. Add the bell peppers and garlic, stirring to combine. Add the broth and cook, stirring occasionally, until the peppers are softened, about 7 minutes. Transfer the mixture to a food processor along with the sun-dried tomatoes, the reserved soaking liquid, the vinegar and salt, and process until smooth, about 1 minute. Transfer the sauce to a large bowl.

3. In a large pot of boiling water, cook the rigatoni until just tender. Add the broccoli to the pot for the last 2 minutes of cooking. Drain well. Add the pasta and the broccoli to the sauce, tossing to combine. Add the olives, toss again, divide among 4 bowls, and serve.

Helpful hint: If you can't find Calamata olives, you can substitute Gaeta olives from Italy, or any other brine-cured (rather than oil-cured) black olives.

FAT: 8G/16%
CALORIES: 459
SATURATED FAT: 1G
CARBOHYDRATE: 81G
PROTEIN: 16G
CHOLESTEROL: 0MG
SODIUM: 587MG

STRAW AND HAY WITH PESTO ALLA GENOVESE

SERVES: 4
WORKING TIME: 25 MINUTES
TOTAL TIME: 40 MINUTES

The gold (straw) and green (hay) fettuccines are bathed here in a creamy pesto. In Genoa (pesto's "hometown"), pasta is combined with potatoes and green beans, then tossed with the basil sauce. Here, asparagus makes a delicious substitute for the beans. Follow the main dish with a classic Italian dessert of fresh figs and grapes.

3 cloves garlic, peeled

2 cups firmly packed fresh basil leaves

1 tablespoon olive oil

1 tablespoon pine nuts

¼ cup grated Parmesan cheese

2 tablespoons reduced-fat cream cheese (Neufchâtel)

⅔ cup reduced-sodium chicken broth, defatted

1 teaspoon salt

¼ teaspoon freshly ground black pepper

5 ounces plain fettuccine

5 ounces spinach fettuccine

½ pound all-purpose potatoes, peeled and cut into 1-inch cubes

¾ pound asparagus, tough ends trimmed, cut on the diagonal into 2-inch pieces

1. In a large pot of boiling water, cook the garlic for 2 minutes to blanch. With a slotted spoon, transfer the garlic to a food processor along with the basil, oil, pine nuts, Parmesan, cream cheese, broth, ¾ teaspoon of the salt, and the black pepper. Process to a smooth purée and transfer the pesto to a large bowl.

2. In the same pot, cook the fettuccine and potatoes with the remaining ¼ teaspoon salt until just tender. Add the asparagus to the pot for the last 2 minutes of cooking. Drain well and transfer to the bowl with the pesto, tossing to combine. Divide the mixture among 4 bowls and serve.

Helpful hint: If you're using fresh fettuccine, add it to the pot along with the asparagus in step 2 rather than with the potatoes, to avoid overcooking the pasta.

FAT: 11G/22%
CALORIES: 453
SATURATED FAT: 3.2G
CARBOHYDRATE: 73G
PROTEIN: 20G
CHOLESTEROL: 75MG
SODIUM: 832MG

SUMMER PASTA WITH UNCOOKED TOMATO SAUCE

SERVES: 4
WORKING TIME: 25 MINUTES
TOTAL TIME: 25 MINUTES

*M*eaty, ripe tomatoes (plum or beefsteak) and fresh mint or basil are necessities for this midsummer specialty.

4 cloves garlic, peeled

12 ounces spaghetti

2 pounds tomatoes, seeded and chopped

3 tablespoons balsamic vinegar

2 teaspoons olive oil

2 teaspoons firmly packed brown sugar

¾ teaspoon dried tarragon

½ teaspoon salt

¼ teaspoon freshly ground black pepper

½ cup chopped fresh basil or mint

⅓ cup grated Parmesan cheese

1. In a large pot of boiling water, cook the garlic for 2 minutes to blanch. With a slotted spoon, transfer the garlic to a cutting board and mince. Add the spaghetti to the boiling water and cook until just tender.

2. Meanwhile, in a large bowl, combine the garlic and the tomatoes. Add the vinegar, oil, sugar, tarragon, salt, and pepper, stirring to combine. When the pasta is done, drain and transfer to the bowl with the tomato mixture. Add the basil and Parmesan and toss well. Divide among 4 bowls and serve.

Helpful hint: Other long pastas, such as perciatelli (thick, hollow spaghetti), vermicelli, linguine, or fettuccine can be substituted for the spaghetti.

FAT: 6G/13%
CALORIES: 426
SATURATED FAT: 1.8G
CARBOHYDRATE: 77G
PROTEIN: 16G
CHOLESTEROL: 5MG
SODIUM: 423MG

ARTICHOKE-PARMESAN SAUCE

SERVES: 4
WORKING TIME: 25 MINUTES
TOTAL TIME: 30 MINUTES

10 ounces fettuccine

2 teaspoons olive oil

2 ribs celery, finely chopped

2 carrots, finely chopped

Two 9-ounce packages frozen artichoke hearts

½ cup dry white wine

½ cup reduced-sodium chicken broth, defatted

5 cups packed torn spinach leaves

4 scallions, thinly sliced

¼ teaspoon salt

⅛ teaspoon freshly ground black pepper

2 teaspoons cornstarch mixed with 1 tablespoon water

⅓ cup grated Parmesan cheese plus ½ cup shaved Parmesan

3 tablespoons reduced-fat sour cream

1 tablespoon fresh lemon juice

1. In a large pot of boiling water, cook the pasta until just tender. Drain well.

2. Meanwhile, in a large nonstick skillet, heat the oil until hot but not smoking over medium heat. Add the celery and carrots and cook, stirring frequently, until the carrots are softened, about 6 minutes.

3. Add the artichokes, wine, and broth to the pan and bring to a simmer. Cover and cook until the artichokes are tender, about 6 minutes. Stir in the spinach, scallions, salt, pepper, and cornstarch mixture. Bring to a simmer and cook, stirring, until slightly thickened, about 2 minutes.

4. Remove the pan from the heat and stir in the grated Parmesan, the sour cream, and lemon juice. Toss the sauce with the hot pasta. Divide among 4 plates, sprinkle with the ½ cup shaved Parmesan, and serve.

Helpful hints: To make Parmesan shavings, draw a vegetable peeler slowly across the side of a wedge of Parmesan. You can substitute ⅓ cup grated Parmesan for the shaved, if you like.

FAT: 12G/22%
CALORIES: 493
SATURATED FAT: 4.4G
CARBOHYDRATE: 73G
PROTEIN: 24G
CHOLESTEROL: 82MG
SODIUM: 653MG

Velvety artichoke hearts jazz up this simple meal. The frozen ones are ready to use and have no added oil or salt.

ealth
experts single out
Fettuccine Alfredo as
the most "dangerous"
pasta dish of all: The
sauce—simply butter,
heavy cream, and
Parmesan—packs an
astonishing payload of
fat and cholesterol. But
you're perfectly safe
with our pasta-and-
zucchini creation. The
predominant sauce
ingredients are
evaporated skimmed
milk and part-skim
ricotta cheese.

ZUCCHINI ALFREDO

SERVES: 4
WORKING TIME: 20 MINUTES
TOTAL TIME: 30 MINUTES

*10 ounces medium strand pasta,
such as linguine, spaghetti, or
long fusilli*

1 tablespoon olive oil

*2 zucchini, cut into 2 x ¼-inch
julienne strips (see tip)*

½ cup chopped fresh basil

¾ teaspoon salt

*¼ teaspoon freshly ground black
pepper*

¾ cup evaporated skimmed milk

½ cup part-skim ricotta cheese

¼ cup grated Parmesan cheese

1 egg

2 tablespoons flour

1. In a large pot of boiling water, cook the pasta until just tender. Drain well.

2. In a large nonstick skillet, heat the oil until hot but not smoking over medium heat. Add the zucchini, basil, salt, and pepper and cook, stirring frequently, until the zucchini is tender, about 5 minutes.

3. Meanwhile, in a blender or food processor, combine the evaporated milk, ricotta, Parmesan, egg, and flour and process until very smooth, about 1 minute. Stir the milk mixture into the skillet and cook, stirring constantly, until the sauce is piping hot and thickened, about 2 minutes. Toss the sauce with the hot pasta, divide among 4 plates, and serve.

Helpful hint: To reduce the fat even further, you can substitute low-fat (1%) cottage cheese for the ricotta,.

FAT: 10G/20%
CALORIES: 446
SATURATED FAT: 3.5G
CARBOHYDRATE: 67G
PROTEIN: 22G
CHOLESTEROL: 69MG
SODIUM: 623MG

TIP

To cut a zucchini into julienne strips, first cut the zucchini crosswise into 2-inch pieces. Then cut the pieces into ¼-inch-wide slices. Stack the slices and cut into ¼-inch-wide sticks.

BROCCOLI-TOMATO SAUCE

SERVES: 4
WORKING TIME: 35 MINUTES
TOTAL TIME: 35 MINUTES

One of the most nutritious vegetables you can eat, broccoli originated in Italy, so it's a natural for a pasta dish. Here, penne is tossed with broccoli in a hearty tomato sauce made with garlic and anchovy paste. The pasta is topped with provolone, a sweet, mellow Italian cheese that's sold sliced in most supermarkets. You could substitute smoked provolone for a change of pace.

10 ounces medium tube pasta, such as penne or ziti

2 teaspoons olive oil

2 onions, coarsely chopped

¼ cup dry sherry

1 teaspoon anchovy paste, or 1 tablespoon grated Parmesan cheese

3 cloves garlic, minced

2 teaspoons dried basil

14½-ounce can no-salt-added stewed tomatoes

8-ounce can no-salt-added tomato sauce

4 cups broccoli florets

¾ teaspoon salt

¼ teaspoon freshly ground black pepper

4 ounces thinly sliced provolone cheese, cut into 2 x ¼-inch-wide strips

1. In a large pot of boiling water, cook the pasta until just tender. Drain well.

2. Meanwhile, in a large nonstick skillet, heat the oil until hot but not smoking over medium heat. Add the onions and cook, stirring frequently, until softened, about 6 minutes. Add the sherry, anchovy paste, garlic, and basil and bring to a simmer. Cook until reduced by half, about 3 minutes.

3. Stir the tomatoes, tomato sauce, broccoli, salt, and pepper into the skillet and bring to a simmer. Cook, stirring occasionally, until the broccoli is crisp-tender, about 12 minutes. Divide the pasta among 4 plates. Spoon the sauce over the hot pasta, top with the provolone, and serve.

Helpful hint: If you like, you can top the pasta with white Cheddar, Gruyère, or Monterey jack cheese instead of provolone.

FAT: 12G/21%
CALORIES: 509
SATURATED FAT: 5.4G
CARBOHYDRATE: 77G
PROTEIN: 23G
CHOLESTEROL: 20MG
SODIUM: 774MG

ots of lively flavors fill this dish: pleasantly bitter Swiss chard, sweet-sharp sun-dried tomatoes, a hot chili pepper, and black pepper. A sturdy pasta such as orecchiette is best for absorbing all that flavor; shells and rotini are other fine choices. If chard is unavailable, substitute an equal amount of fresh spinach, or a ten-ounce package of thawed frozen spinach.

ORECCHIETTE WITH SWISS CHARD

SERVES: 4
WORKING TIME: 20 MINUTES
TOTAL TIME: 30 MINUTES

¼ cup sun-dried (not oil-packed) tomato halves

½ cup boiling water

2 tablespoons olive oil

1 red bell pepper, diced

3 cloves garlic, minced

1 teaspoon minced fresh chili pepper (use gloves)

½ pound Swiss chard, finely chopped (about 4 cups; see tip)

½ cup reduced-sodium chicken broth, defatted

¾ teaspoon salt

½ teaspoon freshly ground black pepper

12 ounces orecchiette pasta

¼ cup grated Parmesan cheese

1. In a small bowl, combine the sun-dried tomatoes and the boiling water. Let stand until the tomatoes have softened, about 20 minutes. Drain, reserving the soaking liquid, and coarsely chop the tomatoes.

2. Meanwhile, start heating a large pot of water to boiling for the pasta. In a large nonstick skillet, heat the oil until hot but not smoking over medium heat. Add the bell pepper and cook, stirring frequently, until the bell pepper begins to soften, about 5 minutes. Stir in the garlic and chili pepper and cook until the garlic is tender, about 3 minutes.

3. Add the Swiss chard and cook, stirring frequently, until the chard is tender, about 5 minutes. Stir in the tomatoes and their soaking liquid, the broth, salt, and black pepper and cook until the sauce is slightly thickened, about 5 minutes longer.

4. Meanwhile, cook the orecchiette in the boiling water until just tender. Drain well. Transfer the chard mixture to a large bowl, add the orecchiette, and toss to combine. Spoon the pasta mixture into 4 shallow bowls, sprinkle with the Parmesan, and serve.

Suggested accompaniments: Crusty bread, and fresh strawberries sprinkled with orange liqueur for dessert.

TIP

To prepare Swiss chard, first rinse the leaves well and blot dry. Stack the leaves and, stabilizing the end of a chef's knife with one hand, chop across the chard. Then chop at right angles to the first chop until the chard is as fine as desired.

FAT: 10G/21%
CALORIES: 439
SATURATED FAT: 2.1G
CARBOHYDRATE: 72G
PROTEIN: 15G
CHOLESTEROL: 4MG
SODIUM: 720MG

SPICY SESAME NOODLES

SERVES: 4
WORKING TIME: 25 MINUTES
TOTAL TIME: 25 MINUTES

You can make these mouth-watering Szechuan noodles, with tender strips of chicken and tender-crisp vegetables, in practically no time.

½ cup reduced-sodium chicken broth, defatted

¼ cup reduced-sodium soy sauce

3 tablespoons rice vinegar

3 tablespoons creamy peanut butter

1 tablespoon honey

1 tablespoon dark Oriental sesame oil

1 scallion, cut into 1-inch pieces

1 tablespoon slivered fresh ginger

½ teaspoon hot pepper sauce

12 ounces angel hair pasta, broken in half

1 green bell pepper, thinly sliced

1 cup shredded carrots

½ pound skinless, boneless chicken breasts, cut crosswise into thin strips

1. In a blender or food processor, combine the broth, soy sauce, vinegar, peanut butter, honey, sesame oil, scallion, ginger, and hot pepper sauce. Process until smooth and transfer to a large serving bowl.

2. In a large pot of boiling water, cook the pasta, bell pepper, carrots, and chicken until the chicken is cooked through and the pasta is just tender, about 4 minutes. Drain well and add to the bowl of sauce, tossing to combine. Divide the pasta mixture among 4 bowls and serve.

Helpful hint: You can make the sauce in advance and keep it refrigerated overnight, but it may separate; be sure to stir it well to recombine it before adding the chicken, vegetables, and noodles.

FAT: 12G/21%
CALORIES: 528
SATURATED FAT: 1.9G
CARBOHYDRATE: 76G
PROTEIN: 29G
CHOLESTEROL: 33MG
SODIUM: 807MG

PESTO WITH POTATOES

SERVES: 4
WORKING TIME: 25 MINUTES
TOTAL TIME: 35 MINUTES

2 teaspoons olive oil

½ pound red potatoes, cut into ½-inch cubes

4 cloves garlic, halved lengthwise

¾ cup reduced-sodium chicken broth, defatted

2 cups packed fresh basil leaves

¼ cup pine nuts, toasted

6 tablespoons grated Parmesan cheese

1 tablespoon fresh lemon juice

¼ teaspoon salt

¼ teaspoon freshly ground black pepper

10 ounces shaped pasta, such as orecchiette or farfalle (bow ties)

1 cup frozen peas

1. Bring a large pot of water to a boil for the pasta. In a large non-stick skillet, heat the oil until hot but not smoking over medium heat. Add the potatoes, cover, and cook, stirring occasionally, until firm-tender, about 10 minutes. Remove from the heat.

2. Meanwhile, in a small saucepan, combine the garlic and broth, bring to a simmer, and cook until the garlic is tender, about 5 minutes. Transfer to a food processor and add the basil, pine nuts, 3 tablespoons of the Parmesan, the lemon juice, salt, and pepper. Process to a smooth purée.

3. Cook the pasta in the boiling water until just tender, adding the peas during the last 1 minute of cooking. Drain well. In a large bowl, toss the pasta and peas with the pesto and potatoes. Divide among 4 plates, sprinkle the remaining 3 tablespoons Parmesan over, and serve.

Helpful hint: To toast the pine nuts, place them in a small, dry skillet and cook over medium heat, stirring and shaking the pan, for 3 minutes, or until golden. Immediately transfer the toasted pine nuts to a plate to cool.

Pesto *is served over a combination of pasta and potatoes here, making for an extra-hearty dish.*

FAT: 11G/20%
CALORIES: 491
SATURATED FAT: 2.6G
CARBOHYDRATE: 82G
PROTEIN: 21G
CHOLESTEROL: 6MG
SODIUM: 437MG

AMATRICIANA SAUCE

SERVES: 4
WORKING TIME: 30 MINUTES
TOTAL TIME: 30 MINUTES

The central-Italian valley town of Amatrice gave birth to a pasta dish now served—with variations—all over Italy. The original is a lusty dish of strand pasta sauced with a rich blend of tomatoes, bacon, and onions, liberally topped with sharp Romano cheese. Our interpretation is no less robust; brine-cured olives give it extra zip. A cool, crisp salad makes the perfect accompaniment.

10 ounces fine strand pasta, such as capellini or spaghettini

2 teaspoons olive oil

2 onions, coarsely chopped

2 cloves garlic, minced

¼ cup dry red wine

28-ounce can no-salt-added tomatoes, drained and chopped, juices reserved

¼ teaspoon red pepper flakes

¼ cup plus 2 tablespoons diced Canadian bacon (2 ounces)

2 tablespoons pitted, chopped Calamata or other brine-cured black olives

½ teaspoon salt

3 tablespoons grated Parmesan cheese

1. In a large pot of boiling water, cook the pasta until just tender. Drain well.

2. Meanwhile, in a large nonstick skillet, heat the oil until hot but not smoking over medium heat. Add the onions and cook, stirring frequently, until barely softened, about 4 minutes. Add the garlic and cook, stirring, until the garlic is softened, about 2 minutes.

3. Add the wine, the juices from the canned tomatoes, and the red pepper flakes to the skillet. Bring to a boil and cook, stirring occasionally, for 8 minutes, to thicken the sauce. Add the tomatoes, Canadian bacon, olives, and salt. Reduce to a simmer and cook until heated through, about 2 minutes. Divide the pasta among 4 plates. Spoon the sauce over the hot pasta, sprinkle with the Parmesan, and serve.

Helpful hint: If you like, you can substitute Romano for the Parmesan; it's sharper and saltier.

FAT: 7G/15%
CALORIES: 420
SATURATED FAT: 1.7G
CARBOHYDRATE: 71G
PROTEIN: 17G
CHOLESTEROL: 10MG
SODIUM: 653MG

SWEET PEPPER AND ONION SAUCE

SERVES: 4
WORKING TIME: 35 MINUTES
TOTAL TIME: 35 MINUTES

The warm autumn color of this hearty pasta sauce helps remind you that early fall—when red and yellow peppers are ripe for picking—is the perfect time to make this dish. The peppers are covered and cooked slowly, to concentrate their flavor. If you've made the sauce in an attractive skillet, you can use it as a serving dish: Stir the pasta into the sauce rather than vice versa.

2 tablespoons olive oil

1 onion, halved and thinly sliced

2 cloves garlic, minced

3 red bell peppers, cut into ½-inch-wide strips

2 yellow bell peppers, cut into ½-inch-wide strips

10 ounces medium strand pasta, such as long fusilli, linguine, or spaghetti

2 cups canned no-salt-added tomatoes, chopped with their juices

¾ teaspoon salt

⅓ cup chopped fresh parsley

1. In a large nonstick skillet, heat the oil until hot but not smoking over medium heat. Add the onion and garlic and cook, stirring frequently, until the onion is softened, about 7 minutes.

2. Add the bell peppers to the skillet, stir to coat, cover, and cook, stirring occasionally, until the peppers are very tender, about 15 minutes.

3. Meanwhile, in a large pot of boiling water, cook the pasta until just tender. Drain well.

4. Add the tomatoes and salt to the skillet and cook, uncovered, stirring frequently, until the sauce is richly flavored and slightly thickened, about 8 minutes. Stir in the parsley, toss the sauce with the hot pasta, and serve.

FAT: 8G/18%
CALORIES: 392
SATURATED FAT: 1.1G
CARBOHYDRATE: 69G
PROTEIN: 12G
CHOLESTEROL: 0MG
SODIUM: 438MG

ASIAN VEGETABLE-PLUM SAUCE

SERVES: 4
WORKING TIME: 25 MINUTES
TOTAL TIME: 25 MINUTES

10 ounces medium strand pasta, such as long fusilli, spaghetti, or linguine

½ cup plum jam

½ cup reduced-sodium chicken broth, defatted

2 tablespoons dry sherry

2 teaspoons dark Oriental sesame oil

1 tablespoon vegetable oil

1 clove garlic, minced

1 tablespoon minced fresh ginger

2 carrots, cut into 2 x ¼-inch julienne strips

1 red bell pepper, cut into thin strips

¼ pound snow peas, trimmed and cut into thin strips

1 cup baby corn, halved lengthwise

1 tablespoon cornstarch mixed with 2 tablespoons water

1. In a large pot of boiling water, cook the pasta until just tender. Drain well.

2. Meanwhile, in a small bowl, combine the jam, broth, ¼ cup of water, the sherry, and sesame oil.

3. In a large nonstick skillet, heat the vegetable oil until hot but not smoking over medium heat. Add the garlic and ginger and cook, stirring, until the garlic is golden, about 2 minutes. Add the carrots, bell pepper, and snow peas. Increase the heat to high and cook, stirring constantly, until the carrots are softened, about 3 minutes.

4. Add the jam mixture to the skillet along with the baby corn. Stir in the cornstarch mixture and bring to a boil. Cook, stirring, until the sauce is slightly thickened, about 2 minutes. Toss the sauce with the hot pasta, divide among 4 bowls, and serve.

Helpful hint: White wine can be substituted for the sherry, if you like.

FAT: 8G/15%
CALORIES: 484
SATURATED FAT: 0.9G
CARBOHYDRATE: 91G
PROTEIN: 12G
CHOLESTEROL: 0MG
SODIUM: 120MG

Plum sauce is a tangy Chinese condiment made from plums, chilies, vinegar, and sugar. But you don't have to go hunting for exotic ingredients, because we've created our own version of the sauce, using plum jam, broth, sherry, and sesame oil. Garlic and fresh ginger add pungency to this wonderfully unique sauce.

PUTTANESCA SAUCE

SERVES: 4
WORKING TIME: 10 MINUTES
TOTAL TIME: 40 MINUTES

This time-honored Neapolitan sauce has many variations. Ours, which can probably be made without a trip to the grocery store, has a bold, spicy flavor—the cumulative effect of black olives, capers, anchovy paste, and red pepper flakes. Brine-cured olives make a striking difference here; if at all possible, avoid using domestic canned black olives.

1½ pounds tomatoes, coarsely chopped

⅓ cup chopped fresh parsley

¼ cup Calamata or other brine-cured black olives, pitted and finely chopped

3 tablespoons capers, rinsed and drained

2 tablespoons extra-virgin olive oil

2 tablespoons balsamic vinegar

1 tablespoon anchovy paste, or 2 tablespoons grated Parmesan cheese

1 teaspoon firmly packed light brown sugar

½ teaspoon red pepper flakes

½ teaspoon salt

10 ounces shaped pasta, such as small shells, ruote (wagon wheels), or radiatore

1. In a large bowl, combine the tomatoes, parsley, olives, capers, oil, vinegar, anchovy paste, brown sugar, red pepper flakes, and salt. Cover and let stand for 30 minutes at room temperature.

2. Meanwhile, in a large pot of boiling water, cook the pasta until just tender. Drain well.

3. Toss the sauce with the hot pasta and serve.

Helpful hints: This recipe calls for extra-virgin olive oil because the flavor of the oil is especially important in an uncooked sauce. Buy a small bottle of extra-virgin oil if you don't use it often, and store it in a cool, dark spot or in the refrigerator. You can substitute the same amount of canned no-salt-added tomatoes, with their juices, for the fresh tomatoes, if you like.

FAT: 11G/25%
CALORIES: 401
SATURATED FAT: 1.6G
CARBOHYDRATE: 64G
PROTEIN: 12G
CHOLESTEROL: 3MG
SODIUM: 778MG

CREAMY PRIMAVERA SAUCE

SERVES: 4
WORKING TIME: 25 MINUTES
TOTAL TIME: 30 MINUTES

Sugar snap peas are sweeter than just about any other kind of peas, but unfortunately, they have a teasingly short season. Catch them while you can and cook up a pasta dinner that celebrates the garden's bounty. Along with the peas, this dish features asparagus, carrots, and cherry tomatoes in a cream sauce light enough to let the vegetables shine through.

10 ounces shaped pasta, such as ruote (wagon wheels), medium shells, or radiatore

1 tablespoon olive oil

4 scallions, thinly sliced

3 carrots, cut into ½-inch cubes

½ pound asparagus, tough ends trimmed, cut on the diagonal into 1½-inch lengths

¼ pound sugar snap or snow peas, strings removed

1 pint cherry tomatoes, halved

½ teaspoon dried thyme

½ teaspoon salt

¼ teaspoon freshly ground black pepper

1½ cups reduced-sodium chicken broth, defatted

2 teaspoons cornstarch mixed with 1 tablespoon water

2 tablespoons reduced-fat cream cheese (Neufchâtel), at room temperature

1. In a large pot of boiling water, cook the pasta until just tender. Drain well.

2. Meanwhile, in a large nonstick skillet, heat the oil until hot but not smoking over medium heat. Add the scallions and carrots and cook, stirring occasionally, until the carrots are softened, about 5 minutes. Add the asparagus and snap peas and cook, stirring, until the asparagus is almost tender, about 5 minutes.

3. Add the tomatoes, thyme, salt, and pepper to the pan. Increase the heat to high and cook until the tomatoes are softened, about 3 minutes. Add the broth and bring to a boil. Add the cornstarch mixture and cook, stirring, until the sauce is slightly thickened, about 2 minutes. Whisk in the cream cheese until well blended. Toss the sauce with the hot pasta, divide among 4 bowls, and serve.

Helpful hint: To string sugar snap peas, pinch off the stem and pull the string from the front of the pod. If the sugar snaps are on the large side (making the strings tougher), you may want to pull the string from the back side of the pod as well.

FAT: 6G/14%
CALORIES: 386
SATURATED FAT: 1.5G
CARBOHYDRATE: 69G
PROTEIN: 15G
CHOLESTEROL: 4MG
SODIUM: 583MG

HERBED TOMATO SAUCE

SERVES: 4
WORKING TIME: 15 MINUTES
TOTAL TIME: 20 MINUTES

The flavor of fresh herbs dissipates if they're cooked for more than a few minutes, so the tastiest sauce may well be one where they're not cooked at all. Here, basil, rosemary, and chives are stirred together with tomatoes and sautéed shallots and garlic. The herbs' flavors are released in a delicious waft of steam when you pour the sauce over the hot pasta.

2 tablespoons olive oil, preferably extra-virgin

3 shallots or 1 small onion, finely chopped

3 cloves garlic, minced

1½ pounds tomatoes, finely chopped

2 tablespoons no-salt-added tomato paste

½ cup chopped fresh basil

2 teaspoons chopped fresh rosemary, or ¾ teaspoon dried, crumbled

2 tablespoons snipped fresh chives or minced scallion greens

1¼ teaspoons salt

¼ teaspoon cayenne pepper

10 ounces medium tube pasta, such as ziti or penne

1. In a large nonstick skillet, heat 2 teaspoons of the oil until hot but not smoking over medium heat. Add the shallots and garlic and cook, stirring frequently, until the shallots are tender, about 5 minutes. Transfer to a large bowl.

2. Add the tomatoes, tomato paste, basil, rosemary, chives, salt, and cayenne to the bowl, stirring well to combine.

3. Meanwhile, in a large pot of boiling water, cook the pasta until just tender and drain well. Toss the hot pasta with the sauce and the remaining 4 teaspoons oil. Divide among 4 bowls and serve.

Helpful hint: Shallots are a member of the onion family with a mild, slightly garlicky flavor. Like garlic, shallots separate into cloves. Store shallots as you would onions, in a cool, dry place.

FAT: 9G/21%
CALORIES: 381
SATURATED FAT: 1.3G
CARBOHYDRATE: 66G
PROTEIN: 12G
CHOLESTEROL: 0MG
SODIUM: 713MG

Eggplant, the colorful star of this dish, cooks in a flavorful sauce with balsamic vinegar to create a satisfying, meat-like texture. Fine Italian balsamic vinegar, made from white Trebbiano grape juice, derives its distinctive taste and dark red color from the wood casks in which it is aged. Balsamic vinegar lasts almost indefinitely and does not need refrigeration.

RADIATORE ALLA NORMA

SERVES: 4
WORKING TIME: 20 MINUTES
TOTAL TIME: 30 MINUTES

2 tablespoons olive oil
1 large onion, finely chopped
3 cloves garlic, minced
1 pound eggplant, cut into ½-inch-wide strips (see tip)
¼ cup balsamic vinegar
1 tablespoon sugar
2 cups canned crushed tomatoes
2 tablespoons chopped fresh basil, or ½ teaspoon dried
½ teaspoon salt
¼ teaspoon freshly ground black pepper
12 ounces radiatore pasta
½ cup part-skim ricotta cheese

1. Start heating a large pot of water to boiling for the pasta. In a large nonstick skillet, heat the oil until hot but not smoking over medium heat. Add the onion and garlic and cook, stirring frequently, until the onion has softened, about 7 minutes.

2. Stir in the eggplant, vinegar, sugar, and ½ cup of water, bring to a boil, reduce to a simmer, and cover. Cook until the eggplant is tender, about 7 minutes. Stir in the tomatoes and cook, uncovered, stirring frequently, until the sauce is flavorful and slightly thickened, about 5 minutes longer. Remove from the heat. Stir in the basil, salt, and pepper.

3. Meanwhile, cook the radiatore in the boiling water until just tender. Drain well. Transfer the radiatore to a large bowl, add the eggplant mixture, and toss to combine. Spoon the pasta mixture into 4 shallow bowls and serve with a dollop of the ricotta.

Suggested accompaniments: Thin bread sticks, followed by dark raisins plumped in dark rum and served over vanilla ice milk for dessert.

FAT: 11G/20%
CALORIES: 505
SATURATED FAT: 2.7G
CARBOHYDRATE: 86G
PROTEIN: 17G
CHOLESTEROL: 10MG
SODIUM: 521MG

TIP

To slice an eggplant, first cut it crosswise into ½-inch-thick slices. Stack several slices, and then cut through the stack to create ½-inch-wide strips. Use this technique for other vegetables as well, such as zucchini.

POTATO-SCALLION SAUCE WITH OLIVES

SERVES: 4
WORKING TIME: 25 MINUTES
TOTAL TIME: 25 MINUTES

10 ounces shaped pasta, such as rotini or radiatore

1 tablespoon olive oil

¾ pound red potatoes, cut into ½-inch cubes

4 scallions, thickly sliced

2 teaspoons dried rosemary, crumbled

4 cups coarsely diced fresh plum tomatoes, or 3½ cups canned no-salt-added tomatoes, chopped with their juices

3 tablespoons chopped green olives plus 2 teaspoons brine from the olive jar

¼ cup reduced-sodium chicken broth, defatted

½ teaspoon hot pepper sauce

¼ teaspoon salt

1. In a large pot of boiling water, cook the pasta until just tender. Drain well.

2. Meanwhile, in a large nonstick skillet, heat the oil until hot but not smoking over medium heat. Add the potatoes, cover, and cook, stirring occasionally, until they begin to brown, about 6 minutes. Add the scallions and rosemary and cook, stirring occasionally, until the potatoes are tender, about 4 minutes.

3. Stir the tomatoes into the skillet and cook until heated through, about 3 minutes. Stir in the olives, olive brine, broth, hot pepper sauce, and salt. Toss the sauce with the hot pasta and serve.

Helpful hint: The liquid (brine) from the olive jar partially salts the sauce and also intensifies the olive flavor. If you can't get 2 teaspoons of brine from the jar, use a little extra chicken broth instead.

If your "starch alarm" sounds at the thought of potatoes and pasta in a single dish, remember that carbohydrates should make up most of your daily food intake. Because the red-skinned potatoes are left unpeeled, they add an extra bit of color to the dish; for a golden touch, try Yellow Finn or Yukon Gold potatoes, which have buttery-yellow flesh.

FAT: 6G/13%
CALORIES: 415
SATURATED FAT: 0.8G
CARBOHYDRATE: 78G
PROTEIN: 13G
CHOLESTEROL: 0MG
SODIUM: 390MG

VEGETABLE-CHEESE SAUCE

SERVES: 4
WORKING TIME: 20 MINUTES
TOTAL TIME: 30 MINUTES

The trick to making a delicious low-fat cheese sauce is to start with a thick white sauce and then melt the cheese into it, instead of relying on the cheese itself for the desired creaminess. If the white sauce is savory and a bit spicy (ours is made with chili powder, mustard, and cayenne), you'll have a head start on flavor, and the cheese doesn't have to do all the work there, either.

10 ounces small tube pasta, such as elbow macaroni or ditalini

1½ cups evaporated skimmed milk

3 tablespoons flour

1 cup reduced-sodium chicken broth, defatted

1 teaspoon chili powder

¾ teaspoon dry mustard

⅛ teaspoon cayenne pepper

2 cups broccoli florets

1 red bell pepper, cut into ½-inch squares

2 carrots, quartered lengthwise and cut into ½-inch pieces

1 cup frozen peas

4 scallions, finely chopped

2 ounces reduced-fat cream cheese (Neufchâtel), at room temperature

1 cup shredded Swiss cheese (4 ounces)

¼ teaspoon salt

1. In a large pot of boiling water, cook the pasta until just tender. Drain well.

2. Meanwhile, in a small bowl, whisk together the evaporated milk and flour until smooth. In a large saucepan, combine the broth, chili powder, mustard, and cayenne and bring to a simmer over medium heat. Add the broccoli, bell pepper, and carrots, cover, and cook until the carrots are crisp-tender, about 5 minutes. Stir in the flour mixture and return to a simmer. Cook, stirring, until thickened and no floury taste remains, about 1 minute.

3. Stir the peas and scallions into the saucepan and cook until the scallions are softened and the peas are heated through, about 3 minutes. Remove from the heat and stir in the cream cheese, ½ cup of the Swiss cheese, and the salt until blended. Divide the pasta among 4 bowls. Spoon the sauce over the hot pasta, top with the remaining ½ cup Swiss cheese, and serve.

Helpful hint: For streamlined meal preparation, cut up the broccoli, bell pepper, and carrots up to 8 hours in advance, and refrigerate in a plastic bag until you are ready to use them.

FAT: 12G/19%
CALORIES: 577
SATURATED FAT: 6.9G
CARBOHYDRATE: 85G
PROTEIN: 32G
CHOLESTEROL: 37MG
SODIUM: 608MG

TORTELLINI WITH GAZPACHO SAUCE

SERVES: 4
WORKING TIME: 25 MINUTES
TOTAL TIME: 25 MINUTES

15-ounce package fresh cheese-filled tortellini

1 cup frozen corn kernels

¾ cup mild or medium-hot prepared salsa

8-ounce can no-salt-added tomato sauce

3 scallions, thinly sliced

1 cup peeled, seeded, and diced cucumber

¼ cup chopped fresh parsley

1 tablespoon red wine vinegar

1 teaspoon Worcestershire sauce

1 teaspoon chopped fresh mint

1. In a large pot of boiling water, cook the tortellini until just tender. Place the corn in a colander and drain the cooked pasta into the colander.

2. Meanwhile, in a large bowl, combine the salsa, tomato sauce, scallions, cucumber, parsley, vinegar, Worcestershire sauce, and mint. Add the corn and pasta and toss to combine. Divide the pasta mixture among 4 bowls and serve warm, at room temperature, or chilled.

Helpful hints: To seed a cucumber, halve it lengthwise and scoop out the seeds with the tip of a small spoon. You can substitute other filled pastas, such as ravioli or cappelletti, for the tortellini. For a lighter meal, try an unfilled pasta, such as rotelle or long fusilli.

FAT: 8G/18%
CALORIES: 408
SATURATED FAT: 3.2G
CARBOHYDRATE: 70G
PROTEIN: 16G
CHOLESTEROL: 44MG
SODIUM: 875MG

A Spanish chilled vegetable soup, gazpacho is most commonly made with fresh tomatoes, cucumbers, bell peppers, and herbs. Here, tomato sauce and bottled salsa are the basis for a light, spicy, gazpacho-style sauce served with cheese tortellini. Whole-wheat peasant bread makes a nice accompaniment.

MEDITERRANEAN VEGETABLE SAUCE

SERVES: 4
WORKING TIME: 20 MINUTES
TOTAL TIME: 30 MINUTES

A tomato-based topping for pasta doesn't have to be a smooth, slow-cooked sauce that takes hours to prepare. Here, for instance, fresh tomatoes are chopped and cooked for just a few minutes so they retain their shape. The tomatoes are combined with green beans, bell pepper, zucchini, and a fragrant handful of basil and tossed with a twisty-shaped pasta.

10 ounces shaped pasta, such as radiatore or rotini

4 teaspoons olive oil

1 onion, diced

2 cloves garlic, minced

¼ pound green beans, cut into 1-inch lengths

1 red bell pepper, cut into ½-inch squares

1 zucchini, quartered lengthwise and cut into ½-inch pieces

2 cups coarsely chopped fresh tomatoes, or 1½ cups canned no-salt-added tomatoes, chopped with their juices

⅓ cup chopped fresh basil

1 teaspoon salt

¼ teaspoon freshly ground black pepper

½ cup reduced-sodium chicken broth, defatted

1 tablespoon cornstarch mixed with 2 tablespoons water

1. In a large pot of boiling water, cook the pasta until just tender. Drain well.

2. Meanwhile, in a large nonstick skillet, heat 2 teaspoons of the oil until hot but not smoking over medium heat. Add the onion and garlic and cook, stirring occasionally, until the onion is softened, about 5 minutes. Add the remaining 2 teaspoons oil, the green beans, bell pepper, and zucchini. Cover and cook until the vegetables are crisp-tender, about 5 minutes.

3. Add the tomatoes, basil, salt, and black pepper to the skillet. Increase the heat to high and cook until the tomatoes are softened, about 5 minutes. Add the broth and cornstarch mixture, bring to a boil, and cook, stirring constantly, until slightly thickened, about 2 minutes. Toss the sauce with the hot pasta and serve.

Helpful hint: If the round "slicing" tomatoes in your market don't look promising, see if you can find plum tomatoes, which are meaty and, when fully ripe, deliciously sweet.

FAT: 6G/15%
CALORIES: 373
SATURATED FAT: 0.8G
CARBOHYDRATE: 69G
PROTEIN: 12G
CHOLESTEROL: 0MG
SODIUM: 639MG

Try this rustic Italian dish as a change from run-of-the-mill sauced pastas. The diced fresh tomatoes form just one aspect of the complex sauce—fresh orange juice and zest, sage, and garlic are the counterparts. Subtleties also count in designing an appealing dish: Notice how the shape of the penne echoes that of the cut-up green beans and Parmesan shavings.

PASTA AND BEANS WITH TOMATO-ORANGE SAUCE

SERVES: 4
WORKING TIME: 20 MINUTES
TOTAL TIME: 30 MINUTES

¾ pound green beans, cut into
2-inch lengths

12 ounces penne pasta

1 tablespoon olive oil

4 cloves garlic, minced

1½ teaspoons dried sage

1½ pounds tomatoes, diced

1 tablespoon grated orange zest

¼ cup orange juice

1 tablespoon balsamic vinegar

¾ teaspoon salt

¼ teaspoon freshly ground black
pepper

19-ounce can white kidney beans
(cannellini), rinsed and drained

4 ounces Parmesan cheese,
shaved (see tip)

1. In a large pot of boiling water, cook the green beans until crisp-tender, about 8 minutes. With a slotted spoon, transfer the beans to a bowl. Add the pasta to the boiling water and cook until tender. Drain well.

2. Meanwhile, in a large nonstick skillet, heat the oil until hot but not smoking over medium-low heat. Add the garlic and cook for 1 minute, until fragrant. Add the sage, tomatoes, orange zest, orange juice, vinegar, salt, and pepper. Increase the heat to high and cook, stirring, until heated through, about 2 minutes.

3. Add the green beans and the white beans to the skillet and cook until heated through, about 1 minute. Transfer the bean mixture to a large bowl and add the pasta and all but 1 ounce of the Parmesan. Top with the remaining Parmesan and serve.

Helpful hint: Instead of the Parmesan shavings, you can toss the pasta with 1 cup of grated Parmesan.

TIP

To make Parmesan shavings: Let a block of Parmesan come to room temperature. Use a vegetable peeler to scrape thin, ribbon-like shavings.

FAT: 14G/20%
CALORIES: 628
SATURATED FAT: 5.4G
CARBOHYDRATE: 97G
PROTEIN: 31G
CHOLESTEROL: 19MG
SODIUM: 923MG

MUSHROOM-HERB SAUCE

SERVES: 4
WORKING TIME: 20 MINUTES
TOTAL TIME: 25 MINUTES

M*arsala, with its richly fruity bouquet, points up the earthy flavor of the mushrooms in this delicately creamy four-vegetable sauce.*

10 ounces medium strand pasta, such as spaghetti, linguine, or long fusilli

2 teaspoons olive oil

2 onions, finely chopped

2 carrots, finely chopped

2 ribs celery, finely chopped

½ pound small mushrooms, quartered

3 tablespoons Marsala or dry red wine

2 teaspoons dried basil

2 teaspoons dried rosemary, crumbled

1 cup reduced-sodium chicken broth, defatted

2 teaspoons cornstarch mixed with 1 tablespoon water

½ teaspoon salt

⅓ cup reduced-fat sour cream

3 tablespoons chopped fresh parsley

1. In a large pot of boiling water, cook the pasta until just tender. Drain well.

2. Meanwhile, in a large nonstick skillet, heat the oil until hot but not smoking over medium heat. Add the onions, carrots, and celery and cook, stirring occasionally, until the carrots are softened, about 7 minutes. Increase the heat to medium-high, add the mushrooms, Marsala, basil, and rosemary and cook until the mushroom liquid has evaporated, about 4 minutes.

3. Add the broth to the pan and return to a simmer. Stir in the cornstarch mixture and salt and cook, stirring, until slightly thickened, about 3 minutes. Remove from the heat and stir in the sour cream and parsley. Divide the pasta among 4 bowls, spoon the sauce over the hot pasta, and serve.

Helpful hint: Marsala is a fortified wine from Sicily. Use a dry Marsala for savory dishes such as this one, and save the sweeter Marsalas for desserts.

FAT: 7G/15%
CALORIES: 412
SATURATED FAT: 1.8G
CARBOHYDRATE: 72G
PROTEIN: 14G
CHOLESTEROL: 7MG
SODIUM: 467MG

MACARONI WITH MOZZARELLA AND VEGETABLES

SERVES: 4
WORKING TIME: 25 MINUTES
TOTAL TIME: 25 MINUTES

12 ounces elbow macaroni

2 teaspoons olive oil

1 red onion, coarsely chopped

1 red or yellow bell pepper, diced

1 zucchini, diced

2 cloves garlic, minced

½ cup dry white wine

1 teaspoon paprika

1 teaspoon dried oregano

¾ teaspoon salt

1 cup reduced-sodium chicken broth, defatted

2 teaspoons cornstarch mixed with 1 tablespoon water

1 cup cubed part-skim mozzarella cheese (4 ounces)

1. In a large pot of boiling water, cook the macaroni until just tender. Drain well.

2. Meanwhile, in a large nonstick skillet, heat the oil until hot but not smoking over medium heat. Add the onion and bell pepper and cook until crisp-tender, about 5 minutes. Add the zucchini, garlic, wine, paprika, oregano, and salt and cook until the zucchini is softened, about 5 minutes.

3. Add the broth and cornstarch mixture to the skillet and cook, stirring, until slightly thickened, about 2 minutes. Stir the macaroni into the pan and remove from the heat. Stir in the mozzarella, tossing to combine. Divide the pasta mixture among 4 bowls and serve.

Helpful hint: Any short pasta, such as medium shells, cavatelli, or rotelle would also be great with this sauce.

FAT: 7G/14%
CALORIES: 456
SATURATED FAT: 2.4G
CARBOHYDRATE: 73G
PROTEIN: 20G
CHOLESTEROL: 10MG
SODIUM: 735MG

Melting cubes of mozzarella create rich pockets of flavor here when tossed with hot pasta and sautéed vegetables.

PENNE WITH SPINACH AND CHICK-PEAS

SERVES: 4
WORKING TIME: 35 MINUTES
TOTAL TIME: 40 MINUTES

Y*ou* might not see a lot of sauce in this tricolored pasta dish, but you'll be wowed by the flavor. The pungency of garlic is played against the freshness of orange and the subtlety of sage, while nutmeg brings out the best in the spinach. If you've never cooked with fresh nutmeg, buy yourself a whole nutmeg and a nutmeg grater and prepare for an eye-opener.

10 ounces penne pasta
1 tablespoon olive oil
1 large onion, diced
3 cloves garlic, minced
1 large red bell pepper, diced
16-ounce can chick-peas, rinsed and drained
8 cups torn fresh spinach leaves (about 1 pound)
1 cup reduced-sodium chicken broth, defatted
½ teaspoon grated orange zest
¾ teaspoon salt
¼ teaspoon dried sage
¼ teaspoon nutmeg
1 teaspoon cornstarch mixed with 1 tablespoon water

1. In a large pot of boiling water, cook the penne until just tender. Drain well.

2. Meanwhile, in a large nonstick skillet, heat the oil until hot but not smoking over medium heat. Add the onion and garlic and cook, stirring occasionally, until the onion is softened, about 7 minutes. Add the bell pepper and cook, stirring occasionally, until the bell pepper is softened, about 5 minutes.

3. Stir the chick-peas, spinach, broth, orange zest, salt, sage, and nutmeg into the skillet and simmer gently until the spinach is wilted, about 5 minutes. Bring to a boil, stir in the cornstarch mixture, and cook, stirring constantly, until slightly thickened, about 1 minute. Combine the penne and the chick-pea mixture in a large bowl, tossing to coat. Divide among 4 bowls and serve.

Helpful hint: Chick-peas, which look like small, cream-colored hazelnuts, may also be labeled "garbanzos" (their Spanish name) or "ceci" (their Italian name).

FAT: 7G/15%
CALORIES: 435
SATURATED FAT: .8G
CARBOHYDRATE: 76G
PROTEIN: 18G
CHOLESTEROL: 0MG
SODIUM: 795MG

Spicy Tomato Sauce

SERVES: 4
WORKING TIME: 25 MINUTES
TOTAL TIME: 25 MINUTES

Canned tomatoes should always be on hand in your cupboard. They're a trusty standby for sauce-making when quality fresh tomatoes aren't available. Canned tomatoes do need some dressing up, however. Here, we've added an array of highly flavorful ingredients, from Canadian bacon to capers to cayenne, for a delightfully zesty sauce.

10 ounces medium strand pasta, such as long fusilli, spaghetti, or linguine

2 teaspoons olive oil

¼ cup plus 2 tablespoons finely chopped Canadian bacon (2 ounces)

1 onion, finely chopped

4 cloves garlic, minced

1 rib celery, finely chopped

2½ cups canned no-salt-added tomatoes, chopped with their juices

¼ cup pimiento-stuffed olives, coarsely chopped

1 tablespoon capers, rinsed and drained

½ teaspoon salt

¼ teaspoon cayenne pepper

⅓ cup chopped fresh parsley

⅓ cup grated Parmesan cheese

1. In a large pot of boiling water, cook the pasta until just tender. Drain well.

2. Meanwhile, in a large nonstick skillet, heat the oil until hot but not smoking over medium heat. Add the Canadian bacon, onion, and garlic and cook, stirring frequently, until the onion is tender, about 5 minutes. Add the celery and cook, stirring frequently, until the celery is tender, about 4 minutes.

3. Add the tomatoes, olives, capers, salt, and cayenne to the pan and bring to a boil. Reduce to a simmer and cook, stirring frequently, until the sauce is richly flavored and slightly thickened, about 5 minutes. Stir in the parsley. Toss the sauce with the hot pasta and all but 2 tablespoons of the Parmesan. Divide among 4 bowls, sprinkle the remaining 2 tablespoons Parmesan over, and serve.

Helpful hint: This recipe is a good candidate to make ahead. Don't add the parsley and the remaining 2 tablespoons of Parmesan until after you've reheated the sauce for serving.

FAT: 8G/18%
CALORIES: 399
SATURATED FAT: 2.2G
CARBOHYDRATE: 65G
PROTEIN: 17G
CHOLESTEROL: 12MG
SODIUM: 892MG

VEGETABLE STIR-FRY WITH SATAY SAUCE

SERVES: 4
WORKING TIME: 30 MINUTES
TOTAL TIME: 30 MINUTES

8 ounces fettuccine

2 teaspoons vegetable oil

3 scallions, cut into 1-inch lengths

2 cloves garlic, finely chopped

1 tablespoon finely chopped fresh ginger

1 pickled jalapeño pepper, seeded and finely chopped

2 red bell peppers, cut into thin strips

2 large carrots, cut into 2-by-⅛-inch julienne strips

2 turnips, peeled and cut into 2-by-⅛-inch julienne strips

½ teaspoon salt

1 cucumber, peeled, halved lengthwise, seeded, and cut into thin julienne strips

1 teaspoon cornstarch

1½ cups reduced-sodium chicken broth, defatted

¼ cup fresh lime juice

4 tablespoons creamy peanut butter

1 tablespoon firmly packed brown sugar

1. In a large pot of boiling water, cook the fettuccine until just tender. Drain well.

2. Meanwhile, in a large nonstick skillet or wok, heat the oil until hot but not smoking over medium heat. Add the scallions, garlic, ginger, and jalapeño and stir-fry until the scallions are softened, about 2 minutes. Add the bell peppers, carrots, turnips, and salt and stir-fry until the vegetables are crisp-tender, about 5 minutes. Add the cucumber and cook until the cucumbers are heated through, about 2 minutes.

3. In a small bowl, combine the cornstarch, broth, lime juice, peanut butter, and brown sugar, whisking until well combined. Pour the mixture over the vegetables and bring to a boil. Add the pasta and toss to combine. Divide the pasta mixture among 4 plates and serve.

Helpful hint: To seed a cucumber, halve it lengthwise and scoop out the seeds with the tip of a small spoon.

FAT: 13G/28%
CALORIES: 420
SATURATED FAT: 2.2G
CARBOHYDRATE: 63G
PROTEIN: 16G
CHOLESTEROL: 54MG
SODIUM: 721MG

Satays—miniature kebabs that are a popular snack in Southeast Asia—are traditionally served with a spicy peanut dipping sauce that's tasty enough to eat on its own. We've sauced this colorful noodle-and-vegetable stir-fry with a similar peanut-butter-based sauce. Note the use of cucumbers in the stir-fry: They're just heated through so they still retain a touch of crispness.

One way to enhance asparagus is with its traditional partner, hollandaise sauce. But if you'd rather spare yourself the butter and egg yolks (and the tedious process of making it), try this elegant sauce, which is based on low-fat milk and reduced-fat cream cheese. It's delicately flavored with lemon, tarragon, and a touch of hot pepper sauce.

ASPARAGUS CREAM SAUCE

SERVES: 4
WORKING TIME: 25 MINUTES
TOTAL TIME: 30 MINUTES

10 ounces shaped pasta, such as farfalle (bow ties) or orecchiette

2 teaspoons olive oil

1 red onion, finely chopped

¾ pound asparagus, tough ends trimmed (see tip), cut on the diagonal into 1-inch lengths

½ cup dry white wine

2 tablespoons flour

1 cup low-fat (1%) milk

1 teaspoon dried tarragon

¼ cup reduced-fat cream cheese (Neufchâtel), at room temperature

1 tablespoon fresh lemon juice

¼ teaspoon hot pepper sauce

½ teaspoon salt

3 tablespoons grated Parmesan cheese

1. In a large pot of boiling water, cook the pasta until just tender. Drain well.

2. Meanwhile, in a large nonstick skillet, heat the oil until hot but not smoking over medium heat. Add the onion and cook, stirring frequently, until softened, about 4 minutes. Add the asparagus and wine, bring to a simmer, partially cover, and cook until the asparagus is crisp-tender, about 6 minutes.

3. In a small bowl, combine the flour and milk. Add the milk mixture to the skillet along with the tarragon and cook, stirring, until thickened, about 3 minutes. Stir in the cream cheese, lemon juice, hot pepper sauce, and salt and cook, stirring, until the cream cheese is melted and the sauce is smooth, about 2 minutes. Divide the pasta among 4 bowls. Spoon the sauce over the hot pasta, sprinkle with the Parmesan, and serve.

Helpful hint: You can substitute the same amount of reduced-sodium chicken broth (defatted) for the white wine, if you like.

TIP

To prepare asparagus for cooking, hold each spear in your hands and bend it until the stem snaps off; it should break naturally where the woody base merges into the more tender part of the stalk.

FAT: 8G/17%
CALORIES: 429
SATURATED FAT: 3.4G
CARBOHYDRATE: 67G
PROTEIN: 17G
CHOLESTEROL: 13MG
SODIUM: 470MG

GRILLED VEGETABLE PASTA

SERVES: 4
WORKING TIME: 25 MINUTES
TOTAL TIME: 45 MINUTES PLUS MARINATING TIME

If you're lucky, you've had the opportunity to try a dish something like this in a restaurant. But if you're smart, you'll use our recipe to make it at home, where you can grill the vegetables precisely to your taste. Equally important, you'll know exactly how much olive oil (a mere tablespoon) is in the marinade; restaurant chefs can be a bit heavy-handed with the oil jug.

1 small butternut squash (about 1 pound), peeled, halved lengthwise, seeded, and cut into ½-inch-thick slices

½ cup reduced-sodium vegetable broth

1 tablespoon olive oil

2 teaspoons grated lemon zest

½ teaspoon dried thyme

½ teaspoon dried oregano

¾ teaspoon salt

⅛ teaspoon red pepper flakes

8 plum tomatoes, halved lengthwise

1 red onion, cut into ¼-inch-thick slices

8 ounces penne pasta

¼ cup chopped fresh basil

½ cup grated Parmesan cheese

1 tablespoon chopped fresh parsley (optional)

1. In a large pot of boiling water, cook the butternut squash until tender, 8 to 10 minutes. Drain, rinse under cold water to stop the cooking, and drain again.

2. In a large sturdy plastic bag, combine the broth, oil, lemon zest, thyme, oregano, salt, and red pepper flakes. Add the cooked butternut squash, the tomatoes, and onion. Toss the vegetables gently in the marinade to coat thoroughly and reseal the bag, squeezing out the air. Refrigerate for at least 1 hour or up to 12 hours.

3. Preheat the grill (with a grill topper, if possible). When ready to cook, spray the rack (or grill topper)—off the grill—with nonstick cooking spray. Meanwhile, in a large pot of boiling water, cook the pasta until tender. Drain well and transfer to a large bowl.

4. Reserving the marinade, transfer the vegetables to the grill and cover. Grill at medium, or 6 inches from the heat, turning once and basting with some of the reserved marinade, for 10 to 12 minutes, or until the vegetables are crisp-tender. When they are cool enough to handle, cut the vegetables into bite-size pieces. Add the grilled vegetables to the pasta along with the remaining marinade and the basil, tossing to coat. Divide among 4 plates, sprinkle the Parmesan and parsley over, and serve.

FAT: 8G/19%
CALORIES: 376
SATURATED FAT: 2.5G
CARBOHYDRATE: 64G
PROTEIN: 14G
CHOLESTEROL: 8MG
SODIUM: 651MG

BEAN, TOMATO, AND TORTELLINI CHOWDER

SERVES: 4
WORKING TIME: 20 MINUTES
TOTAL TIME: 45 MINUTES

Filled pasta can turn a simple soup into a hearty meal. Here, cheese-filled tortellini, widely available in fresh or frozen form, go into a savory supper dish. Tomato-vegetable juice is the base for the tasty broth; reduced-fat sour cream adds a smooth richness that's balanced by lively accents of fresh mint and lemon juice. Serve a simple green salad on the side.

2½ cups reduced-sodium tomato-vegetable juice

2 leeks, cut into ½-inch dice, or 4 scallions, cut into ½-inch lengths

2 large carrots, halved lengthwise and thinly sliced

1 turnip (6 ounces), peeled and cut into ½-inch dice

3 cloves garlic, minced

¾ teaspoon ground ginger

½ teaspoon salt

1 pound all-purpose potatoes, peeled and cut into ½-inch dice

¼ cup chopped fresh mint

3 tablespoons fresh lemon juice

¾ pound cheese tortellini

½ pound green beans, cut into 1-inch lengths

3 tablespoons reduced-fat sour cream

1. In a Dutch oven or large saucepan, combine 4½ cups of water, the tomato-vegetable juice, leeks, carrots, turnip, garlic, ginger, and salt and bring to a boil over medium heat. Reduce to a simmer, cover, and cook until the vegetables are crisp-tender and the broth is flavorful, about 12 minutes.

2. Add the potatoes, mint, lemon juice, and tortellini and cook for 5 minutes. Add the green beans and cook until the tortellini are tender and the beans are crisp-tender, about 5 minutes. Remove from the heat, stir in the sour cream, divide among 4 bowls, and serve.

Helpful hints: Frozen tortellini may take 2 to 3 minutes longer to cook than fresh. A leek's many layers trap sand and dirt, and it's tricky to get a whole or split leek really clean. When the recipe calls for sliced leeks, like this one, it's easier to wash the vegetable in a bowl of water after cutting it up.

FAT: 8G/15%
CALORIES: 471
SATURATED FAT: 3.3G
CARBOHYDRATE: 85G
PROTEIN: 17G
CHOLESTEROL: 39MG
SODIUM: 831MG

FUSILLI FLORENTINE

SERVES: 4
WORKING TIME: 20 MINUTES
TOTAL TIME: 20 MINUTES

Pasta with greens and garlic is a beloved Italian dish; bits of pancetta—an unsmoked Italian bacon—may be added for extra savory punch. For a similar flavor, we've used Canadian bacon, which is cut from the lean pork loin and has about one-eighth as much fat as regular bacon, and is readily available in supermarkets.

8 ounces fusilli pasta
1 tablespoon vegetable oil
2 ounces Canadian bacon, diced
1 yellow or red bell pepper, cut into strips
½ cup coarsely chopped scallions
1 clove garlic, minced
½ cup reduced-sodium chicken broth, defatted
¾ pound spinach leaves, torn into large pieces
¼ teaspoon freshly ground black pepper
1 tablespoon slivered Calamata or other brine-cured black olives
1 tablespoon chopped pine nuts

1. In a large pot of boiling water, cook the pasta until just tender. Drain well.

2. Meanwhile, in a large nonstick skillet, heat the oil until hot but not smoking over medium heat. Add the Canadian bacon, bell pepper, scallions, and garlic. Cook, stirring, until the bacon is lightly browned, about 5 minutes. Add the broth, spinach, and black pepper to the skillet and cook until the spinach is wilted, about 2 minutes. Stir in the olives and pine nuts.

3. Transfer the mixture to a large bowl, add the pasta, and toss to combine. Divide the pasta mixture among 4 bowls and serve.

Helpful hint: If you have a few moments to spare, toast the pine nuts to bring out their flavor. Cook them in a dry skillet over medium heat, shaking the pan frequently, for 3 to 4 minutes, or until golden.

FAT: 7G/20%
CALORIES: 312
SATURATED FAT: 1.2G
CARBOHYDRATE: 49G
PROTEIN: 14G
CHOLESTEROL: 7MG
SODIUM: 392MG

FETTUCCINE AL PESTO

SERVES: 4
WORKING TIME: 10 MINUTES
TOTAL TIME: 20 MINUTES

Only fresh basil will do for this classic Italian specialty, which takes little effort to prepare and is a perfect warm-weather supper.

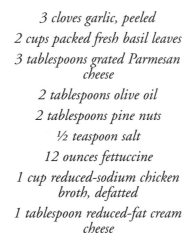

3 cloves garlic, peeled
2 cups packed fresh basil leaves
3 tablespoons grated Parmesan cheese
2 tablespoons olive oil
2 tablespoons pine nuts
½ teaspoon salt
12 ounces fettuccine
1 cup reduced-sodium chicken broth, defatted
1 tablespoon reduced-fat cream cheese

1. Heat a large pot of water to boiling, and cook the garlic until tender, about 3 minutes. Reserve the boiling water for the pasta and, with a slotted spoon, transfer the garlic to a food processor or blender. Add the basil, Parmesan, oil, pine nuts, and salt to the garlic and purée until smooth.

2. Cook the fettuccine in the reserved boiling water until just tender. Drain well.

3. Meanwhile, in a large nonstick skillet, bring the broth to a simmer over medium heat. Whisk in the basil purée and the cream cheese until smooth. Add the fettuccine and cook until just heated through, about 2 minutes. Spoon the fettuccine mixture into 4 shallow bowls and serve.

Suggested accompaniments: Escarole and red bell pepper salad drizzled with a red wine vinaigrette, and fresh cherries for dessert.

FAT: 15G/29%
CALORIES: 463
SATURATED FAT: 3.1G
CARBOHYDRATE: 68G
PROTEIN: 17G
CHOLESTEROL: 86MG
SODIUM: 545MG

SPICY PENNE WITH CAULIFLOWER

SERVES: 4
WORKING TIME: 20 MINUTES
TOTAL TIME: 30 MINUTES

¼ cup golden raisins

2 tablespoons pine nuts

2 tablespoons olive oil

4 cups cauliflower florets

4 cloves garlic, thinly slivered

14½-ounce can no-salt-added stewed tomatoes

8-ounce can no-salt-added tomato sauce

¾ teaspoon salt

½ teaspoon red pepper flakes

½ teaspoon ground ginger

12 ounces penne pasta

¼ cup chopped fresh parsley

1. Start heating a large pot of water to boiling for the pasta. In a small bowl, combine the raisins and ½ cup of hot water. Let stand until the raisins have softened, about 10 minutes. Meanwhile, in a small dry skillet, cook the pine nuts over low heat until lightly toasted, stirring frequently, about 4 minutes. Remove from the heat.

2. In a large nonstick skillet, heat the oil until hot but not smoking over low heat. Add the cauliflower and cook, stirring frequently, until the cauliflower is golden, about 5 minutes. Add the garlic and cook, stirring frequently, until the garlic is lightly golden, about 3 minutes.

3. Add the raisins and their soaking liquid, tomatoes, tomato sauce, salt, pepper flakes, and ginger, breaking up the tomatoes with the back of a spoon. Cook until the cauliflower is tender and the sauce is slightly thickened, about 4 minutes longer.

4. Meanwhile, cook the penne in the boiling water until just tender. Drain well. Transfer the cauliflower mixture to a large bowl, add the penne and parsley, and toss to combine. Spoon the penne mixture into 4 shallow bowls, sprinkle with the pine nuts, and serve.

Suggested accompaniments: Shredded carrot and celery salad tossed with orange juice and drizzled with olive oil. Follow with ripe melon wedges topped with a purée of canned apricots.

FAT: 11G/20%
CALORIES: 504
SATURATED FAT: 1.5G
CARBOHYDRATE: 89G
PROTEIN: 16G
CHOLESTEROL: 0MG
SODIUM: 466MG

A*t work in this fragrant dish are some enticing flavors—ginger, hot pepper, sweet raisins, and pine nuts.*

Leeks, Spanish onions, and scallions are three members of the onion family that add up to a splendidly full-flavored sauce. The leek and onions are sautéed in olive oil to golden sweetness; the scallions are added toward the end of the cooking time so that they retain a touch of their fresh "green" flavor. Bread crumbs render the sauce thick and "clingy."

THREE-ONION SAUCE

SERVES: 4
WORKING TIME: 30 MINUTES
TOTAL TIME: 30 MINUTES

10 ounces shaped pasta, such as farfalle (bow ties) or orecchiette

1 tablespoon olive oil

1 small Spanish onion, coarsely chopped

1 leek, halved lengthwise and sliced (see tip)

½ cup reduced-sodium beef broth, defatted

4 scallions, thinly sliced

1 teaspoon dried marjoram or oregano

1½ cups coarsely chopped no-salt-added canned tomatoes

¼ teaspoon salt

¼ teaspoon freshly ground black pepper

¼ cup grated Parmesan cheese

1 slice (1 ounces) firm-textured white sandwich bread, torn into bread crumbs

1. In a large pot of boiling water, cook the pasta until just tender. Drain well.

2. Meanwhile, in a large nonstick skillet, heat the oil until hot but not smoking over medium heat. Add the onion and leek and cook, stirring occasionally, until the onion is softened and lightly golden, about 12 minutes.

3. Stir the broth, scallions, and marjoram into the skillet and bring to a boil. Reduce to a simmer and cook for 4 minutes to reduce slightly. Stir in the tomatoes, salt, and pepper and return to a simmer. Remove from the heat and stir in the Parmesan and bread crumbs. Toss the sauce with the hot pasta, divide among 4 plates, and serve.

Helpful hint: If leeks are not available, you can substitute 2 more scallions.

FAT: 7G/16%
CALORIES: 395
SATURATED FAT: 1.7G
CARBOHYDRATE: 70G
PROTEIN: 14G
CHOLESTEROL: 4MG
SODIUM: 374MG

TIP

When a recipe calls for leeks to be sliced, first trim the root end and the dark green leaves, then cut the leeks as directed. Place the cut leeks in a bowl of tepid water, let them sit for 1 to 2 minutes, then lift the leeks out of the water, leaving any dirt and grit behind in the bowl. This is easier and faster than splitting and washing whole leeks before slicing them.

PASTA WITH MINESTRONE SAUCE

SERVES: 4
WORKING TIME: 20 MINUTES
TOTAL TIME: 30 MINUTES

This lovely dish, brimming with vegetables and two kinds of beans, is a delicious favorite even when canned whole tomatoes (about two cups) and dried basil are substituted for fresh. Feel free to replace the pintos with other varieties, such as cannellini or red kidney beans.

2 tablespoons olive oil

1 medium red onion, diced

4 cloves garlic, minced

1 zucchini, halved lengthwise, and thinly sliced

½ pound green beans, cut diagonally into 1-inch pieces

¾ cup reduced-sodium chicken broth, defatted

2 tomatoes, coarsely chopped

1 cup canned pinto beans, rinsed and drained

⅓ cup chopped fresh basil, or 1 teaspoon dried

¼ teaspoon salt

¼ teaspoon freshly ground black pepper

12 ounces rotini pasta

½ cup grated Parmesan cheese

1. Start heating a large pot of water to boiling for the pasta. In a large nonstick skillet, heat the oil until hot but not smoking over medium heat. Add the onion and garlic and cook, stirring frequently, until the onion has softened, about 7 minutes.

2. Stir in the zucchini and cook until the zucchini begins to soften, about 2 minutes. Add the green beans and broth and cook, stirring occasionally, until the green beans are almost tender, about 3 minutes. Stir in the tomatoes, pinto beans, basil, salt, and pepper and cook until the green beans are tender and the sauce is slightly thickened, about 4 minutes longer.

3. Meanwhile, cook the rotini in the boiling water until just tender. Drain well. Transfer the vegetable mixture to a large bowl, add the rotini, and toss to combine. Spoon the pasta mixture into 4 shallow bowls, sprinkle with the Parmesan, and serve.

Suggested accompaniments: Italian or French bread, followed by ripe Bartlett pears.

FAT: 12G/20%
CALORIES: 527
SATURATED FAT: 3.1G
CARBOHYDRATE: 84G
PROTEIN: 21G
CHOLESTEROL: 8MG
SODIUM: 592MG

FRESH FETTUCCINE WITH TOMATO CREAM SAUCE

SERVES: 4
WORKING TIME: 20 MINUTES
TOTAL TIME: 30 MINUTES

1 red bell pepper, halved lengthwise and seeded

1 cup evaporated low-fat milk

¼ cup grated Parmesan cheese

½ teaspoon salt

½ teaspoon freshly ground black pepper

1 teaspoon olive oil

3 tablespoons finely chopped prosciutto or Canadian bacon (1 ounce)

2 cups canned no-salt-added tomatoes, coarsely chopped with their juices

1 cup frozen peas, thawed

1 pound fresh fettuccine

1. Preheat the broiler. Place the bell pepper halves, cut-sides down, on the broiler rack. Broil the pepper 4 inches from the heat for 10 minutes, or until the skin is blackened. When the peppers are cool enough to handle, peel them and cut into thin strips. Start heating a large pot of water to boiling for the pasta.

2. Meanwhile, in a large bowl, combine the evaporated milk, Parmesan, salt, and pepper. Set aside.

3. In a large nonstick skillet, heat the oil until hot but not smoking over medium heat. Add the prosciutto and cook until lightly crisped, about 2 minutes. Add the tomatoes and red pepper strips and cook, stirring occasionally, until flavorful and lightly thickened, about 5 minutes. Add the peas and cook until heated through, about 2 minutes.

4. Cook the fettuccine in the boiling water until just tender. Drain and add to the milk and Parmesan mixture, tossing well to coat and to melt the cheese. Transfer the pasta to the tomato sauce in the skillet, toss to coat, and serve.

Helpful hint: You can substitute 12 ounces of dried fettuccine for the fresh pasta.

FAT: 10G/15%
CALORIES: 593
SATURATED FAT: 2.4G
CARBOHYDRATE: 98G
PROTEIN: 28G
CHOLESTEROL: 128MG
SODIUM: 823MG

The "cream" in this recipe is really evaporated low-fat milk. Here are the impressive figures on this "miracle" ingredient: Evaporated low-fat milk has a mere 3 grams of fat per cup, while the same amount of heavy cream has a whopping 90 grams! It's one of the more dramatic ways to cut fat in a sauce without sacrificing luxurious richness.

NEAPOLITAN EGGPLANT SAUCE

SERVES: 4
WORKING TIME: 35 MINUTES
TOTAL TIME: 35 MINUTES

One of the best things about eggplant is its meaty texture, which makes any dish seem more substantial. One disadvantage is its tendency to soak up every bit of oil in the pan—but that's not a problem here, since the oil in this recipe is minimal and the eggplant is simmered in broth, not fried. A touch of nutmeg and a toss of fresh mint give the vegetables a unique flavor.

10 ounces shaped pasta, such as medium shells, ruote (wagon wheels), or radiatore
2 teaspoons olive oil
1 red onion, cut into thin slivers
½ cup dry white wine
2 carrots, shredded
3 cups peeled, cubed eggplant (½-inch cubes)
½ cup reduced-sodium chicken broth, defatted
1 tablespoon no-salt-added tomato paste
4 cups coarsely diced fresh plum tomatoes, or 3½ cups canned no-salt-added tomatoes, chopped with their juices
¼ cup chopped fresh mint
¾ teaspoon salt
⅛ teaspoon nutmeg
¾ cup shredded part-skim mozzarella cheese (3 ounces)

1. In a large pot of boiling water, cook the pasta until just tender. Drain well.

2. Meanwhile, in a large nonstick skillet, heat the oil until hot but not smoking over medium heat. Add the onion and cook, stirring frequently, until softened, about 5 minutes. Add the wine and bring to a boil over medium-high heat. Add the carrots, eggplant, broth, and tomato paste and cook, stirring occasionally, until the eggplant is almost tender, about 6 minutes. Stir in the tomatoes, mint, salt, and nutmeg and cook until the tomatoes are softened, about 6 minutes.

3. Toss the sauce with the hot pasta and ½ cup of the mozzarella. Sprinkle the remaining ¼ cup mozzarella over, and serve.

Helpful hint: It's easy to peel eggplant with a swivel-bladed vegetable peeler. Cut off the stem end so that you have a cut edge of skin to start on; otherwise it can be tricky to catch the slick skin in the peeler blade.

FAT: 8G/16%
CALORIES: 450
SATURATED FAT: 2.7G
CARBOHYDRATE: 74G
PROTEIN: 18G
CHOLESTEROL: 12MG
SODIUM: 626MG

Ravioli Primavera

SERVES: 4
WORKING TIME: 20 MINUTES
TOTAL TIME: 30 MINUTES

1 teaspoon olive oil

2 cloves garlic, minced

1 carrot, diced

⅓ cup reduced-sodium chicken broth, defatted

3 cups broccoli florets

1¼ pounds plum tomatoes (about 5), coarsely chopped

1½ cups frozen peas

1 cup frozen corn kernels

3 tablespoons chopped fresh basil, or ½ teaspoon dried

2 tablespoons chopped fresh parsley

¾ teaspoon salt

¼ teaspoon freshly ground black pepper

12 ounces refrigerated or frozen cheese ravioli

1. Start heating a large pot of water to boiling for the pasta. In a large nonstick skillet, heat the oil until hot but not smoking over medium heat. Add the garlic and cook, stirring frequently, until tender, about 2 minutes. Stir in the carrot and 2 tablespoons of the broth and cook, stirring frequently, until the carrot is tender, about 5 minutes.

2. Add the broccoli and the remaining broth, stirring to coat. Stir in the tomatoes and ½ cup of water and cook until the broccoli is tender and the sauce is slightly thickened, about 4 minutes. Stir in the peas, corn, basil, parsley, salt, and pepper and cook until the peas and corn are heated through, about 2 minutes longer.

3. Meanwhile, cook the ravioli in the boiling water until just tender. Drain well. Transfer the vegetable mixture to a large bowl, add the ravioli, and toss to combine. Spoon the ravioli primavera into 4 shallow bowls and serve.

Suggested accompaniments: Sesame flat breads and, for dessert, raspberry sherbet topped with diced fresh mango.

This vibrant dish, inspired by the summer garden, can be made all year round, thanks to quality frozen vegetables, such as corn and peas and even chopped broccoli, if fresh is unavailable. Our version of primavera contrasts the chewy tenderness of ravioli with a mix of vegetable textures. Try serving it at room temperature for an easy make-ahead meal.

FAT: 13G/27%
CALORIES: 430
SATURATED FAT: 6.3G
CARBOHYDRATE: 61G
PROTEIN: 22G
CHOLESTEROL: 75MG
SODIUM: 929MG

*T*hose *ivory and orange noodles certainly make a festive dish, don't they? But wait—the orange pasta isn't pasta at all; it's actually wide strips of carrot that have been cooked along with the noodles. Cauliflower, spinach, tomatoes, and peas make this dish a very special pasta primavera; the creamy, low-fat sauce is a blend of tangy goat cheese and sour cream.*

Vegetable "Pasta"

Serves: 4
Working time: 35 minutes
Total time: 35 minutes

4 carrots, peeled

10 ounces pappardelle pasta or wide "yolkless" egg noodles

4 ounces goat cheese

⅓ cup reduced-fat sour cream

2 tablespoons flour

2 teaspoons olive oil

4 scallions, thinly sliced

1½ cups cauliflower florets

2 cups coarsely chopped fresh spinach

1 cup frozen peas

1¼ teaspoons dried tarragon

2 cloves garlic, minced

2 cups cherry tomatoes, halved if large

½ teaspoon salt

1. Bring a large pot of water to a boil for the pasta. With a vegetable peeler, cut the carrots into long thin strips (see tip). Add the pasta to the water and cook until tender, adding the carrot strips for the last 1 minute of cooking. Reserving ¾ cup of the pasta cooking water, drain the pasta and carrots.

2. Meanwhile, in a small bowl, combine the goat cheese, sour cream, and flour, blending until smooth. In a large nonstick skillet, heat the oil until hot but not smoking over medium heat. Add the scallions, cauliflower, and spinach and cook, stirring occasionally, until the scallions and spinach are wilted, about 5 minutes.

3. Add the peas, tarragon, and garlic to the skillet and cook until heated through, about 2 minutes. Add the goat cheese mixture and reserved pasta cooking water, stirring until blended. Add the cherry tomatoes and salt and cook until slightly thickened and heated through, about 2 minutes. Divide the pasta and carrots among 4 plates, spoon the vegetable mixture over, and serve.

Helpful hint: Chèvre (French-style goat cheese) would be a good choice for this recipe, but you can use Greek feta cheese instead. Rinse the feta to remove some of the salty brine, then mash the cheese with a fork before blending it with the sour cream and flour.

Fat: 16g/28%
Calories: 520
Saturated Fat: 7.9g
Carbohydrate: 77g
Protein: 23g
Cholesterol: 29mg
Sodium: 556mg

TIP

Use long, even strokes with a vegetable peeler to create noodle-like strips from the carrots. If you use large carrots, the "noodles" will be nice and wide.

SERVES: 4
WORKING TIME: 30 MINUTES
TOTAL TIME: 45 MINUTES

The squiggly ridges in the rotini pasta are great hiding places for the chunks of vegetables and tangy Cheddar sauce.

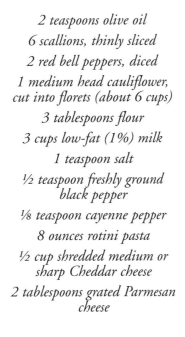

2 teaspoons olive oil

6 scallions, thinly sliced

2 red bell peppers, diced

1 medium head cauliflower, cut into florets (about 6 cups)

3 tablespoons flour

3 cups low-fat (1%) milk

1 teaspoon salt

½ teaspoon freshly ground black pepper

⅛ teaspoon cayenne pepper

8 ounces rotini pasta

½ cup shredded medium or sharp Cheddar cheese

2 tablespoons grated Parmesan cheese

1. In a large nonstick skillet, heat the oil until hot but not smoking over medium heat. Add the scallions and cook, stirring frequently, until the scallions are tender, about 4 minutes. Stir in the bell peppers and cauliflower and cook, stirring frequently, until the cauliflower is lightly browned, about 5 minutes.

2. Add the flour and cook, stirring constantly, until the vegetables are well coated, about 1 minute. Gradually stir in the milk. Stir in the salt, black pepper, and cayenne, reduce the heat to low, and cook until the mixture is slightly thickened and the vegetables are tender, about 5 minutes longer.

3. Meanwhile, in a large pot of boiling water, cook the pasta until just tender. Drain well. Add the pasta to the sauce and toss well to coat. Stir in the Cheddar and Parmesan and cook until the cheese is just melted, about 1 minute longer. Divide the pasta mixture among 4 shallow bowls and serve.

Helpful hints: You can substitute broccoli for the cauliflower, yellow or green bell peppers for the red, and shredded mozzarella or Monterey jack for the Cheddar. Radiatore or farfalle (bow-tie) pasta would be equally appropriate with this sauce.

FAT: 11G/22%
CALORIES: 451
SATURATED FAT: 5.1G
CARBOHYDRATE: 67G
PROTEIN: 22G
CHOLESTEROL: 24MG
SODIUM: 807MG

VEGETABLE AGLIATA

SERVES: 4
WORKING TIME: 35 MINUTES
TOTAL TIME: 35 MINUTES

10 ounces shaped pasta, such as radiatore, farfalle (bow ties), or orecchiette

2 teaspoons olive oil

8 cloves garlic, minced

½ cup reduced-sodium chicken broth, defatted

1 cup jarred roasted red peppers, rinsed and drained

2 tablespoons no-salt-added tomato paste

1 tablespoon walnuts

1 teaspoon chili powder

⅛ teaspoon cayenne pepper

1 zucchini, quartered lengthwise and thinly sliced

1 yellow summer squash, quartered lengthwise and thinly sliced

½ cup evaporated skimmed milk

½ teaspoon salt

¼ cup chopped fresh parsley

1. In a large pot of boiling water, cook the pasta until just tender. Drain well.

2. Meanwhile, in a large nonstick skillet, heat 1 teaspoon of the oil until hot but not smoking over medium heat. Add the garlic, stirring to coat. Add the broth, cover, and cook, stirring occasionally, until the garlic is very tender, about 7 minutes. Transfer the broth mixture to a food processor along with the roasted peppers, tomato paste, walnuts, chili powder, and cayenne and process to a smooth purée.

3. In a medium skillet, heat the remaining 1 teaspoon oil until hot but not smoking over medium heat. Add the zucchini and yellow squash and cook, stirring frequently, until lightly browned and crisp-tender, about 4 minutes. Stir in the red pepper-garlic purée, the evaporated milk, and salt and bring to a boil. Reduce to a simmer and cook, stirring, until the zucchini and yellow squash are tender and the sauce is richly flavored, about 4 minutes. Toss the sauce with the hot pasta and 2 tablespoons of the parsley. Divide among 4 plates, sprinkle the remaining 2 tablespoons parsley over, and serve.

Helpful hint: You could make the roasted-pepper purée up to 8 hours in advance. Refrigerate it in a tightly closed jar so that the garlic aroma does not permeate other foods in the refrigerator.

FAT: 5G/12%
CALORIES: 367
SATURATED FAT: 0.6G
CARBOHYDRATE: 66G
PROTEIN: 14G
CHOLESTEROL: 1MG
SODIUM: 474MG

Agliata means "garlic sauce." Our interpretation is a delicious red pepper-walnut cream sauce with fresh vegetables.

Peasant dishes are typically based on grains and vegetables, with small amounts of meat or cheese as flavorings. These healthy proportions are reflected in this rustic Italian meal: The hearty pasta and lentils are accented with touches of pancetta and Parmesan. Serve a lettuce and tomato salad with balsamic-vinegar dressing alongside.

SHELLS WITH HERBED LENTIL SAUCE

SERVES: 4
WORKING TIME: 20 MINUTES
TOTAL TIME: 50 MINUTES

1 teaspoon olive oil

3 tablespoons finely chopped pancetta or Canadian bacon (1 ounce)

1 large onion, finely chopped

2 cloves garlic, minced

1 large red bell pepper, diced

1 large carrot, halved lengthwise and thinly sliced

¾ cup lentils, rinsed and picked over

1¼ cups reduced-sodium chicken broth, defatted

½ teaspoon dried oregano

¼ teaspoon dried rosemary

¾ teaspoon salt

¼ teaspoon freshly ground black pepper

10 ounces medium pasta shells

¼ cup grated Parmesan cheese

⅓ cup chopped fresh parsley

2 teaspoons unsalted butter

1. In a medium nonstick saucepan, heat the oil until hot but not smoking over medium heat. Add the pancetta and cook until lightly crisped, about 1 minute. Add the onion and garlic and cook, stirring frequently, until the onions are softened, about 7 minutes.

2. Add the bell pepper and carrot to the pan and cook, stirring frequently, until tender, about 5 minutes. Stir in the lentils, broth, ½ cup of water, the oregano, rosemary, salt, and black pepper and bring to a boil. Reduce to a simmer, cover, and cook until the lentils are tender and most of the liquid has been absorbed, about 20 minutes (see tip).

3. Meanwhile, in a large pot of boiling water, cook the shells until just tender. Drain well. Transfer to a large bowl, add the lentil mixture, Parmesan, parsley, and butter. Toss well, divide among 4 plates, and serve.

Helpful hint: Although packaged lentils are usually quite clean, it's a good idea to look them over before cooking them. Pick out and discard any discolored lentils or bits of dirt, rinse thoroughly under cold running water, and drain.

FAT: 7G/13%
CALORIES: 495
SATURATED FAT: 2.7G
CARBOHYDRATE: 84G
PROTEIN: 25G
CHOLESTEROL: 13MG
SODIUM: 828MG

TIP

The lentils should be cooked in a bit more liquid than they will eventually absorb. When they are done, all of the lentils at the top of the pot will seem dry, but there will still be some liquid at the bottom of the pot. The extra liquid, which has a meaty richness from the lentils, combines with the Parmesan, parsley, and butter to create a delicious sauce.

PASTA SALADS

Left, Chinese Pasta Salad with Shredded Chicken.
Above, Mediterranean Pasta Salad.

CHICKEN NOODLE SALAD

SERVES: 4
WORKING TIME: 20 MINUTES
TOTAL TIME: 30 MINUTES

You loved it as a soup, now try it as a salad! Not surprisingly, the combination of tender chicken and ribbony pasta works as well in a main-course salad as in does in a heart-warming soup. All the familiar touches are here: carrots, peas, fresh dill, and—as in the best homemade chicken soup—subtle hints of lemon and ginger.

8 ounces fettuccine

1½ cups reduced-sodium chicken broth, defatted

¼ teaspoon freshly ground black pepper

¼ teaspoon ground ginger

¾ pound skinless, boneless chicken breasts

2 carrots, halved lengthwise and thinly sliced

1 cup frozen peas

⅓ cup reduced-fat sour cream

2 tablespoons reduced-fat mayonnaise

½ teaspoon grated lemon zest

1 tablespoon fresh lemon juice

⅓ cup snipped fresh dill

½ teaspoon salt

2 ribs celery, halved lengthwise and thinly sliced

1. In a large pot of boiling water, cook the fettuccine until just tender. Drain well.

2. Meanwhile, in a large skillet, bring the broth, pepper, and ginger to a boil over medium heat. Reduce to a simmer, add the chicken, cover, and cook, turning once, until the chicken is cooked through, about 10 minutes. Add the carrots for the last 2 minutes of cooking time. Add the peas to the skillet and remove from the heat. Reserving the cooking liquid, drain the chicken and vegetables. When the chicken is cool enough to handle, cut it into ½-inch cubes.

3. In a large bowl, combine ½ cup of the reserved cooking liquid, the sour cream, mayonnaise, lemon zest, lemon juice, dill, and salt. Add the pasta, chicken, carrots, peas, and celery, tossing to combine. Serve at room temperature or chilled.

Helpful hint: You can cook the chicken and vegetables up to 12 hours in advance; refrigerate them in the broth rather than draining them right after cooking.

FAT: 8G/17%
CALORIES: 415
SATURATED FAT: 2.4G
CARBOHYDRATE: 54G
PROTEIN: 32G
CHOLESTEROL: 110MG
SODIUM: 554MG

Garlic is a multi-purpose ingredient in this salad. Of course, it contributes its popular pungent flavor (tempered somewhat by roasting on the grill), but it also serves to thicken the dressing in place of higher-fat ingredients. The basil-garlic vinaigrette coats a medley of radiatore pasta, squash, bell pepper, eggplant, tomatoes, and green olives.

PASTA-VEGETABLE SALAD WITH GARLIC DRESSING

SERVES: 4
WORKING TIME: 40 MINUTES
TOTAL TIME: 40 MINUTES

8 ounces radiatore pasta

9-ounce package frozen artichoke hearts, thawed

6 cloves garlic

¾ cup reduced-sodium chicken broth, defatted

3 tablespoons red wine vinegar

2 scallions, cut into 1-inch lengths

¼ cup chopped fresh basil

1½ tablespoons olive oil

¾ teaspoon salt

2 yellow summer squash, halved lengthwise

1 green bell pepper, seeded and halved lengthwise

1 eggplant (1 pound), peeled and cut lengthwise into ¾-inch pieces

8 plum tomatoes (1 pound total), halved lengthwise

¼ cup chopped pitted green olives

1 ounce shaved Parmesan, or ¼ cup grated Parmesan cheese

1. In a large pot of boiling water, cook the pasta until just tender. Add the artichokes for the last 6 minutes of cooking time. Drain and rinse under cold running water. Place in a large bowl.

2. Meanwhile, preheat the grill (with a grill topper, if possible). Wrap the garlic in foil. In a small bowl, combine the broth and vinegar. Set aside ¼ cup of the broth mixture to use as a baste. Place the remaining broth mixture in a food processor or blender along with the scallions, basil, oil, and salt; set the mixture aside in the processor bowl (or blender container).

3. Spray the rack (or grill topper)—off the grill—with nonstick cooking spray. Place the garlic, squash, bell pepper, and eggplant on the grill. Cover and grill at medium, or 6 inches from the heat, turning occasionally and basting with the reserved basting mixture, for 12 to 14 minutes, or until the vegetables are tender but not falling apart. Place the tomatoes (skin-sides down) on the grill for the last 6 minutes of cooking time.

4. Cut the vegetables into bite-size pieces and add to the bowl with the pasta and artichokes. Squeeze the garlic flesh from the grilled garlic cloves (see tip), add them to the food processor, and process the dressing to a smooth purée. Add the dressing and the olives to the bowl, tossing to coat. Divide among 4 plates, top with the Parmesan, and serve warm or at room temperature.

Unwrap the grilled garlic cloves, then snip off the tip of each clove and squeeze out the roasted garlic, discarding the skin.

FAT: 10G/23%
CALORIES: 396
SATURATED FAT: 2G
CARBOHYDRATE: 66G
PROTEIN: 15G
CHOLESTEROL: 4MG
SODIUM: 866MG

ASIAN-STYLE SCALLOP SALAD

SERVES: 4
WORKING TIME: 15 MINUTES
TOTAL TIME: 35 MINUTES

Poached scallops in a nest of noodles retain their delicate flavor when bathed in a light Japanese-style dressing made with soy sauce, wine vinegar, and sesame oil. We've used vermicelli (very thin spaghetti) instead of Japanese noodles. If you like to experiment, make the dish with Japanese soba, which are thin, buff-colored noodles made with buckwheat flour.

8 ounces vermicelli pasta

2 carrots, cut into 2 x ¼-inch julienne strips

1 red bell pepper, cut into 2-inch julienne strips

½ cup bottled clam juice, or reduced-sodium chicken broth, defatted

2 tablespoons minced fresh ginger

1 clove garlic, minced

1 pound sea scallops, halved

¼ cup reduced-sodium soy sauce

3 tablespoons white wine vinegar

1 tablespoon dark Oriental sesame oil

2 teaspoons Dijon mustard

8-ounce can sliced water chestnuts, drained

1 cup julienne-cut scallions

1 tablespoon sesame seeds, toasted

1. In a large pot of boiling water, cook the pasta until just tender. Add the carrots and bell pepper during the last 1 minute of cooking time. Drain well.

2. Meanwhile, in a medium saucepan, combine the clam juice, 1 tablespoon of the ginger, and the garlic. Bring to a boil over medium heat and add the scallops. Return to a boil and cook until the scallops are just opaque throughout, about 3 minutes. Drain, reserving ⅓ cup of the cooking liquid.

3. In a large bowl, combine the reserved cooking liquid, the soy sauce, vinegar, sesame oil, mustard, and the remaining 1 tablespoon ginger. Add the pasta, carrots, bell pepper, scallops, water chestnuts, and scallions, tossing to coat thoroughly. Divide the salad among 4 plates, sprinkle with the sesame seeds, and serve at room temperature or chilled.

Helpful hint: Toast the sesame seeds in a dry skillet over medium heat: Cook, stirring, for 2 to 3 minutes, until the seeds are golden brown.

FAT: 6G/13%
CALORIES: 416
SATURATED FAT: 0.9G
CARBOHYDRATE: 59G
PROTEIN: 29G
CHOLESTEROL: 38MG
SODIUM: 911MG

SPICY ITALIAN SHRIMP SALAD

SERVES: 4
WORKING TIME: 30 MINUTES
TOTAL TIME: 30 MINUTES

This pasta salad is made pretty much the same way as you would prepare a hot tomato-sauced pasta; however, the sauce is a real quickie rather than a recipe that requires all-day simmering. You can substitute another tube-shaped pasta for the ziti. Penne and elbow macaroni would both work well. Serve the salad with a hearty whole-grain Italian peasant loaf.

8 ounces ziti pasta

1 tablespoon olive oil

3 cloves garlic, minced

2 pickled jalapeños, finely chopped

1 pound medium shrimp, shelled and deveined

⅔ cup bottled clam juice, or reduced-sodium chicken broth, defatted

2 cups no-salt-added canned tomatoes, chopped with their juices

1 teaspoon dried tarragon

¾ teaspoon salt

1 teaspoon cornstarch mixed with 1 tablespoon water

3 ribs celery, halved lengthwise and thinly sliced

1 cucumber, peeled, halved lengthwise, seeded, and cut into ¼-inch dice

½ cup chopped fresh parsley

1. In a large pot of boiling water, cook the pasta until just tender. Drain well.

2. Meanwhile, in a large nonstick skillet, heat the oil until hot but not smoking over medium heat. Add the garlic and jalapeños and cook, stirring frequently, until the garlic is softened, about 3 minutes. Add the shrimp and cook, stirring frequently, until the shrimp are just opaque, about 3 minutes. With a slotted spoon, transfer the shrimp to a plate and when cool enough to handle, halve crosswise.

3. Add the clam juice to the skillet, increase the heat to high, and cook, stirring frequently, until reduced to ½ cup, about 3 minutes. Add the tomatoes, tarragon, and salt. Bring to a boil and cook for 2 minutes, stirring frequently. Add the cornstarch mixture and cook, stirring, until slightly thickened, about 1 minute.

4. Transfer the tomato mixture to a large bowl and add the pasta, shrimp, celery, cucumber, and parsley, tossing well. Serve warm, at room temperature, or chilled.

Helpful hint: For added Italian flavor, you can substitute 1 cup of chopped fresh fennel for the celery.

FAT: 6G/14%
CALORIES: 386
SATURATED FAT: 0.9G
CARBOHYDRATE: 54G
PROTEIN: 28G
CHOLESTEROL: 140MG
SODIUM: 797MG

Dishes called "lo mein" traditionally consist of noodles that have been stir-fried, then combined with vegetables, meat, or seafood, and a savory sauce. Frying the noodles adds quite a bit of fat, so we've eliminated that step. In our version, pasta is tossed with juicy broiled beef strips and a sesame-peanut dressing with a delicious gingery kick.

BEEF LO MEIN SALAD

SERVES: 4
WORKING TIME: 25 MINUTES
TOTAL TIME: 35 MINUTES

8 ounces linguine or spaghetti

3-inch piece fresh ginger

3 tablespoons reduced-sodium soy sauce

2 tablespoons rice vinegar

4 teaspoons dark Oriental sesame oil

1 tablespoon honey

2 teaspoons creamy peanut butter

½ teaspoon salt

¼ teaspoon cayenne pepper

1 yellow bell pepper, cut into ¼-inch-wide strips

1 red bell pepper, cut into ¼-inch-wide strips

1 cucumber, peeled, halved lengthwise, seeded, and cut into 2 x ¼-inch strips

2 scallions, thinly sliced

¼ cup chopped fresh cilantro or parsley

10 ounces well-trimmed top round of beef

1. In a large pot of boiling water, cook the pasta until just tender. Drain well.

2. Meanwhile, preheat the broiler. Grate the ginger into a small bowl (see tip, top photo). Squeeze the ginger to extract as much ginger juice as possible (bottom photo), discarding the solids; you should have about 2 tablespoons of juice. Transfer the ginger juice to a large bowl. Whisk in the soy sauce, vinegar, sesame oil, honey, peanut butter, salt, and cayenne until smooth. Stir in the bell peppers, cucumber, scallions, and cilantro. Add the pasta, tossing well to combine.

3. Broil the beef 6 inches from the heat for about 4 minutes per side, or until medium-rare. Place the beef on a plate and let it stand for 10 minutes. Thinly slice the beef on the diagonal, reserving any juices on the plate. Transfer the beef and juices to the bowl with the pasta, tossing to combine. Serve warm, at room temperature, or chilled.

Helpful hint: If you have a cutting board with a channel or lip to collect the juices, you can transfer the beef to your cutting board, rather than a plate, to let it stand for 10 minutes before slicing.

FAT: 9G/20%
CALORIES: 402
SATURATED FAT: 1.8G
CARBOHYDRATE: 54G
PROTEIN: 26G
CHOLESTEROL: 40MG
SODIUM: 783MG

TIP

To make ginger juice, grate the unpeeled fresh ginger on the fine side of a grater. Then scoop up a palm-size amount of the ginger and squeeze it—first in the palm of your hand, then between your fingers—to release the juice.

PASTA-CHEESE SALAD WITH SUN-DRIED TOMATOES

SERVES: 4
WORKING TIME: 20 MINUTES
TOTAL TIME: 30 MINUTES

The modernization of the macaroni salad required a change of pasta (to thimble-shaped ditalini), a nutritional boost (we added broccoli and raisins), and a flavor makeover (accomplished with sun-dried tomatoes, Parmesan, garlic, and fresh basil). The result is quite a spiffy update of good old macaroni with mayonnaise!

¼ cup (not oil-packed) sun-dried tomatoes
3 cloves garlic, peeled
10 ounces ditalini pasta
3 cups broccoli florets
⅔ cup part-skim ricotta cheese
⅓ cup low-fat (1%) cottage cheese
⅔ cup low-fat (1%) milk
¼ cup grated Parmesan cheese
2 teaspoons olive oil
½ teaspoon salt
¼ teaspoon freshly ground black pepper
½ cup raisins
⅓ cup chopped fresh basil
¼ cup coarsely chopped pecans

1. In a large pot of boiling water, cook the sun-dried tomatoes for about 5 minutes to soften. Add the garlic for the last 2 minutes of cooking. With a slotted spoon, remove the sun-dried tomatoes and garlic. When the sun-dried tomatoes are cool enough to handle, coarsely chop them.

2. Add the pasta to the boiling water and cook until just tender. Add the broccoli during the last 2 minutes of cooking time. Drain. Rinse under cold water, drain again.

3. In a food processor, combine the blanched garlic, ricotta, cottage cheese, milk, Parmesan, oil, salt, and pepper and process to a smooth purée. Transfer the purée to a large bowl, fold in the sun-dried tomatoes, raisins, basil, pecans, broccoli, and pasta. Divide among 4 plates and serve.

Helpful hint: This salad is best served warm or at room temperature; you can refrigerate it for an hour or so, but longer chilling will cause the dressing to thicken, changing the texture of the salad.

FAT: 14G/23%
CALORIES: 545
SATURATED FAT: 4.3G
CARBOHYDRATE: 83G
PROTEIN: 25G
CHOLESTEROL: 19MG
SODIUM: 569MG

SHRIMP AND ORZO SALAD

SERVES: 4
WORKING TIME: 20 MINUTES
TOTAL TIME: 25 MINUTES

*O*rzo *has a tendency to absorb flavors, and is well placed in this unique salad with seasoned shrimp and a spicy lemon dressing.*

12 ounces orzo pasta
3 ribs celery, thinly sliced
3 cloves garlic, peeled
3 thin slices fresh ginger
1 carrot, thinly sliced
1 small yellow onion, sliced
1 bay leaf
8 black peppercorns
10 ounces medium shrimp, shelled and deveined
½ cup fresh lemon juice
3 tablespoons olive oil
1 tablespoon grated lemon zest
1 teaspoon salt
¾ teaspoon allspice
½ teaspoon freshly ground black pepper
½ teaspoon hot pepper sauce
1 small red onion, diced
1 yellow summer squash, halved lengthwise and cut into thin slices
½ cup snipped fresh dill
12 green-leaf lettuce leaves

1. Heat a large pot of water to boiling, and cook the orzo until just tender. Drain well.

2. Meanwhile, in a large saucepan, combine 1 rib of the celery, the garlic, ginger, carrot, yellow onion, bay leaf, peppercorns, and 3 cups of water. Bring to a boil over high heat and cook for 5 minutes. Reduce to a simmer, add the shrimp, and cook until the shrimp are just opaque, about 3 minutes. With a slotted spoon, transfer the shrimp to a cutting board. Strain the cooking liquid, discarding the solids. Reserve ½ cup of the cooking liquid. Cut each shrimp in half lengthwise.

3. In a large bowl, whisk together the lemon juice, oil, zest, salt, allspice, pepper, pepper sauce, and the reserved ½ cup cooking liquid. Stir in the remaining 2 ribs celery, the red onion, squash, dill, and shrimp. Add the orzo and toss to combine. Serve immediately, or cover and refrigerate for up to 4 hours. May be served chilled or at room temperature. Place the lettuce on 4 plates, place the shrimp and orzo salad on top, and serve.

Suggested accompaniments: Toasted pita bread wedges and, for dessert, fat-free chewy fig cookies served with cappuccino.

FAT: 13G/22%
CALORIES: 524
SATURATED FAT: 1.8G
CARBOHYDRATE: 78G
PROTEIN: 25G
CHOLESTEROL: 87MG
SODIUM: 697MG

PASTA WHEEL SALAD MEXICANA

SERVES: 4
WORKING TIME: 15 MINUTES
TOTAL TIME: 20 MINUTES

1 cup frozen corn kernels

8 ounces ruote (wagon wheel) pasta

¼ cup fresh lime juice

1 tablespoon olive oil

1 teaspoon grated lime zest

1 teaspoon minced jalapeño pepper (use gloves)

½ teaspoon ground cumin

½ teaspoon salt

¾ pound plum tomatoes (about 3), diced

¾ cup diced mango

⅔ cup diced avocado

⅔ cup thinly sliced scallions

⅓ cup chopped fresh cilantro or parsley

1. Heat a large pot of water to boiling, and blanch the corn in the boiling water for 30 seconds. Reserve the water for the pasta and, with a slotted spoon, transfer the corn to a colander to drain. Cook the ruote in the reserved boiling water until just tender. Drain well.

2. Meanwhile, in a large serving bowl, whisk together the lime juice, oil, zest, jalapeño, cumin, and salt. Stir in the corn, tomatoes, mango, avocado, scallions, and cilantro. Add the ruote, toss gently to combine, and serve.

Suggested accompaniment: Chunks of cantaloupe and honeydew melon tossed with lime juice and brown sugar for dessert.

FAT: 9G/22%
CALORIES: 371
SATURATED FAT: 1.4G
CARBOHYDRATE: 65G
PROTEIN: 10G
CHOLESTEROL: 0MG
SODIUM: 293MG

This refreshing pasta salad, sharpened with tangy lime juice and accented with avocado, is a snap to prepare.

Picnic planners, take note: This snappy-tasting macaroni salad puts the bland original in the shade, and is no mere side dish but a meal in itself. The macaroni is tossed with turkey, corn, and cubed tomato; the robust dressing is made with tomato-vegetable juice and balsamic vinegar. And once the pasta's cooked, the salad is a simple one-bowl proposition.

SUMMER TURKEY SALAD

SERVES: 4
WORKING TIME: 15 MINUTES
TOTAL TIME: 25 MINUTES

4 ounces elbow macaroni

½ cup low-sodium tomato-
vegetable juice

2 tablespoons balsamic vinegar

2 tablespoons olive oil, preferably
extra-virgin

1 tablespoon no-salt-added
tomato paste

½ teaspoon dried oregano

½ teaspoon salt

¼ teaspoon freshly ground black
pepper

¾ pound cooked turkey breast
(see tip), cut into 2 x ½-inch
julienne strips

2 cups frozen corn kernels,
thawed

1 tomato, cut into ½-inch cubes

4 scallions, thinly sliced

⅓ cup chopped fresh parsley

1. In a large pot of boiling water, cook the pasta until just tender. Drain well.

2. In a large bowl, whisk together the tomato-vegetable juice, vinegar, oil, tomato paste, oregano, salt, and pepper. Add the pasta, turkey, corn, tomato, scallions, and parsley, tossing well to combine. Serve at room temperature or chilled.

Helpful hint: Tomato-vegetable juice comes in big bottles, but it's also sold in six-packs of 6-ounce cans—a useful size for recipes. Tomato-vegetable juice is also a refreshing, low-calorie snack.

FAT: 9G/21%
CALORIES: 378
SATURATED FAT: 1.4G
CARBOHYDRATE: 44G
PROTEIN: 33G
CHOLESTEROL: 71MG
SODIUM: 354MG

TIP

You can buy cooked turkey breast for this recipe, or poach turkey cutlets yourself using the following method: Bring 2 cups of water or broth to a boil in a large skillet over medium heat. Reduce to a simmer, add 1 pound of turkey breast cutlets, and cook, turning once, until the turkey is cooked through, 3 to 4 minutes.

Vegetable Pasta Salad

SERVES: 4
WORKING TIME: 15 MINUTES
TOTAL TIME: 25 MINUTES

Perfect for the winter months, this pasta salad, lightly dressed in a tangy herbed Dijon mustard vinaigrette, takes advantage of frozen vegetables as well as potatoes and carrots. It would also be delicious with sweet potatoes in place of the red potatoes, and rotini could be substituted for the shells.

10 ounces medium pasta shells

½ pound small red potatoes, cut into ½-inch chunks

10-ounce package frozen artichoke hearts, thawed and halved

1 bay leaf

¼ teaspoon red pepper flakes

2 carrots, quartered lengthwise and cut into ¼-inch pieces

½ cup frozen peas

3 tablespoons red wine vinegar

3 tablespoons Dijon mustard

2 tablespoons olive oil

½ teaspoon salt

¼ cup snipped fresh chives or finely chopped scallions

2 tablespoons chopped fresh parsley

1 teaspoon dried tarragon

1. Heat a large pot of water to boiling, and cook the pasta shells until just tender. Drain well.

2. Meanwhile, in a large skillet, combine the potatoes, artichoke hearts, bay leaf, pepper flakes, and 2 cups of water. Bring to a boil over high heat and reduce to a simmer. Cover and cook until the potatoes and artichokes are almost tender, about 8 minutes. Add the carrots, cover, and cook until the carrots are almost tender, about 3 minutes. Add the peas and cook, uncovered, until the vegetables are tender, about 1 minute longer. Drain the vegetables, reserving ¾ cup of the cooking liquid. Discard the bay leaf.

3. In a large bowl, whisk together the vinegar, mustard, oil, salt, and reserved ¾ cup cooking liquid. Whisk in the chives, parsley, and tarragon. Gently stir in the vegetable mixture. Add the pasta shells and toss to combine. Serve immediately, or cover and refrigerate for up to 8 hours. May be served chilled or at room temperature. Spoon the vegetable pasta salad into 4 bowls and serve.

Suggested accompaniments: Canned sliced beets topped with nonfat sour cream. For dessert, part-skim ricotta cheese puréed and mixed with chopped candied orange peel and a little grated semisweet chocolate, then layered between thin slices of sponge cake.

FAT: 9G/18%
CALORIES: 439
SATURATED FAT: 1.3G
CARBOHYDRATE: 77G
PROTEIN: 14G
CHOLESTEROL: 0MG
SODIUM: 497MG

PENNE CAPRESE

SERVES: 4
WORKING TIME: 10 MINUTES
TOTAL TIME: 20 MINUTES

Using just a few plump Calamata olives lends a mellow richness to this fresh-tasting combination of ripe tomatoes, pasta, mild cheese, and herbs— without adding excessive fat. French Niçoise olives would be another good choice. For a stronger flavored cheese, try Greek feta. And for an alternate pasta shape, use ziti or medium shells instead of the penne.

12 ounces penne pasta

2 teaspoons olive oil

3 cloves garlic, minced

1 pound plum tomatoes (about 4), coarsely chopped

½ cup diced cucumber

⅓ cup diced red onion

3 tablespoons chopped fresh basil

3 tablespoons chopped fresh parsley

½ teaspoon dried tarragon

½ teaspoon salt

6 ounces part-skim mozzarella cheese, diced (about 1½ cups)

¼ cup coarsely chopped, pitted brine-cured black olives (such as Calamata)

1. Heat a large pot of water to boiling, and cook the penne until just tender. Drain well.

2. Meanwhile, in a small nonstick skillet, heat the oil until hot but not smoking over low heat. Add the garlic and cook, stirring frequently, until tender, about 4 minutes. Transfer the garlic and oil to a large bowl. Add the tomatoes, cucumber, onion, basil, parsley, tarragon, and salt and toss to coat. Stir in the mozzarella and olives.

3. Add the penne and toss to combine. Serve immediately, or cover and refrigerate for up to 4 hours. May be served chilled or at room temperature. Spoon the penne salad into 4 bowls and serve.

FAT: 12G/22%
CALORIES: 491
SATURATED FAT: 4.9G
CARBOHYDRATE: 74G
PROTEIN: 23G
CHOLESTEROL: 25MG
SODIUM: 565MG

SHRIMP AND ROTINI WITH PINEAPPLE SALSA

SERVES: 4
WORKING TIME: 20 MINUTES
TOTAL TIME: 25 MINUTES

8 ounces rotini pasta

1 pound small shrimp, shelled and deveined

½ teaspoon salt

½ teaspoon freshly ground black pepper

½ teaspoon ground ginger

20-ounce can pineapple chunks in unsweetened juice

1 red bell pepper, finely diced

1 green bell pepper, finely diced

1 large red onion, finely diced

3 tablespoons fresh lemon juice

2 tablespoons olive oil

2 tablespoons low-sodium ketchup

1 tablespoon honey

1. Heat a large pot of water to boiling, and cook the rotini until just tender. Drain well.

2. Meanwhile, in a shallow bowl, combine the shrimp, ¼ teaspoon of the salt, ¼ teaspoon of the black pepper, and ¼ teaspoon of the ginger and toss to coat. Let stand for 10 minutes.

3. Preheat the broiler. Drain the pineapple, reserving ¼ cup of the juice. In a large serving bowl, combine the pineapple, reserved ¼ cup juice, bell peppers, onion, lemon juice, oil, ketchup, honey, remaining ¼ teaspoon salt, remaining ¼ teaspoon black pepper, and remaining ¼ teaspoon ginger and stir to blend.

4. Place the shrimp on the broiler rack and broil 4 inches from the heat for about 2 minutes, or until the shrimp are just opaque and the edges are lightly browned. Add the shrimp and rotini to the pineapple mixture, toss to combine, and serve.

Suggested accompaniments: Crusty rolls and, for dessert, reduced-calorie vanilla pudding layered in parfait glasses with toasted coconut.

FAT: 10G/18%
CALORIES: 509
SATURATED FAT: 1.4G
CARBOHYDRATE: 79G
PROTEIN: 28G
CHOLESTEROL: 140MG
SODIUM: 479MG

384

The liveliness of salsa marries well with pasta and tender broiled shrimp in this Caribbean-inspired specialty. This is one pasta salad that is at its flavorful best if served soon after preparation. For a tasty variation, weather permitting, grill the shrimp as well as the bell peppers for the salsa, peeling off the blackened skin of the peppers.

ASIAN-STYLE GRILLED VEGETABLE SALAD

SERVES: 4
WORKING TIME: 40 MINUTES
TOTAL TIME: 40 MINUTES PLUS MARINATING TIME

1 small head Napa cabbage (¾ pound), trimmed and quartered lengthwise

¼ cup reduced-sodium soy sauce

¼ cup chili sauce

¼ cup reduced-sodium vegetable broth

3 tablespoons fresh lime juice

2 tablespoons grated fresh ginger

1 clove garlic, minced

4 teaspoons dark Oriental sesame oil

1 pound firm, low-fat tofu, cut into 2 large pieces

½ pound asparagus, ends trimmed

1 red bell pepper, cut into quarters

6 scallions, trimmed

8 ounces linguine

1. In a large pot of boiling water, cook the Napa cabbage for 1 minute to blanch. Drain well. In a large bowl, combine the soy sauce, chili sauce, broth, lime juice, ginger, garlic, and sesame oil, whisking until well blended. Add the blanched cabbage, tofu, asparagus, bell pepper, and scallions. Toss the vegetables in the marinade to coat thoroughly and refrigerate for at least 1 hour or up to 12 hours.

2. In a large pot of boiling water, cook the linguine until just tender. Drain well.

3. Meanwhile, preheat the grill (with a grill topper, if possible). Spray the rack (or grill topper)—off the grill—with nonstick cooking spray. Reserving the marinade, transfer the vegetables and tofu to the grill and cover. Grill at medium, or 6 inches from the heat, turning once and basting with some of the reserved marinade, for 10 to 12 minutes, or until the vegetables are crisp-tender. When they are cool enough to handle, cut the vegetables and tofu into bite-size pieces.

4. Transfer the remaining marinade to a bowl. Add the linguine, grilled vegetables, and tofu, tossing to combine. Divide among 4 plates and serve.

Helpful hint: Napa, a Chinese cabbage, comes in a compact oblong head. The leaves are a greenish-cream color with delicately frilled edges.

FAT: 5G/14%
CALORIES: 325
SATURATED FAT: 0.7G
CARBOHYDRATE: 57G
PROTEIN: 14G
CHOLESTEROL: 0MG
SODIUM: 951MG

You can practically see the vibrant flavors in this delectable warm pasta salad. Asparagus, Napa cabbage, bell pepper, scallions, and tofu, marinated in a pungent Asian-inspired sauce, are grilled and then tossed with linguine. The rest of the marinade—a lively blend of chili sauce, soy sauce, sesame oil, lime juice, ginger, and garlic—serves as the salad dressing.

The sunny flavors of tomatoes, fresh orange, and ginger make this salad a sensational winter meal. If you can't find good-quality fresh basil (which is now available year round), substitute a pinch of dried basil and oregano. Garnish the salad with celery leaves and thin orange slices, cut into quarters.

ROTINI SALAD WITH BASIL, PARSLEY, AND MOZZARELLA

SERVES: 4
WORKING TIME: 15 MINUTES
TOTAL TIME: 30 MINUTES

10 ounces rotini pasta

2 cups canned crushed tomatoes

½ cup orange juice

2 cloves garlic, minced

3 tablespoons chopped fresh basil

¾ teaspoon grated orange zest

¾ teaspoon ground ginger

½ teaspoon salt

¼ teaspoon freshly ground black pepper

2 teaspoons olive oil

6 ounces part-skim mozzarella cheese, diced (about 1½ cups)

1 cup thinly sliced celery

1 cup diced orange segments (see tip)

2 tablespoons chopped fresh parsley

1. Heat a large pot of water to boiling, and cook the rotini until just tender. Drain well.

2. Meanwhile, in a medium saucepan, combine the tomatoes, orange juice, garlic, basil, zest, ginger, salt, and pepper. Bring to a boil over high heat and reduce to a simmer. Cover and cook until the garlic is tender and the flavors have blended, about 5 minutes. Remove from the heat and stir in the oil. Transfer the tomato mixture to a large serving bowl. Cool to room temperature.

3. Add the rotini and toss to combine. Add the mozzarella, celery, orange, and parsley and toss again. Serve immediately, or cover and refrigerate for up to 4 hours. May be served chilled or at room temperature. Spoon the rotini salad into 4 bowls and serve.

Suggested accompaniments: Thin bread sticks. Follow with toasted fat-free pound cake slices topped with warm raspberry jam and a few toasted sliced almonds.

TIP

To prepare the orange, remove the peel and, using a small knife, trim away all the bitter white pith. Working over a sieve set over a bowl to catch the juices, cut between the membranes to release the orange segments. Cut the segments crosswise into uniform dice.

FAT: 11G/21%
CALORIES: 462
SATURATED FAT: 4.8G
CARBOHYDRATE: 70G
PROTEIN: 22G
CHOLESTEROL: 25MG
SODIUM: 700MG

CURRIED CHICKEN AND PASTA SALAD

SERVES: 4
WORKING TIME: 15 MINUTES
TOTAL TIME: 25 MINUTES

Fragrant curry powder and turmeric color this pasta salad its characteristic yellow-orange—and fill it with wonderful flavor.

10 ounces elbow macaroni

1 cup reduced-sodium chicken broth, defatted

4 cloves garlic, peeled

½ teaspoon turmeric

¼ teaspoon ground ginger

½ pound skinless, boneless chicken breasts

⅔ cup plain nonfat yogurt

⅓ cup light sour cream

3 tablespoons chopped mango chutney

2 tablespoons fresh lemon juice

2 teaspoons mild curry powder

½ teaspoon salt

2 ribs celery, cut into thin 1-inch-long strips

1 Granny Smith apple, cored and diced

½ cup dark raisins

⅓ cup thinly sliced scallions

1. Heat a large pot of water to boiling, and cook the macaroni until just tender. Drain well.

2. Meanwhile, in a medium skillet, combine the broth, garlic, turmeric, and ginger. Bring to a boil over high heat, add the chicken, and reduce to a simmer. Cover and cook until the chicken is cooked through, about 7 minutes. With a slotted spoon, transfer the chicken to a cutting board. Strain the cooking liquid, discarding the garlic. Reserve ⅔ cup of the cooking liquid. Cut the chicken into ¾-inch chunks.

3. In a large serving bowl, whisk together the yogurt, sour cream, chutney, lemon juice, curry powder, salt, and reserved ⅔ cup cooking liquid. Stir in the celery, apple, raisins, scallions, and chicken. Add the macaroni and toss gently to combine. Serve immediately, or cover and refrigerate for up to 8 hours. May be served chilled or at room temperature.

Suggested accompaniments: Bagel crisps, and chilled stewed prunes topped with a dollop of lemon nonfat yogurt for dessert.

FAT: 5G/9%
CALORIES: 511
SATURATED FAT: 1.8G
CARBOHYDRATE: 89G
PROTEIN: 27G
CHOLESTEROL: 40MG
SODIUM: 659MG

Farfalle and Black Bean Salad

Serves: 4
Working time: 15 minutes
Total time: 25 minutes

8 ounces farfalle (bow-tie) pasta

⅔ cup reduced-sodium chicken broth, defatted

3 cloves garlic, slivered

1½ cups canned black beans, rinsed and drained

½ cup packed fresh cilantro or parsley leaves

3 tablespoons fresh lime juice

2 tablespoons olive oil

1 tablespoon no-salt-added tomato paste

1½ teaspoons dried oregano

¾ teaspoon salt

1 red bell pepper, diced

1 green bell pepper, diced

1 zucchini, diced

⅓ cup diced red onion

12 chicory lettuce leaves

1. Heat a large pot of water to boiling, and cook the farfalle until just tender. Drain well.

2. Meanwhile, in a small saucepan, combine the broth and garlic. Bring to a boil over high heat, reduce to a simmer, and cook until the garlic is tender, about 5 minutes. Transfer the broth mixture to a food processor or blender. Add ¼ cup of the black beans, the cilantro, lime juice, oil, tomato paste, oregano, and salt and purée until smooth.

3. Transfer the purée to a large bowl. Add the remaining 1¼ cups black beans, the bell peppers, zucchini, and onion and toss gently to combine. Add the farfalle and toss again. Place the lettuce on 4 plates, spoon the farfalle salad on top, and serve.

Suggested accompaniments: Sliced tomatoes sprinkled with chopped fresh parsley and a little grated Parmesan cheese. For dessert, cubed fresh pineapple served with nonfat chocolate syrup for dipping.

Fat: 10g/23%
Calories: 383
Saturated Fat: 1.5g
Carbohydrate: 60g
Protein: 15g
Cholesterol: 54mg
Sodium: 745mg

We've puréed black beans with tomato paste and other seasonings to create a zesty low-fat dressing for this salad.

ITALIAN BEEF SALAD

SERVES: 4
WORKING TIME: 30 MINUTES
TOTAL TIME: 30 MINUTES

With its pasta, tomatoes, green beans, and its sassy dressing—a blend of balsamic vinegar, olive oil, and fresh basil—this salad is brimming with Italian character. The broad shavings of cheese that top the salad are another authentic touch: You can cut the Parmesan shavings with a swivel-bladed vegetable peeler or a sharp paring knife.

8 ounces penne pasta

10-ounce package frozen Italian green beans, thawed

4 teaspoons olive oil

¾ pound well-trimmed sirloin, cut into 2 x ¼-inch strips

1 onion, finely chopped

3 cloves garlic, minced

1 carrot, halved lengthwise and thinly sliced

1½ pounds tomatoes, finely chopped

½ cup chopped fresh basil

2 tablespoons balsamic vinegar

½ teaspoon salt

2 ounces shaved Parmesan cheese

1. In a large pot of boiling water, cook the pasta until just tender. Add the green beans during the last 2 minutes of cooking time. Drain well.

2. Meanwhile, in a large nonstick skillet, heat the oil until hot but not smoking over medium heat. Add the beef and cook, stirring frequently, until no longer pink, about 3 minutes. With a slotted spoon, transfer the beef to a plate.

3. Add the onion and garlic to the pan and cook, stirring frequently, until the onion is tender, about 5 minutes. Add the carrot and cook, stirring frequently, until the carrot is crisp-tender, about 4 minutes. Transfer the vegetables to a large bowl and add the tomatoes, basil, vinegar, and salt.

4. Add the pasta, green beans, and beef to the bowl, tossing well to coat. Cool to room temperature, divide evenly among 4 plates, top with the Parmesan, and serve.

Helpful hint: You can make the salad up to 8 hours ahead of time; do not add the shaved Parmesan until just before serving.

FAT: 14G/24%
CALORIES: 521
SATURATED FAT: 4.9G
CARBOHYDRATE: 65G
PROTEIN: 35G
CHOLESTEROL: 63MG
SODIUM: 617MG

SICILIAN-STYLE CHICKEN SALAD

SERVES: 4
WORKING TIME: 20 MINUTES
TOTAL TIME: 30 MINUTES

The time-honored Italian marriage of pasta and tomatoes is the starting point for this multi-flavored salad. Wine vinegar, olive oil, and sage would be at home in Italian dishes from many regions, but the influence of sunny Sicily is clearly indicated through the inclusion of orange juice, fennel, raisins, and pine nuts. Accompany the salad with grissini (pencil-thin bread sticks).

8 ounces farfalle (bow-tie) pasta
¾ pound skinless, boneless chicken breasts
¾ teaspoon salt
½ teaspoon dried sage
½ teaspoon grated orange zest
¾ cup orange juice
3 tablespoons red wine vinegar
2 tablespoons no-salt-added tomato paste
2 tablespoons olive oil, preferably extra-virgin
½ teaspoon cayenne pepper
2 cups thinly sliced fennel or celery
1 cup coarsely chopped tomatoes
¼ cup golden or regular raisins
4 teaspoons pine nuts

1. In a large pot of boiling water, cook the pasta until just tender. Drain well.

2. Meanwhile, preheat the broiler. Sprinkle the chicken with ¼ teaspoon of the salt and the sage. Broil 6 inches from the heat for 4 minutes per side, or until cooked through.

3. In a large bowl, combine the orange zest, orange juice, vinegar, tomato paste, oil, cayenne, and the remaining ½ teaspoon salt. Add the fennel, tomatoes, raisins, and pasta, tossing well to combine. Slice the chicken crosswise on the diagonal into ½-inch slices. Add the chicken to the bowl and toss to combine.

4. Divide the chicken mixture among 4 plates, sprinkle with the pine nuts, and serve at room temperature or chilled.

Helpful hint: Fennel looks like the flattened base of a head of celery; the vegetable has a mild anise flavor. Look for a firm, unblemished fennel bulb; cut off the stalks and trim the root end before slicing it.

FAT: 11G/22%
CALORIES: 456
SATURATED FAT: 1.7G
CARBOHYDRATE: 61G
PROTEIN: 29G
CHOLESTEROL: 49MG
SODIUM: 534MG

PASTA MARINARA SALAD

SERVES: 4
WORKING TIME: 15 MINUTES
TOTAL TIME: 20 MINUTES

mong the most beloved pasta toppings is marinara, a zesty tomato sauce. And here's the easiest marinara you'll ever make—an uncooked version with fresh tomatoes and basil that's puréed in the food processor. Along with the pasta, the sauce dresses crisp asparagus and snow peas, meaty kidney beans, and cubes of mozzarella.

3 cloves garlic, peeled

10 ounces spinach fusilli

1 pound asparagus, tough ends trimmed and cut on the diagonal into 1-inch lengths

½ pound snow peas, strings removed

1 pound tomatoes, quartered

½ cup packed fresh basil leaves

½ cup low-sodium tomato-vegetable juice

2 tablespoons balsamic vinegar

1 tablespoon olive oil

¾ teaspoon salt

19-ounce can red kidney beans, rinsed and drained

6 ounces part-skim mozzarella, cut into ½-inch cubes

1. In a large pot of boiling water, cook the garlic for 2 minutes to blanch. Remove with a slotted spoon. Add the fusilli to the water and cook until tender, adding the asparagus and snow peas during the last 1 minute of cooking time. Drain well.

2. Meanwhile, in a food processor, combine the tomatoes, basil, tomato-vegetable juice, vinegar, oil, salt, and blanched garlic and process to a smooth purée, about 30 seconds.

3. Transfer the dressing to a large bowl and add the kidney beans, mozzarella, pasta, asparagus, and snow peas. Toss well and serve at room temperature or chill for up to 8 hours.

Helpful hint: Spinach pasta, which is colored and flavored with spinach, is actually no more or less nutritious than regular pasta. You can substitute plain fusilli, if you like.

FAT: 13G/20%
CALORIES: 581
SATURATED FAT: 5.1G
CARBOHYDRATE: 86G
PROTEIN: 33G
CHOLESTEROL: 25MG
SODIUM: 841MG

HOT AND TANGY PASTA SALAD WITH SCALLOPS

SERVES: 4
WORKING TIME: 20 MINUTES
TOTAL TIME: 25 MINUTES

10 ounces ziti pasta

2 tablespoons olive oil

3 cloves garlic, minced

6 ounces bay scallops, or sea scallops cut into quarters (see tip)

1¼ cups unsweetened pineapple juice

¼ cup fresh lime or lemon juice

3 tablespoons no-salt-added tomato paste

1¼ teaspoons medium-hot chili powder

½ teaspoon salt

¼ teaspoon red pepper flakes

1 red bell pepper, cut into thin slivers

1 green bell pepper, cut into thin slivers

1 cucumber, peeled, halved lengthwise, seeded, and diced

¼ cup minced red onion

¼ cup chopped fresh parsley

1. Heat a large pot of water to boiling, and cook the ziti until just tender. Drain well.

2. Meanwhile, in a large nonstick skillet, heat 1 tablespoon of the oil until hot but not smoking over low heat. Add the garlic and cook, stirring frequently, until softened, about 3 minutes. Add the scallops, cover, and cook until the scallops are just opaque, about 2 minutes. With a slotted spoon, transfer the scallops to a large serving bowl.

3. Add the pineapple juice, lime juice, tomato paste, remaining 1 tablespoon oil, chili powder, salt, and pepper flakes to the skillet. Bring to a boil over high heat and cook until the mixture is slightly thickened, about 2 minutes. Pour the mixture over the scallops. Add the bell peppers, cucumber, onion, and parsley and toss to combine. Add the ziti, toss again, and serve.

Suggested accompaniments: Thin baguette, and broiled peach halves sprinkled with crumbled gingersnaps for dessert.

FAT: 9G/18%
CALORIES: 443
SATURATED FAT: 1.1G
CARBOHYDRATE: 74G
PROTEIN: 18G
CHOLESTEROL: 14MG
SODIUM: 373MG

Cooking the scallops in their own juices over a low flame keeps them tender, juicy, and succulent. The citrusy dressing, spiked with hot red pepper flakes, partners well with the sweet scallops. For added zip, accompany this salad with lime wedges to bring out maximum flavor. Penne, medium rigatoni, or rotini may stand in for the ziti.

CHICKEN CAPRESE

SERVES: 4
WORKING TIME: 15 MINUTES
TOTAL TIME: 25 MINUTES

The popular Italian appetizer of sliced tomatoes, mozzarella, and basil leaves drizzled with olive oil is properly known as "insalata caprese" (it's named for the island of Capri). We've rounded out this flavor-packed quartet of ingredients with chicken, pasta, and greens for a terrific main course. You can substitute another pasta for the small, tube-shaped ditalini.

5 ounces ditalini pasta or elbow macaroni (about 1¼ cups)

10 ounces skinless, boneless chicken breasts

¾ teaspoon salt

½ teaspoon dried oregano

2 cups cherry tomatoes, halved

½ cup chopped fresh basil

3 ounces part-skim mozzarella, cut into ½-inch cubes

2 tablespoons balsamic vinegar

1 tablespoon olive oil, preferably extra-virgin

4 cups mesclun or mixed greens

1. In a medium pot of boiling water, cook the pasta until just tender. Drain well.

2. Meanwhile, preheat the broiler. Rub the chicken with ¼ teaspoon of the salt and the oregano. Broil 6 inches from the heat for 4 minutes per side, or until just cooked through. Set the chicken aside and when cool enough to handle, cut it into 1-inch pieces.

3. In a large bowl, combine the tomatoes, basil, mozzarella, vinegar, oil, and the remaining ½ teaspoon salt. Add the chicken and pasta, tossing to combine. Place the greens on 4 plates, top with the chicken mixture, and serve at room temperature or chilled.

Helpful hint: For a more colorful salad, use half red cherry tomatoes and half yellow pear tomatoes.

FAT: 10G/29%
CALORIES: 316
SATURATED FAT: 3.6G
CARBOHYDRATE: 31G
PROTEIN: 26G
CHOLESTEROL: 58MG
SODIUM: 553MG

TURKEY-PASTA SALAD WITH PESTO DRESSING

SERVES: 4
WORKING TIME: 30 MINUTES
TOTAL TIME: 35 MINUTES

What a terrific buffet centerpiece this salad would make (and you can easily double the recipe if necessary). The pesto dressing boasts a full, true basil flavor, but is much lower in fat than a traditional pesto. The secret lies in replacing much of the oil with chicken broth—a trick that works with many types of salad dressing.

4 cloves garlic, peeled
8 ounces ziti pasta
3 cups broccoli florets
4 teaspoons olive oil
¾ pound turkey cutlets, cut into
2 x ½-inch strips
¾ cup reduced-sodium chicken
broth, defatted
1½ cups packed fresh basil leaves
½ teaspoon salt
⅓ cup grated Parmesan cheese
1 red bell pepper, cut into
½-inch-wide strips
1 yellow bell pepper, cut into
½-inch-wide strips

1. In a large pot of boiling water, cook the garlic for 2 minutes to blanch. With a slotted spoon, remove the garlic and set aside. Add the ziti to the boiling water and cook until just tender, adding the broccoli for the last 1 minute of cooking time. Drain well.

2. Meanwhile, in a large nonstick skillet, heat 2 teaspoons of the oil until hot but not smoking over medium heat. Add the turkey and cook, stirring frequently, until cooked through, about 4 minutes. With a slotted spoon, transfer the turkey to a plate. Add the broth to the skillet and bring to a boil, scraping up any browned bits that cling to the pan.

3. In a food processor, combine the broth from the skillet, the blanched garlic, basil, salt, and the remaining 2 teaspoons oil and process until smooth, about 1 minute. Transfer to a large bowl and whisk in the Parmesan until well combined. Add the pasta, broccoli, turkey, and bell peppers, stirring to coat. Serve at room temperature or chilled.

Helpful hints: As is true of many pasta salads, this dish actually benefits from being made up to 8 hours in advance. The extra time allows the pasta to absorb more of the dressing. You can use 2 red or yellow bell peppers instead of 1 of each, if you like.

FAT: 9G/18%
CALORIES: 456
SATURATED FAT: 2.2G
CARBOHYDRATE: 59G
PROTEIN: 37G
CHOLESTEROL: 58MG
SODIUM: 595MG

THAI NOODLES WITH TOFU

SERVES: 4
WORKING TIME: 25 MINUTES
TOTAL TIME: 35 MINUTES

This easy-to-prepare recipe nicely shows off the complex sweet, hot, and tangy flavors of the Pacific rim. Chili sauce is enlivened with fresh lime juice, cilantro, and mint, while mild-tasting tofu rounds out the flavors. Garnish with sprigs of fresh mint and serve with rice cakes, if desired, for a little crunch.

8 ounces linguine

⅓ cup chili sauce

3 tablespoons reduced-sodium soy sauce

2 tablespoons fresh lime juice

1 tablespoon honey

2 tablespoons chopped fresh cilantro

2 tablespoons chopped fresh mint

2 carrots, shredded

2 red bell peppers, slivered

1 rib celery, cut into 2-inch julienne strips

4 ounces firm tofu, diced

2 tablespoons coarsely chopped unsalted peanuts

1. In a large pot of boiling water, cook the linguine until just tender. Drain well and set aside.

2. Meanwhile, in a large bowl, whisk together the chili sauce, soy sauce, lime juice, honey, and 2 tablespoons of water. Whisk in the cilantro and mint.

3. Add the carrots, bell peppers, and celery to the dressing and stir well to coat. Add the linguine and toss to combine. Add the tofu and gently toss again. Divide the salad among 4 plates, sprinkle the peanuts on top, and serve.

Helpful hint: If cilantro is not available, substitute 1 teaspoon ground coriander and 2 tablespoons chopped fresh flat-leaf Italian parsley. You can also eliminate the cilantro altogether.

FAT: 7G/17%
CALORIES: 379
SATURATED FAT: 1G
CARBOHYDRATE: 66G
PROTEIN: 16G
CHOLESTEROL: 0MG
SODIUM: 787MG

MEDITERRANEAN PASTA SALAD

SERVES: 4
WORKING TIME: 10 MINUTES
TOTAL TIME: 20 MINUTES

We've deliciously updated this classic warm-weather pasta salad with water-packed tuna for less fat, and enlivened it with a simple red wine vinaigrette. If fresh basil is not on hand, you may substitute a teaspoon of dried. Blanched broccoli florets or sliced raw zucchini may replace the green beans, and farfalle or rotini would be fine instead of the shells.

½ pound green beans, trimmed and cut lengthwise in half

8 ounces medium pasta shells

1 pound plum tomatoes (about 4), diced

1 cup thinly sliced red onion

⅓ cup red wine vinegar

2 tablespoons olive oil

½ teaspoon salt

¼ teaspoon freshly ground black pepper

12½-ounce can water-packed tuna, drained and flaked

¼ cup chopped fresh basil

1. Heat a large pot of water to boiling, and cook the green beans until crisp-tender, about 3 minutes. Reserve the boiling water for the pasta and, with a slotted spoon, transfer the green beans to a colander. Rinse under cold water and drain. Cook the pasta shells in the reserved boiling water until just tender. Drain well.

2. Meanwhile, in a large bowl, combine the green beans, tomatoes, onion, vinegar, oil, salt, and pepper. Add the tuna and basil and toss to combine. Add the pasta shells and toss again. Serve immediately, or cover and refrigerate for up to 4 hours. May be served chilled or at room temperature. Spoon the pasta salad onto 4 plates and serve.

Suggested accompaniments: Iced lemon-flavored seltzer, and sesame flat breads. Follow with raspberry sorbet garnished with fresh raspberries.

FAT: 9G/19%
CALORIES: 435
SATURATED FAT: 1.2G
CARBOHYDRATE: 56G
PROTEIN: 33G
CHOLESTEROL: 33MG
SODIUM: 576MG

CHICKEN PASTA SALAD PRIMAVERA

SERVES: 4
WORKING TIME: 30 MINUTES
TOTAL TIME: 30 MINUTES

Bright and colorful with its whimsical zucchini and carrot ribbons, this salad is sure to inspire smiles of appreciation. The sweet-tart dressing is a subtle blend of apple and lemon juices, with a splash of hot pepper sauce and a deep background note of roasted garlic. Serve with crunchy bread sticks.

3 tablespoons fresh lemon juice
½ teaspoon dried rosemary
½ teaspoon dried sage
1 pound skinless, boneless chicken breasts
4 cloves garlic, peeled
8 ounces rotini pasta
1 red onion, halved and thinly sliced
1 cup frozen peas
1 teaspoon salt
½ cup apple juice
¼ cup red wine vinegar
2 tablespoons olive oil
½ teaspoon hot pepper sauce
1 zucchini
2 carrots, peeled

1. Preheat the oven to 375°. In a small bowl, combine 2 tablespoons of the lemon juice, the rosemary, and sage. Place the chicken on a baking sheet and rub with the herbed lemon juice. Place the garlic on the baking sheet and bake for 20 minutes, or until the chicken is cooked through. Set the garlic aside. When cool enough to handle, cut the chicken into strips.

2. Meanwhile, in a large pot of boiling water, cook the pasta until tender. Add the onion and peas during the last 1 minute of cooking. Drain and rinse under cold water.

3. In a large bowl, mash the garlic with the salt. Stir in the apple juice, vinegar, oil, hot pepper sauce, and the remaining 1 tablespoon lemon juice. Add the pasta mixture and the chicken and toss to coat.

4. With a vegetable peeler, make long strips of zucchini and carrots and add to the pasta mixture, tossing to coat. Divide the salad among 4 bowls and serve warm, at room temperature, or chilled.

Helpful hint: You can substitute other similar-sized pasta shapes, such as ruote, penne, or radiatore.

FAT: 9G/17%
CALORIES: 486
SATURATED FAT: 1.5G
CARBOHYDRATE: 62G
PROTEIN: 37G
CHOLESTEROL: 66MG
SODIUM: 705MG

Spicy Tuna-Pasta Salad

Serves: 4
Working time: 20 minutes
Total time: 20 minutes

Instead of a tuna sandwich, enjoy this lemony tuna-and-orzo salad with unexpected hints of hot pepper and cumin.

8 ounces orzo pasta

⅔ cup plain nonfat yogurt

¼ cup reduced-fat sour cream

2 tablespoons reduced-fat mayonnaise

1 teaspoon grated lemon zest

3 tablespoons fresh lemon juice

½ teaspoon hot pepper sauce

½ teaspoon salt

1 teaspoon ground cumin

Two 6½-ounce cans water-packed tuna, drained and flaked

1 cup diced celery

½ cup chopped scallions

¼ cup chopped fresh cilantro or parsley

6 cups mixed torn greens

4 tomatoes, cut into wedges

¼ cup diced avocado

1. In a large pot of boiling water, cook the pasta until just tender. Drain well.

2. Meanwhile, in a large bowl, combine the yogurt, sour cream, mayonnaise, lemon zest, lemon juice, hot pepper sauce, salt, and cumin, whisking to blend. Stir in the pasta, tuna, celery, scallions, and cilantro.

3. Arrange the greens and tomatoes on 4 plates, top with the tuna mixture, sprinkle with the avocado, and serve at room temperature or chilled.

Helpful hints: The salad can be made up to 8 hours in advance; don't spoon it over the greens or add the tomato and avocado until serving time. Read labels carefully when buying canned tuna: Some national brands of water-packed solid white tuna have as much as 5 grams of fat in 2 ounces. Look for a brand with no more than 1 gram of fat in 2 ounces.

Fat: 7g/14%
Calories: 454
Saturated Fat: 1.9g
Carbohydrate: 60g
Protein: 38g
Cholesterol: 40mg
Sodium: 731mg

PASTA SALAD WITH SUN-DRIED TOMATO VINAIGRETTE

SERVES: 4
WORKING TIME: 20 MINUTES
TOTAL TIME: 30 MINUTES

½ cup sun-dried (not oil-packed) tomatoes

1 cup boiling water

½ cup reduced-sodium vegetable broth

½ cup packed fresh basil leaves

¼ cup balsamic or red wine vinegar

2 tablespoons extra-virgin olive oil

¼ teaspoon salt

10-ounce package frozen Italian flat green beans

10 ounces medium pasta shells

4 cups cherry tomatoes, halved

19-ounce can chick-peas, rinsed and drained

1 red onion, cut into ¼-inch dice

1. In a small bowl, combine the sun-dried tomatoes and boiling water. Let stand at room temperature until softened, about 15 minutes. When softened, transfer the tomatoes and their soaking liquid to a food processor and process to a smooth purée, about 1 minute. Add the broth, basil, vinegar, oil, and salt and process until well combined. Transfer to a large bowl.

2. Meanwhile, in a large pot of boiling water, cook the green beans until crisp-tender, about 2 minutes. With a slotted spoon, transfer the beans to the bowl with the dressing; set aside. Add the pasta to the boiling water and cook until tender. Drain well and add to the bowl along with the cherry tomatoes, chick-peas, and onion, tossing to combine. Serve at room temperature or chill for up to 4 hours.

Helpful hint: If you can get fresh Italian flat green beans, use them in place of the frozen. The cooking time will be approximately the same, depending on the size of the fresh beans. Test them after 2 minutes and if they are still too raw, continue cooking them.

FAT: 11G/18%
CALORIES: 544
SATURATED FAT: 1.3G
CARBOHYDRATE: 94G
PROTEIN: 21G
CHOLESTEROL: 0MG
SODIUM: 352MG

R*ed, white, and green—the colors of the Italian flag—are fitting colors for this sensational Italian salad.*

THAI CHICKEN AND PEANUT SALAD

SERVES: 4
WORKING TIME: 25 MINUTES
TOTAL TIME: 35 MINUTES

It's nice to be able to fix an exotic-tasting Asian-style dinner without having to shop around for obscure ingredients. We've made some clever substitutions in this recipe that let you create true Thai taste using standard supermarket items. The dressing is made with fresh basil, plum jam, ketchup, lime juice, and that all-American staple, peanut butter.

1 cup reduced-sodium chicken broth, defatted
¾ pound skinless, boneless chicken breasts
⅓ cup chopped fresh basil or mint
2 tablespoons plum jam
2 tablespoons ketchup
2 tablespoons creamy peanut butter
2 tablespoons fresh lime juice
½ teaspoon hot pepper sauce
½ teaspoon salt
8 ounces fettuccine, broken into thirds
6 ounces green beans, halved crosswise
1 red bell pepper, cut into ¼-inch-wide strips
1 yellow bell pepper, cut into ¼-inch-wide strips
1 cucumber, peeled, halved lengthwise, seeded, and thinly sliced
1 tablespoon chopped peanuts

1. In a medium skillet, bring the broth to a boil. Reduce to a simmer, add the chicken, cover, and cook until the chicken is cooked through, about 10 minutes. With a slotted spoon, transfer the chicken to a plate; reserve the cooking liquid. When cool enough to handle, shred the chicken with your fingers.

2. In a large bowl, combine ¼ cup of the reserved cooking liquid, the basil, plum jam, ketchup, peanut butter, lime juice, hot pepper sauce, and salt.

3. Meanwhile, in a large pot of boiling water, cook the pasta and green beans until the pasta is just tender. Add the bell peppers for the last 1 minute of cooking time. Drain well.

4. Add the chicken, pasta, green beans, bell peppers, and cucumber to the bowl with the basil mixture, tossing well to combine. Divide the salad among 4 plates, sprinkle the peanuts over, and serve warm, at room temperature, or chilled.

Helpful hints: You can prepare the salad up to 8 hours in advance; do not sprinkle the peanuts over until just before serving. You can use 2 red or yellow bell peppers instead of 1 of each, if you like.

FAT: 9G/18%
CALORIES: 441
SATURATED FAT: 1.6G
CARBOHYDRATE: 59G
PROTEIN: 33G
CHOLESTEROL: 103MG
SODIUM: 565MG

PENNE AND SMOKED TURKEY SALAD

SERVES: 4
WORKING TIME: 15 MINUTES
TOTAL TIME: 25 MINUTES

Robust winter flavors make this smoky-sweet salad quite at home as a fireside supper. If you prefer to microwave the sweet potato, place the diced potato in a microwave-safe bowl and tightly cover. Microwave on full power for four to five minutes, stirring once or twice. For an easy variation, replace the smoked turkey with three-quarter cup of diced cooked turkey or chicken.

1 sweet potato, peeled and diced

10 ounces penne pasta

2 tablespoons olive oil

1 medium onion, diced

3 cloves garlic, minced

14½-ounce can no-salt-added stewed tomatoes

⅓ cup apple juice

1 tablespoon cider vinegar

2 teaspoons reduced-sodium soy sauce

6 ounces smoked turkey, diced

1 Granny Smith apple, cored and diced

3 tablespoons finely chopped fresh basil

½ teaspoon freshly ground black pepper

¼ teaspoon cayenne pepper

1. Heat a large pot of water to boiling, and cook the sweet potato until tender, about 5 minutes. Reserve the boiling water for the pasta and, with a slotted spoon, transfer the sweet potato to a colander to drain. Cook the penne in the reserved boiling water until just tender. Drain well.

2. Meanwhile, in a large nonstick skillet, heat 1 tablespoon of the oil until hot but not smoking over medium heat. Add the onion and garlic and cook, stirring frequently, until the onion has softened, about 7 minutes. Add the remaining 1 tablespoon oil and the tomatoes, breaking them up with the back of a spoon. Cook until the mixture is slightly thickened, about 4 minutes longer. Stir in the apple juice and bring to a boil. Remove from the heat and stir in the vinegar and soy sauce. Transfer to a large serving bowl.

3. Add the sweet potato, turkey, apple, basil, black pepper, and cayenne and toss gently to coat. Add the penne and toss again. Serve immediately, or cover and refrigerate for up to 4 hours. May be served chilled or at room temperature.

Suggested accompaniments: Mixed green salad drizzled with balsamic vinegar, and a dessert of frozen vanilla yogurt topped with a sauce of puréed canned apricots and honey.

FAT: 10G/19%
CALORIES: 486
SATURATED FAT: 1.7G
CARBOHYDRATE: 81G
PROTEIN: 20G
CHOLESTEROL: 22MG
SODIUM: 560MG

COLD SESAME NOODLES WITH CHICKEN

SERVES: 4
WORKING TIME: 15 MINUTES
TOTAL TIME: 25 MINUTES

The peanut butter dressing for this noodle salad is a tantalizing interplay of sweet, smoky, and hot. To enhance the taste of the chicken poaching liquid, we've flavored it with scallions and thin slices of ginger. Cilantro adds a special fragrance but could easily be replaced with parsley.

8 ounces fettuccine

3 thin slices fresh ginger

1 cup thinly sliced scallions

½ pound skinless, boneless chicken breasts

3 tablespoons creamy peanut butter

1 tablespoon plus 1 teaspoon Oriental sesame oil

2 tablespoons reduced-sodium soy sauce

2 tablespoons chopped fresh cilantro

1 tablespoon honey

2 teaspoons rice vinegar

1 clove garlic, peeled

¼ teaspoon red pepper flakes

¼ teaspoon salt

2 cups halved cherry tomatoes

2 carrots, grated

1. Heat a large pot of water to boiling, and cook the fettuccine until just tender. Drain well. Transfer to a large bowl.

2. Meanwhile, in a medium skillet, combine the ginger, ½ cup of the scallions, and 1 cup of water. Bring to a boil over high heat, add the chicken, and reduce to a simmer. Cover and cook until the chicken is cooked through, about 7 minutes. With a slotted spoon, transfer the chicken to a cutting board. Strain the cooking liquid, discarding the solids. Reserve ½ cup of the cooking liquid. When cool enough to handle, shred the chicken.

3. In a blender or food processor, combine the peanut butter, sesame oil, soy sauce, cilantro, honey, vinegar, garlic, pepper flakes, and salt. Purée until smooth, adding enough of the reserved ½ cup cooking liquid to thin slightly.

4. Add the tomatoes, carrots, remaining ½ cup scallions, and chicken to the fettuccine. Pour the peanut butter dressing on top and toss well to combine. Serve immediately, or cover and refrigerate for up to 8 hours. May be served chilled or at room temperature. Spoon the sesame noodles into 4 bowls and serve.

Suggested accompaniments: Orange wedges, and fortune cookies.

FAT: 11G/23%
CALORIES: 424
SATURATED FAT: 1.9G
CARBOHYDRATE: 57G
PROTEIN: 26G
CHOLESTEROL: 87MG
SODIUM: 568MG

DITALINI AND BULGHUR SALAD

SERVES: 4
WORKING TIME: 15 MINUTES
TOTAL TIME: 30 MINUTES

In this vibrantly flavored Middle Eastern salad, the cool tastes of lemon, mint, and scallions shine in every bite. The tiny ditalini pair well with the bulghur, keeping the texture grain like. Bulghur, also known as cracked wheat, is available in three textures: fine, medium, and coarse. Medium and coarse are the best for salads.

2 tablespoons olive oil
1 large onion, diced
3 cloves garlic, minced
1 cup bulghur
⅔ cup reduced-sodium chicken broth, defatted
8 ounces ditalini pasta
1 cup canned chick-peas, rinsed and drained
½ pound plum tomatoes (about 2), diced
½ cup thinly sliced scallions
¼ cup fresh lemon juice
¼ cup chopped fresh mint or basil
2 teaspoons grated lemon zest
½ teaspoon allspice
½ teaspoon salt
¼ teaspoon freshly ground black pepper

1. In a large nonstick skillet, heat 1 tablespoon of the oil until hot but not smoking over medium heat. Add the onion and garlic and cook, stirring frequently, until the onion has softened, about 7 minutes. Add the bulghur, stirring to coat. Remove from the heat and stir in the broth and ⅔ cup of water. Transfer to a large serving bowl. Let stand until the bulghur is softened and the liquid is absorbed, about 15 minutes.

2. Meanwhile, heat a large pot of water to boiling, and cook the ditalini until just tender. Drain well.

3. Add the chick-peas, tomatoes, scallions, lemon juice, mint, zest, allspice, salt, pepper, and the remaining 1 tablespoon oil to the bulghur mixture and toss gently to combine. Add the ditalini and toss again. Serve immediately, or cover and refrigerate for up to 8 hours. May be served chilled or at room temperature.

Suggested accompaniments: Steamed broccoli tossed with grated orange zest. For dessert, fat-free gingerbread topped with a dollop of nonfat sour cream.

FAT: 10G/19%
CALORIES: 486
SATURATED FAT: 1.2G
CARBOHYDRATE: 87G
PROTEIN: 16G
CHOLESTEROL: 0MG
SODIUM: 377MG

APPLE AND PLUM PASTA SALAD

SERVES: 4
WORKING TIME: 25 MINUTES
TOTAL TIME: 30 MINUTES

The apple slices, walnuts, and mayonnaise dressing reveal the inspiration for this dish: It's Waldorf salad, an American tradition since the 1890s. We've introduced pasta to the mix—bow ties seem appropriate to the formality of the Waldorf. The plums, red cabbage, and hard-cooked eggs are innovations, too; we've also lightened (and spiced up) the dressing.

8 ounces farfalle (bow ties) or rotini pasta

1½ cups plain nonfat yogurt

½ cup frozen apple juice concentrate, thawed

3 tablespoons reduced-fat mayonnaise

1 teaspoon ground ginger

½ teaspoon salt

2 cups shredded red cabbage

2 large red plums (6 ounces each), thinly sliced

1 McIntosh apple, halved, cored, and thinly sliced

1 Granny Smith apple, halved, cored, and thinly sliced

3 ribs celery, thinly sliced

2 hard-cooked eggs, peeled and coarsely chopped

2 tablespoons coarsely chopped walnuts

1. In a large pot of boiling water, cook the pasta until tender. Drain well.

2. In a large bowl, combine the yogurt, apple juice concentrate, mayonnaise, ginger, and salt. Add the pasta, cabbage, plums, apples, and celery, stirring to coat. Divide among 4 plates, sprinkle with the eggs and walnuts, and serve.

Helpful hints: We use two types of apples here, 1 red and 1 green. You can use all of one kind, if you like. Although we call for red plums, you can use almost any plum variety for this recipe. For perfect hard-cooked eggs, place the eggs in a small pot with cold water to cover. Bring to a boil, turn off the heat, cover, and let stand for 15 minutes. Peel the eggs under cold running water.

FAT: 9G/16%
CALORIES: 519
SATURATED FAT: 1.7G
CARBOHYDRATE: 94G
PROTEIN: 18G
CHOLESTEROL: 108MG
SODIUM: 503MG

PASTA-VEGETABLE SALAD WITH PESTO DRESSING

SERVES: 4
WORKING TIME: 30 MINUTES
TOTAL TIME: 30 MINUTES

6 cloves garlic, peeled

¾ pound fusilli

1½ cups packed fresh basil leaves

½ cup canned white kidney beans (cannellini), rinsed and drained

¼ cup grated Parmesan cheese

1 tablespoon olive oil

2 teaspoons pine nuts

½ teaspoon salt

2 red bell peppers, cut into ½-inch squares

½ pound mushrooms, thickly sliced

¾ pound asparagus, tough ends trimmed and cut on the diagonal into 1-inch lengths

6 Calamata or other brine-cured black olives, pitted and coarsely chopped

1. In a large pot of boiling water, cook the garlic for 2 minutes to blanch. With a slotted spoon, remove the garlic and set aside. Add the fusilli to the pot and cook until tender. Drain well and transfer to a large bowl.

2. Meanwhile, in a food processor, combine the garlic, basil, beans, Parmesan, 1 teaspoon of the oil, the pine nuts, and salt and process to a smooth purée. Add ⅓ cup of water and process until creamy. Pour the dressing over the pasta, tossing to combine.

3. In a large nonstick skillet, heat the remaining 2 teaspoons oil until hot but not smoking over medium heat. Add the bell peppers and cook, stirring frequently, until crisp-tender, about 4 minutes. Add the mushrooms and asparagus and cook, stirring frequently, until the asparagus is crisp-tender, about 4 minutes. Add to the bowl with the pasta. Add the olives, tossing to combine. Serve at room temperature or chill for up to 8 hours.

Helpful hint: Penne rigate (ridged penne) could be substituted for the fusilli; penne's shape, like that of fusilli, suits the other ingredients in the dish.

FAT: 10G/18%
CALORIES: 507
SATURATED FAT: 2.0G
CARBOHYDRATE: 87G
PROTEIN: 21G
CHOLESTEROL: 4MG
SODIUM: 561MG

If you're looking for a healthy pasta sauce, steer clear of the supermarket dairy case—the sauces found there are often loaded with fat. A commercial pesto sauce may have as much as 30 grams of fat in a quarter-cup serving! By comparison, our bean-based pesto, made with modest amounts of cheese, oil, and pine nuts, is a minor miracle.

ROTINI SALAD WITH WHITE BEANS AND HERBS

SERVES: 4
WORKING TIME: 15 MINUTES
TOTAL TIME: 25 MINUTES

Serve this salad, dressed in a deliciously tangy tomato vinaigrette, for a light summer luncheon or a change-of-pace Sunday supper.

½ pound green beans, trimmed and cut lengthwise in half

10 ounces tricolor rotini pasta

5.5-ounce can reduced-sodium tomato-vegetable juice

2 tablespoons fresh lemon juice

2 tablespoons Dijon mustard

2 tablespoons olive oil

¾ teaspoon dried sage

¾ teaspoon dried oregano

¾ teaspoon salt

¼ teaspoon freshly ground black pepper

¾ pound plum tomatoes (about 3), diced

⅔ cup thinly sliced scallions

¾ cup canned cannellini beans, rinsed and drained

12 Boston lettuce leaves

1. Heat a large pot of water to boiling, and cook the green beans until crisp-tender, about 3 minutes. Reserve the boiling water for the pasta and, with a slotted spoon, transfer the green beans to a colander. Rinse under cold water and drain. Cook the rotini in the reserved boiling water until just tender. Drain well.

2. Meanwhile, in a large bowl, whisk together the tomato-vegetable juice, lemon juice, mustard, oil, sage, oregano, salt, and pepper. Stir in the green beans, tomatoes, and scallions. Add the cannellini beans and rotini and toss gently to combine. Place the lettuce on 4 plates, spoon the rotini salad on top, and serve.

Suggested accompaniments: Crusty Italian bread, followed by tapioca pudding made with low-fat milk and flavored with cinnamon.

FAT: 9G/20%
CALORIES: 414
SATURATED FAT: 1.1G
CARBOHYDRATE: 71G
PROTEIN: 15G
CHOLESTEROL: 0MG
SODIUM: 650MG

CHUNKY CHICKEN AND MACARONI SALAD

SERVES: 4
WORKING TIME: 15 MINUTES
TOTAL TIME: 25 MINUTES

10 ounces elbow macaroni

1 teaspoon mild paprika

¾ teaspoon dried rosemary

½ teaspoon dried thyme

½ pound skinless, boneless chicken breasts

⅓ cup reduced-fat mayonnaise

¼ cup plain nonfat yogurt

1 tablespoon plus 1 teaspoon Dijon mustard

1 tablespoon plus 1 teaspoon cider vinegar

½ teaspoon freshly ground black pepper

½ teaspoon salt

1 red bell pepper, cut into thin slivers

1 green bell pepper, cut into thin slivers

½ cup frozen peas, thawed, rinsed, and drained

½ cup thinly sliced scallions

1. Heat a large pot of water to boiling, and cook the macaroni until just tender. Drain well.

2. Meanwhile, in a medium skillet, combine the paprika, rosemary, thyme, and 1 cup of water. Bring to a boil over high heat, add the chicken, and reduce to a simmer. Cover and cook until the chicken is cooked through, about 7 minutes. With a slotted spoon, transfer the chicken to a cutting board. Reserve ½ cup of the cooking liquid. Cut the chicken into ¾-inch chunks.

3. In a large bowl, whisk together the mayonnaise, yogurt, mustard, vinegar, black pepper, salt, and reserved ½ cup cooking liquid. Stir in the bell peppers, peas, scallions, and chicken. Add the macaroni and toss gently to combine. Serve immediately, or cover and refrigerate for up to 8 hours. May be served chilled or at room temperature. Spoon the macaroni salad onto 4 plates and serve.

Suggested accompaniments: Curly chicory and leafy green lettuce drizzled with an herb vinaigrette, and sliced apples sautéed with brown sugar and apple brandy for dessert.

FAT: 6G/13%
CALORIES: 423
SATURATED FAT: 1.1G
CARBOHYDRATE: 65G
PROTEIN: 25G
CHOLESTEROL: 33MG
SODIUM: 628MG

This hearty favorite gets extra goodness from tender chicken poached with spices—for flavor without fat.

CHINESE PASTA SALAD WITH SHREDDED CHICKEN

SERVES: 4
WORKING TIME: 15 MINUTES
TOTAL TIME: 25 MINUTES

This exotically spiced dish marries tender chicken and pasta strands with a mix of colorful vegetables for delectable crunch. We've kept the fat low in the honey-ginger dressing by whisking in some of the flavorful poaching liquid from the chicken, reducing the need for oil. Regular white mushrooms could easily replace the shiitakes for a milder taste.

8 ounces angel hair or capellini pasta

¼ pound fresh shiitake mushrooms, trimmed

3 cloves garlic, minced

2 thin slices fresh ginger

8 scallions, cut into 2-inch julienne strips (about 1 cup)

½ pound skinless, boneless chicken breasts

¼ cup reduced-sodium soy sauce

2 tablespoons honey

2 tablespoons Oriental sesame oil

1 teaspoon ground ginger

2 carrots, cut into 2-inch julienne strips

1 red bell pepper, cut into 2-inch julienne strips

1 cucumber, halved lengthwise, seeded, and cut into 2-inch julienne strips

1. Heat a large pot of water to boiling, and cook the angel hair pasta until just tender. Drain well.

2. Meanwhile, in a medium skillet, combine the mushrooms, garlic, fresh ginger, ⅓ cup of the scallions, and 1 cup of water. Bring to a boil over high heat, add the chicken, and reduce to a simmer. Cover and cook until the chicken is cooked through and the mushrooms are tender, about 7 minutes. With a slotted spoon, transfer the chicken and mushrooms to a cutting board. Strain the cooking liquid, discarding the solids. Reserve ⅓ cup of the cooking liquid. When cool enough to handle, shred the chicken and cut the mushrooms into thin slivers.

3. In a large bowl, whisk together the soy sauce, honey, sesame oil, ground ginger, and reserved ⅓ cup cooking liquid. Stir in the carrots, bell pepper, cucumber, remaining ⅔ cup scallions, chicken, and mushrooms. Add the angel hair pasta and toss to combine. Spoon the pasta salad onto 4 plates and serve.

Suggested accompaniments: Herb tea, and sautéed banana chunks served over vanilla ice milk for dessert.

FAT: 9G/19%
CALORIES: 424
SATURATED FAT: 1.3G
CARBOHYDRATE: 64G
PROTEIN: 23G
CHOLESTEROL: 33MG
SODIUM: 661MG

Couscous Salad

Serves: 4
Working time: 20 minutes
Total time: 30 minutes

Here's a novel pasta salad made with couscous— a Middle Eastern pasta that takes the form of tiny beads—instead of the traditional macaroni. The couscous is steeped with raisins and then combined with roasted bell pepper strips, parsley, cucumber, scallions and a light citrusy dressing. It's served on a bed of mixed greens and topped with crumbled feta cheese.

2 red bell peppers
2 yellow bell peppers
½ cup fresh lemon juice
2 tablespoons extra-virgin olive oil
1 teaspoon paprika
¾ teaspoon ground ginger
½ teaspoon salt
½ teaspoon freshly ground black pepper
1½ cups couscous
4 cups boiling water
¾ cup raisins
⅓ cup chopped fresh parsley
1 cucumber, peeled, halved lengthwise, seeded, and cut into ½-inch cubes
3 scallions, thinly sliced
4 cups watercress, tough stems removed
4 cups torn Boston lettuce
½ cup crumbled feta cheese (2 ounces)

1. Preheat the broiler. Cut off the 4 sides of each bell pepper and remove the ribs. Broil the bell peppers, cut-sides down, for about 10 minutes, or until the skin is blackened. When cool enough to handle, peel and cut into ½-inch-wide strips.

2. Meanwhile, in a medium bowl, combine the lemon juice, oil, paprika, ginger, salt, and black pepper. In another medium bowl, combine the couscous and boiling water. Add the raisins, cover, and let stand until the couscous is tender, about 5 minutes. Drain the couscous if any liquid remains.

3. Transfer the couscous and raisins to the bowl with the dressing. Add the roasted pepper strips, parsley, cucumber, and scallions, tossing to combine. Serve at room temperature or chill for up to 8 hours. To serve, place the watercress and Boston lettuce on 4 plates, top with the couscous mixture, and sprinkle with the feta.

Helpful hints: To seed a cucumber, cut it in half lengthwise and use the tip of a spoon to scrape out the seeds. You can substitute dried figs for the raisins: Plump 6 ounces of figs in boiling water for about 15 minutes, then drain and coarsely chop.

Fat: 11g/20%
Calories: 505
Saturated Fat: 3.3g
Carbohydrate: 91g
Protein: 15g
Cholesterol: 13mg
Sodium: 471mg

RADIATORE SALAD WITH ROASTED RED PEPPERS

SERVES: 4
WORKING TIME: 20 MINUTES
TOTAL TIME: 30 MINUTES

3 red bell peppers, each cut in half

3 cloves garlic, peeled

1 pound tomatoes

8 ounces radiatore pasta

3 tablespoons red wine vinegar

3 tablespoons chopped fresh mint

2 tablespoons olive oil

1 teaspoon salt

¼ teaspoon freshly ground black pepper

1 zucchini, quartered lengthwise and cut into thin slices

1. Preheat the broiler. Place the pepper halves, cut-sides down, on the broiler rack. Broil the peppers 4 inches from the heat for 10 minutes, or until the skin is charred. Transfer the pepper halves to a small bowl, cover with plastic wrap, and let stand for 5 minutes. Transfer the peppers to a cutting board, remove the skin and any seeds, and cut into thick slices. Set aside.

2. Meanwhile, heat a large pot of water to boiling, and blanch the garlic in the boiling water for 3 minutes. Reserve the boiling water for the tomatoes and, with a slotted spoon, transfer the garlic to a cutting board. Blanch the tomatoes in the reserved boiling water for 30 seconds. Reserve the boiling water again and, with a slotted spoon, transfer the tomatoes to a cutting board. Using a paring knife, peel the tomatoes and coarsely chop. Mince the garlic. Set the tomatoes and garlic aside.

3. Cook the radiatore in the reserved boiling water until just tender. Drain well.

4. In a large serving bowl, whisk together the vinegar, mint, oil, salt, and black pepper. Stir in the roasted peppers, garlic, tomatoes, and zucchini. Add the radiatore and toss to combine. Serve immediately, or cover and refrigerate for up to 4 hours. If chilled, bring to room temperature before serving.

Suggested accompaniment: A fresh fruit salad in a lemon-sugar syrup.

FAT: 8G/23%
CALORIES: 320
SATURATED FAT: 1.1G
CARBOHYDRATE: 54G
PROTEIN: 9G
CHOLESTEROL: 0MG
SODIUM: 567MG

430

This summery salad relies on the best tomatoes, zucchini, and red bell peppers for its garden-fresh flavor. Cook's trick: Blanching the garlic sweetens its taste. The mint adds a lovely fragrance but if unavailable, you may use fresh basil or flat-leaf Italian parsley. Rotini, ruote, elbows, or ziti would all be good substitutes for the radiatore.

GLOSSARY

Artichoke—The bud of a thistle-like plant, this delicious vegetable is extremely popular in Italy. The bases of the leaves and the fleshy bottom, or heart, of the artichoke are edible; the tough parts of the leaves and the fuzzy interior "choke" are discarded. Select heavy artichokes with tight leaves and fresh-looking stems; refrigerate them in a plastic bag for no longer than three to four days.

Avocado—A fruit with a nutty flavor and a smooth, buttery consistency. The flesh of the pebbly textured, black Hass variety is richer and meatier than the larger, smooth-skinned, green Fuerte. Select firm avocados that yield slightly to pressure without being mushy; avoid rock-hard fruit. To ripen, store in a loosely closed brown paper bag at room temperature. Because avocados are high in fat, they should be used in small amounts.

Balsamic vinegar—A dark red vinegar made from the unfermented juice of pressed grapes, most commonly the white Trebbiano, and aged in wooden casks. The authentic version is produced in a small region in Northern Italy, around Modena, and tastes richly sweet with a slight sour edge. Balsamic vinegar adds a pleasant tang to pasta sauces.

Basil—An herb with a flavor somewhere between clove and licorice. Fresh basil will maintain more fragrance and flavor if added toward the end of cooking. Dried basil is a good deal milder than fresh, but can still be used to good advantage in pasta sauces as well as salads. To store, refrigerate fresh basil, unwashed, stem ends in a jar of water and tops loosely covered with a plastic bag, for up to 3 days.

Bay leaf—The dried, whole leaf of the evergreen European laurel tree. The herb adds a distinctive, pungent flavor to soups, stews, and casseroles; the Turkish variety is milder than the somewhat harsh California bay leaves. Always remove bay leaves before serving food.

Beans, black—Pea-sized oval black legumes much used in Latin American cuisine. Black beans, also called turtle beans, are fairly soft, with an earthy flavor. They come in both dried and canned (rehydrated, ready-to-use) forms. Black beans, like all canned beans, should be rinsed and drained before using to remove the high-sodium canning liquid and freshen the beans' flavor.

Beans, cannellini—Large white kidney beans often used in Italian cooking. Cannellini are sold both dried and canned. Like all canned beans, cannellini should be rinsed and drained before use; this removes much of the sodium present in the canning liquid and also gives the beans a fresher flavor. Look for cannellini in the canned vegetable or Italian foods section of your supermarket.

Bok choy—A type of Chinese cabbage with crisp, white stalks and dark green, crinkled leaves. It has a much milder flavor than regular green cabbage, and is good added to pasta sauces with stir-fried vegetables for an Asian touch. Look for heads with firm leaves free of blemished edges and refrigerate, unwashed, in a plastic bag for no more than a few days.

Canadian bacon—A lean smoked meat, similar to ham. This bacon is precooked, so it can be used as is. (For extra flavor, cook it in a skillet until the edges are lightly crisped.) Just a small amount adds big flavor to sauces and soups, but with much less fat than regular bacon.

Capers—The flower buds of a small bush found in Mediterranean countries. To make capers, the buds are dried and then pickled in vinegar with some salt: To reduce saltiness, rinse before using. The piquant taste of capers permeates any sauce quickly, and just a few supply a big flavor boost.

Cayenne pepper—A hot spice ground from dried red chili peppers. Add cayenne to taste when preparing Mexican, Tex-Mex, Indian, Chinese, and Caribbean dishes; start with just a small amount, as cayenne is fiery-hot.

Chili powder—A commercially prepared seasoning mixture made from ground dried chilies, oregano, cumin, coriander, salt, and dehydrated garlic, and sometimes cloves and allspice, used in pasta salads, sauces, and baked pasta dishes for a Southwestern punch. Pure ground chili powder, without any added spices, is also available as cayenne. Chili powders can range in strength from mild to very hot; for proper potency, use within 6 months of purchase.

Chives—A mild-flavored member of the onion family distinguished by long, green shoots. Because their subtle flavor is quickly lost when heated, it is best to add chives to a cooked dish at the last minute. Snip rather than chop chives to avoid crushing the delicate herb.

Chop—To roughly cut an ingredient into small pieces—not as uniform as a dice and not as fine as a mince. Flavor will permeate a dish with still a hint of texture. Anchor the tip of a knife with your hand, keeping fingers away from the sharp edge, and quickly lift and lower the knife handle, slowly swinging the blade across the food.

Cilantro/Coriander—A lacy-leaved green herb (called by both names). The plant's seeds are dried and used as a spice (known as coriander). The fresh herb, much used in Mexican and Asian cooking, looks like pale flat-leaf parsley and is strongly aromatic. Store fresh cilantro by placing the stems in a container of water and covering the leaves loosely with a plastic bag. Coriander seeds are important in Mexican and Indian cuisines; sold whole or ground, they have a somewhat citrusy flavor that complements both sweet and savory dishes.

Clams—A shellfish with sweet, slightly chewy flesh. The small hard-shell littlenecks are preferred for sweetness, but the soft-shell varieties—steamers and West Coast razors—are also delicious. Fresh clams must be purchased live. The hard-shell variety should be tightly closed or, if open, should close when lightly tapped; the neck of a soft-shell clam should move when lightly touched. Discard clams that remain unopened after cooking. Use as soon after purchase as possible.

Cornstarch—A fine flour made from the germ of the corn. Cornstarch, like flour, is used as a fat-free sauce thickener; cornstarch-thickened sauces are lighter, glossier, and more translucent than those made with flour. To prevent lumps, combine cornstarch with a cold liquid before adding it to a hot sauce; bring it gently to a boil and don't stir too vigorously or the sauce may thin.

Couscous—Fine granules of pasta made from semolina flour. Of North African origin, couscous is traditionally cooked by steaming it over boiling water or a pot of stew. The couscous sold in boxes in American markets is quick cooking ("instant"): It requires only a few minutes of steeping in boiling water or broth. Couscous can be served as a side dish, like rice, or used as the basis for a hearty main dish.

Crabmeat—The meat from various varieties of hard-shell crabs, the tastiest part being from lump or backfin meat. Crab is most conveniently purchased in "lump" form, which is meat picked from the crab, cleaned, cooked, and packed fresh or frozen. Crabmeat can also be purchased canned, but the canned is often flaked meat and is not as flavorful. Add crabmeat toward the end of the cooking time, since overcooking makes it tough.

Cream cheese, reduced-fat—A light cream cheese, commonly called Neufchâtel, with about one-third less fat than regular cream cheese. It can be used as a substitute for regular cream cheese. A small amount used in sauces duplicates the richness of full-fat cheese or heavy cream.

Curry powder—Not one spice but a mix of spices, commonly used in Indian cooking to flavor a dish with sweet heat and add a characteristic yellow-orange color. While curry blends vary (consisting of as many as 20 herbs and spices), they typically include turmeric (for its vivid yellow color), fenugreek, ginger, cardamom, cloves, cumin, coriander, and cayenne pepper. Commercially available Madras curry is hotter than other store-bought types.

Dice—To cut food into small, uniform squares of ⅛ to ¼ inch, adding visual interest and texture to a dish. To dice, cut the ingredient into uniform strips, depending on how small or large you want the dice. Then cut the strips crosswise.

Dill—A name given to both the fresh herb and the small, hard seeds that are used as a spice. Add the light, lemony, fresh dill leaves (also called dillweed) toward the end of cooking. Dill seeds provide a pleasantly distinctive bitter taste and marry beautifully with sour cream- or yogurt-based sauces.

Egg noodles—Egg noodles are distinct from pasta because eggs have been added to the basic concoction of flour and water. In addition what is simply called egg noodles, fettuccine is also an egg noodle. Also available are yolk-free egg noodles, which, because they are made without the yolk, have almost no fat or cholesterol.

Eggplant—An oval-, pear-, or zucchini-shaped vegetable with deep purple or white skin and porous pale-green flesh. Since the spongy flesh readily soaks up oil, it's better to bake, broil, or grill eggplant; the last two methods give this vegetable a deep, smoky flavor as well. Choose a firm, glossy, unblemished eggplant that seems heavy for its size. Don't buy eggplant too far in advance—it will turn bitter if kept too long. Store eggplant in the refrigerator for 3 to 4 days.

Evaporated milk, skimmed and low-fat—Canned, unsweetened, homogenized milk that has had most of its fat removed: In the skimmed version, 100 percent of the fat has been removed; the low-fat version contains 1 percent fat. Used in sauces, these products add a creamy richness with almost no fat. Store at room temperature for up to 6 months until opened, then refrigerate for up to 1 week.

Fennel—A vegetable resembling a flattened head of celery, with a subtle licorice flavor. The feathery fronds that top the stalks are used as an herb, and the bulb is used raw and cooked, like celery. Choose firm, unblemished fennel bulbs with fresh green fronds. Store in the refrigerator in a plastic bag for three to four days. Fennel seeds, which come from a slightly different plant, have an almost sweet, licorice-like taste; they are often used in Italian dishes and with fish.

Fennel seed—A seed from the fennel plant with a slightly sweet, licorice-like taste, often used to season Italian-style sausages. The spice is used in pasta sauces, especially with meat, to add a mellow flavor.

Feta cheese—A soft, crumbly, cured Greek cheese, traditionally made from sheep's or goat's milk. White and rindless, feta is usually available in squares packed in its own brine, and can always be recognized in a dish by its somewhat salty, tangy flavor. Used in pasta salads or crumbled over hot baked pastas as the final garnish.

Garlic—The edible bulb of a plant closely related to onions, leeks, and chives. Garlic can be pungently assertive or sweetly mild, depending on how it is prepared: Minced or crushed garlic yields a more powerful flavor than whole or halved cloves. Whereas sautéing turns garlic rich and savory, slow simmering or roasting produces a mild, mellow flavor. Select firm, plump bulbs with dry skins; avoid bulbs that have begun to sprout. Store garlic in an open or loosely covered container in a cool, dark place for up to 2 months.

Ginger—A thin-skinned root used as a fragrant seasoning. Rather than peeling and mincing fresh ginger, it's easier to grate it, unpeeled. Toss grated ginger into a pasta sauce for a peppery note. Tightly wrapped, unpeeled fresh ginger can be refrigerated for 1 week or frozen for up to 2 months. Ground ginger is not a true substitute for fresh, but it will enliven pasta salads and baked pastas.

Goat cheese—A variety of cheeses made from goat's milk; often called by the French name, chèvre. You can choose from mild, spreadable types; firm, tangy ones; or assertive, well-aged chèvres. A fairly young cheese in log form is just the thing for general cooking purposes. (Small logs are sold whole, large ones by the slice.) Some examples are Montrachet, Chevrotin, Banon, Chabis, Ste. Maure, and Bucheron. Feta cheese is a reliable substitute in most recipes.

Green chili—A pungent, pod-shaped fruit produced by numerous pepper plants. Green chilies can range in heat from relatively mild to hot to wildly fiery. The jalapeño (see below) is perhaps the most well known of the hot to medium-hot chilies. There is also a type of canned chili pepper labeled simply "mild green chilies." They are available either whole or chopped and can be used to add a gentle bite to Mexican and Southwestern dishes.

Hot pepper sauce—A highly incendiary sauce made from a variety of hot peppers flavored with vinegar and salt. This sauce comes into play in Caribbean and Tex-Mex dishes as well as Creole and Cajun cuisines. Use sparingly, drop by drop, to introduce a hot edge to any dish.

Jalapeño peppers—Hot green chili peppers about two inches long and an inch in diameter, with rounded tips. Most of the heat resides in the membranes (ribs) of the pepper, so remove them for a milder effect—wear gloves to protect your hands from the volatile oils. Jalapeños are also sold whole or chopped in small cans, although the canned version is not nearly as arresting as the fresh. Toss a little jalapeño into soups, sautés, baked dishes, or anywhere you want to create some fire. When buying fresh, look for tight, glossy skins, and store in a brown paper bag in the refrigerator for several weeks.

Juice, citrus—The flavorful liquid component of oranges, lemon, limes, tangerines, and the like. Freshly squeezed citrus juice has an inimitable freshness that livens up low-fat foods. Frozen juice concentrates make a tangy base for sweet or savory sauces. An inexpensive hand reamer makes quick work of juicing citrus fruits.

Julienne—Thin, uniform, matchstick-size pieces of an ingredient, usually a vegetable, typically 2 inches long. Cut the food into long, thin slices. Stack the slices and cut lengthwise into sticks, and then crosswise into the desired length.

Leek—A member of the onion family, resembling a giant scallion. To prepare, trim the root end and any blemished dark green ends. Slit lengthwise from the root end to the top, leaving the root end intact, and then rinse thoroughly to remove any dirt trapped between the leaves. Use leeks in pasta sauces, especially seafood sauces, for their light, almost sweet onion flavor.

Lentil—A tiny, flat pulse (the dried seed of a legume), distinguished by a mild, nutty flavor and a starchy texture. The advantage of using lentils is that, unlike dried beans, they require no presoaking. They do require careful cooking, however, since overcooking makes them mushy. Beside the familiar brown variety, also try colorful green and red lentils in soups and stews.

Marjoram—A member of the mint family that tastes like mildly sweet oregano. Fresh marjoram should be added at the end of the cooking so the flavor doesn't vanish. Dried marjoram, sold in leaf and ground form (the more intense leaf being preferable), stands up to longer cooking.

Marsala—A sweet, nutty, fortified wine made in Sicily. To make Marsala, sweet concentrated grape juice is added to strong white wine; the wine is then aged for several years and, in some cases, blended. Marsala is much used in cooking: Sweet Marsala is good for dessert-making, but a dry version should be used in savory sauces.

Mince—To cut an ingredient into very small pieces, finer than a chop, so its flavor infuses the dish and the pieces themselves practically disappear when cooked. Mincing is usually done to foods that provide background flavor, such as scallions, garlic, chilies, and onions. The technique of stabilizing the point end and rocking the knife on the work surface is the same as for chopping.

Mint—A large family of herbs used to impart a perfumy, heady flavor and a cool aftertaste to foods, the most common being spearmint. Fresh mint is best added toward the end of cooking. Since the dried is fairly intense, a pinch is usually all that is needed in cooking. Store fresh mint the same way as basil.

Mozzarella—A soft, fresh cheese with great melting properties, originally made from water-buffalo's milk, but now more commonly from cow's milk, both in whole-milk and part-skim milk varieties. Its mild flavor can be used to good advantage in strongly flavored pasta salads and baked pasta.

Olive oil—A fragrant oil pressed from olives. Olive oil is one of the signature ingredients of Italian cuisine. This oil is rich in monounsaturated fats, which make it more healthful than butter and other solid shortenings. Olive oil comes in different grades, reflecting the method used to refine the oil and the resulting level of acidity. The finest, most expensive oil is cold-pressed extra-virgin, which should be reserved for flavoring uncooked or lightly cooked sauces. "Virgin" and "pure" olive oils are slightly more acidic with less olive flavor, and are fine for most types of cooking.

Olives—Small, oval fruits native to the Mediterranean region with an intense, earthy taste. Olives are picked green (unripe) or black (ripe) and then must be cured—in oil or brine—to mellow their natural bitterness and develop their flavor; herbs and other seasonings are added to create a wide variety of olives. Spanish olives—green olives sold whole, pitted, or pimiento-stuffed—add jazzy color as well as piquant flavor.

Olives, Calamata—A purple-black, brine-cured olive. The Calamata is a full-flavored Greek-style olive that works well in pasta sauces. Use all olives sparingly since they are high in fat (olive oil).

Onions, red—Medium- to large-sized spherical onions with purplish-red skins. Red onions are somewhat milder than yellow or white globe onions; they don't require long cooking to mellow their flavor, so they're perfect for briefly cooked (or uncooked) sauces. Bermuda onions or Spanish onions can be substituted for red onions.

Oregano—A member of the mint family characterized by small, green leaves. Prized for its pleasantly bitter flavor, oregano is essential to many Mediterranean-style pasta sauces and baked pasta dishes and is used in Mexican cooking as well. The dried version is actually more potent than the fresh.

Orzo—A small pasta shape that resembles large grains of rice. Orzo is popular in Greece and makes a delicious alternative to rice, especially with Mediterranean-inspired meals.

Paprika—A spice ground from a variety of red peppers and used in many traditional Hungarian and Spanish preparations, equally good in pasta salads and sauces. Paprika colors food a characteristic brick-red hue and flavors dishes from sweet to hot, depending on the pepper potency.

Parmesan cheese—An intensely flavored, hard grating cheese, ideal for low-fat cooking because a little goes a long way. Genuine Italian Parmesan, stamped "Parmigiano-Reggiano" on the rind, is produced in the Emilia-Romagna region, and tastes richly nutty with a slight sweetness. Buy Parmesan in blocks and grate it as needed for best flavor and freshness. For a fine, fluffy texture that melts into hot foods, use a hand-cranked grater.

Parsley—A popular herb available in two varieties: Curly parsley, with lacy, frilly leaves, is quite mild and is preferred for garnishing, while flat-leaf Italian parsley has a stronger flavor and is better for cooking. Store parsley as you would basil. Since fresh parsley is so widely available, there is really no reason to use dried, which has very little flavor.

Peanut oil—A clear, mild-tasting oil pressed from peanuts, composed mainly of monounsaturated fat and some polyunsaturated. Used for sautéing as well as in salad dressings.

Peppercorns, black—The whole dried berries of a tropical vine, *piper nigrum*. A touch of this hot, pungent seasoning enlivens just about any savory dish, and the flavor of freshly ground pepper is so superior to pre-ground that no cook should be without a pepper grinder filled with peppercorns.

Peppers, bell—The large, sweet members of the Capsicum family. Green peppers are most common; red peppers are riper and sweeter. You can also buy yellow, orange, purple, and brown bell peppers. Choose well-colored, firm peppers that are heavy for their size; these will have thick, juicy flesh. Store refrigerated in a plastic bag for up to a week. To trim peppers, remove the stem, spongy ribs, and seeds.

Pine nuts—The seed of certain pine trees. Also called *pignoli*, the nuts are widely known for their role in pesto, the classic Italian basil sauce. Use sparingly, since they are high in fat, in a pasta sauce, or sprinkle over a dish as a garnish. Toast them first for maximum flavor. Store pine nuts in the freezer for up to 6 months.

Prosciutto—A salt-cured, air-dried Italian ham that originated in the area around the city of Parma. This dense-textured, intensely flavored ham is served as an appetizer with melon or figs and also used in cooking, often to flavor sauces. Prosciutto has been produced in the United States for years, but imported Italian prosciutto is also available; the finest is labeled "Prosciutto di Parma." Our recipes should be made with very thinly sliced prosciutto crudo (raw) rather than prosciutto cotto (cooked).

Provolone cheese—A cow's milk Italian cheese that has a slightly salty, smoky flavor, and can range from mellow to sharp, depending on how long the cheese is aged. Layered into a casserole sparingly, the cheese adds a wonderful richness, or it can be sprinkled on top and lightly browned.

Red pepper flakes—A spice made from a variety of dried red chili peppers. Pepper flakes will permeate a sauce or stew with a burst of heat and flavor during the cooking and eating. Begin with a small amount—you can always add more.

Rice vinegar—A pale-colored vinegar made from fermented rice, typically more sweet and mild flavored than other more familiar vinegars. Use in stir-fried meat or vegetable combinations for pasta sauces, or in dressings for pasta salads.

Ricotta cheese—A fresh, creamy white cheese, smoother than cottage cheese, with a slightly sweet flavor. Available in whole-milk and part-skim milk versions, ricotta is often used in lasagna and stuffed pastas, and a little can be stirred into a sauce to add richness as well as creamy body. Refrigerate and use within a week.

Romano cheese—A hard, salty grating cheese. Pecorino Romano is the best known, and is made with sheep's milk, while many other types, especially in this country, are made with cow's milk or a blend of cow's and goat's milk. Grate as you would Parmesan and use as a tangy accent for pasta dishes.

Rosemary—An aromatic herb with needle-like leaves and a sharp pine-citrus flavor. Rosemary's robust flavor complements lamb particularly well, and it stands up to long cooking better than most herbs. If you can't get fresh rosemary, use whole dried leaves, which retain the flavor of the fresh herb quite well. Crush or chop rosemary leaves with a mortar and pestle or a chef's knife.

Sage—An intensely fragrant herb with grayish-green leaves. Sage will infuse a dish with a pleasant, musty mint taste. In its dried form, sage is sold as whole leaves and in a crumbly version. Dried sage is actually more flavorful than fresh, and is especially good added to meatballs, baked pastas, and pasta-vegetable salads.

Scallions—Immature onions (also called green onions) with a mild and slightly sweet flavor. Both the white bulb and the green tops can be used in cooking; the green tops make an attractive garnish. To prepare, trim off the base of the bulb or root end and any withered ends of the green tops. Remove the outermost, thin skin from around the bulb. Cut the white portion from the green tops and use separately, or use together in the same dish.

Scallops—A sweet, mild-flavored shellfish with a delicate texture, at its best when quickly cooked to avoid a rubbery texture. Bay scallops and calicos are the smaller varieties, while sea scallops grow large, and may be quartered or halved to approximate the size of the bays. Refrigerate scallops and use within a day of purchase.

Sesame oil, Oriental—A dark, polyunsaturated oil, pressed from toasted sesame seeds, used as a flavor enhancer in many Asian and Indian dishes. Do not confuse the Oriental oil with its lighter colored counterpart, which is cold-pressed from untoasted sesame seeds and imparts a much milder flavor. Store either version in the refrigerator for up to 6 months.

Shallot—A member of the onion family, looking rather like large cloves of garlic. Shallots are used to infuse savory dishes with a mild, delicate onion flavor. Refrigerate for no more than 1 week to maintain maximum flavor.

Sherry—A fortified wine, originally made in Spain but now produced elsewhere as well. Sherries range in sweetness from quite dry (labeled fino, manzanillo, or simply "dry") to medium-dry (labeled amontillado or "milk sherry") to sweet (oloroso, also called "cream" or "golden"). Use a dry sherry to add a fragrant bouquet to savory sauces.

Shiitake mushroom—A meaty, Oriental variety of mushroom with an almost steak-like flavor, used in pasta sauces and salads for depth. Choose fresh shiitakes that are plump and unblemished, and avoid broken or shriveled caps, a sign of age. Remove the tough part of the stem before slicing. Dried shiitakes, which must be reconstituted in warm water before using, are also available.

Snow pea—A flat pea pod that is fully edible, even uncooked. Slightly sweet and very tender, snow peas need only quick cooking and add both crunch and color to vegetable mixtures. Select crisp, bright green pods, and refrigerate in a plastic bag for up to 3 days. Remove papery tips and strings before using.

Sour cream—A soured dairy product, resulting from treating sweet cream with a lactic acid culture. Regular sour cream contains at least 18 percent milk fat by volume; reduced-fat sour cream contains 4 percent fat; nonfat sour cream is, of course, fat-free. In cooking, the reduced-fat version can be substituted for regular sour cream; use the nonfat cautiously since it behaves differently in some types of recipes. To avoid curdling, do not subject sour cream to high heat.

Sun-dried tomatoes—Plum tomatoes that have been dried slowly to produce a chewy, intensely flavorful sauce ingredient. Although oil-packed tomatoes are widely available, the dry-packed type are preferred for their lower fat content. For many recipes, the dried tomatoes must be soaked in hot water to soften them before using.

Thyme—A lemony-tasting member of the mint family frequently paired with bay leaves in Mediterranean-style dishes and rice-based preparations. The dried herb, both ground and leaf, is an excellent substitute for the fresh.

Tomato paste—A concentrated essence of cooked tomatoes, sold in cans and tubes. Tomato paste is commonly used to thicken and accent the flavor and color of sauces; however, it is slightly bitter and should not be used alone or in large quantities. Cooking tomato paste mellows it. If you're using only part of a can of tomato paste, save the remainder by freezing it in a plastic bag.

Tomato sauce—A cooked, seasoned purée of fresh tomatoes, sold in cans or jars. Tomato sauce is usually seasoned with salt, spices, and corn syrup; some brands come in Italian- or Mexican-style versions with more assertive flavorings. The recipes in this book call for "no-salt-added" tomato sauce, because the regular sauce is quite high in sodium.

Tomatoes, canned—Fresh tomatoes processed and packed for easy use and reliable year-round quality. Canned tomatoes are definitely preferable when the only available fresh tomatoes are hard, pale, and lacking in flavor. Canned whole peeled plum tomatoes, often imported from Italy, are especially tasty; they can be packed with or without added salt and are sometimes packed with herbs. You can also buy canned crushed tomatoes, packed with no added liquid, or with tomato juice, purée, or paste. The recipes in this book call for "no-salt-added" tomatoes. Some no-salt-added brands are not labeled as such—check the ingredient list.

Tomatoes, cherry—Round tomatoes roughly the size of ping-pong balls; may be red or yellow. These bite-size tomatoes add a colorful touch to pasta dishes and are great for salads. Cherry tomatoes are usually sold in baskets. Choose well-colored specimens and store them at room temperature to preserve their flavor.

Tomatoes, plum—Smallish, egg-shaped or oblong tomatoes. Sometimes called Roma tomatoes, these are meatier (thicker fleshed, with less liquid inside) than most globe tomatoes, which makes them excellent for cooking. They are a good choice when vine-ripened local tomatoes are not available.

Tomatoes, stewed—Canned tomatoes that have been cooked with seasonings and other vegetables, such as onions, green peppers, or celery. Stewed tomatoes add an extra touch of flavor to pasta sauces, soups, and stews.

Turkey sausage, hot—A spicy sausage filled with ground turkey meat. It can be used to great advantage in low-fat cooking since ground turkey is much lower in fat than the ground pork used in Italian hot sausage. It is available in links and patties, and also comes in a milder, sweeter version, similar to Italian sweet sausage.

Wine, dry white—A non-sweet alcoholic beverage made from fermented grape juice. White wine may be made from white grapes, or from red grapes with their skins and seeds removed. Dry white wine lends a unique fragrance and flavor to sauces. Avoid the so-called "cooking wines" sold in supermarkets: These are of poor quality and may have added salt. Instead, buy an inexpensive but drinkable white. Once opened, recork and refrigerate the bottle.

Yogurt, nonfat and low-fat—Delicately tart cultured milk products made from low-fat or skim milk. Plain yogurt adds creamy richness (but little or no fat) to pasta sauces. Be careful when cooking with yogurt, as it will curdle if boiled or stirred too vigorously: Adding flour or cornstarch to the yogurt before adding it to a hot sauce helps stabilize it.

Zest, citrus—The thin, outermost colored part of the rind of citrus fruits that contains strongly flavored oils. Zest imparts an intense flavor that makes a refreshing contrast to the richness of meat, poultry, or fish. Remove the zest with a grater, citrus zester, or vegetable peeler; be careful to remove only the colored layer, not the bitter white pith beneath it.

INDEX

Time-Life Books is a division of Time Life Inc.

TIME LIFE INC.

PRESIDENT and CEO: George Artandi

TIME-LIFE CUSTOM PUBLISHING

VICE PRESIDENT and PUBLISHER: Terry Newell

Vice President of Sales and Marketing: Neil Levin
Director of Special Markets: Liz Ziehl
Managing Editor: Donia Steele
Production Manager: Carolyn Clark
Quality Assurance Manager: James D. King

Interior design by David Fridberg of Miles Fridberg
    Molinaroli, Inc.
Cover design by Christopher M. Register

TIME-LIFE BOOKS

PRESIDENT: Stephen R. Frary
PUBLISHER/MANAGING EDITOR: Neil Kagan

Director of Finance: Christopher Hearing
Directors of Book Production: Marjann Caldwell;
    Patricia Pascale
Director of Publishing Technology: Betsi McGrath
Director of Photography and Research: John Conrad Weiser
Director of Editorial Administration: Barbara Levitt
Chief Librarian: Louise D. Forstall

Books produced by Time-Life Custom Publishing are
available at special bulk discount for promotional and
premium use. Custom adaptations can also be created to
meet your specific marketing goals.
Call 1-800-323-5255

 REBUS, INC.
PUBLISHER: Rodney M. Friedman

Editorial Staff for *Pasta Light*
Director, Recipe Development and Photography:
    Grace Young
Editorial Director: Kate Slate
Senior Recipe Developer: Sandra Rose Gluck
Recipe Developers: Helen Jones, Paul Piccuito,
    Marianne Zanzarella
Managing Editor: Julee Binder Shapiro
Writers: Bonnie J. Slotnick, David J. Ricketts
Editorial Assistant: James W. Brown, Jr.
Nutritionists: Hill Nutrition Associates

Art Director: Timothy Jeffs
Photographers: Lisa Koenig, Vincent Lee, Corinne Colen,
    René Velez, Edmund Goldspink
Photographers' Assistants: Alix Berenberg, Bill Bies, Bain
    Coffman, Eugene DeLucie, Russell Dian, Katie Bleacher
    Everard, Petra Liebetanz, Rainer Fehringer, Robert
    Presciutti, Val Steiner
Food Stylists: A.J. Battifarano, Helen Jones, Catherine
    Paukner, Karen Pickus, Roberta Rall, Andrea B.
    Swenson, Karen J.M. Tack
Assistant Food Stylists: Mako Antonishek, Catherine
    Chatham, Charles Davis, Tracy Donovan, Susan Kadel,
    Amy Lord, Ellie Ritt
Prop Stylists: Sara Abalan, Debra Donahue
Prop Coordinator: Karin Martin